EXPONENTIAL ORGANIZATIONS

Why new organizations are ten times
better, faster, and cheaper than yours
(and what to do about it)

SALIM ISMAIL

with **MICHAEL S. MALONE** and **YURI VAN GEEST**

FOREWORD and AFTERWORD by PETER H. DIAMANDIS

DIVERSIONBOOKS

Diversion Books
A Division of Diversion Publishing Corp.
443 Park Avenue South, Suite 1008
New York, New York 10016
www.DiversionBooks.com

For more information, email info@diversionbooks.com

First Diversion Books edition October 2014.
Print ISBN: 978-1-62681-423-3
eBook ISBN: 978-1-62681-358-8

CONTENTS

FOREWORD

Welcome to a time of exponential change, the most amazing time ever to be alive.

In the pages that follow, Salim Ismail, my colleague, friend and one of the leading thinkers and practitioners on the future of organizations, offers you a first look at what this new world will look like—and how it will change the way you work and live. Salim has studied and interviewed CEOs and entrepreneurs whose companies are leveraging a newly available set of externalities and, as a result, scaling their organizations at many times the normal rate of typical companies. More important, he's thought deeply about and analyzed how existing organizations need to adapt. For this reason, I can't think of a more perfect guide to those CEOs and executives interested in thriving during this time of disruptive change.

Have no doubt, *Exponential Organizations: Why New Organizations are Ten Times Better, Faster and Cheaper Than Yours (And What To Do About It)* is both a roadmap and a survival guide for the CEO, the entrepreneur and, most of all, the executive of the future. Congratulations on the successes that got you to this point in your career, but let me forewarn you that those skills are already out of date. The concepts in this book and the conversations that they spark are the new *lingua franca* for anyone wanting to remain competitive and stay in the game. In today's corporate world there is a new breed of institutional organism—the Exponential Organization—loose on Earth, and if you don't understand it, prepare for it and, ultimately, *become* it, you will be disrupted.

The concept of the Exponential Organization (ExO) first arose at Singularity University, which I co-founded in 2008 with noted futurist, author, entrepreneur-turned-AI director at Google, Ray Kurzweil. The goal was to create a new kind of university, one whose curriculum was constantly being updated. For that reason SU was never accredited—not because we didn't care, but because the curriculum was changing too fast. SU would focus only on the exponentially growing (or accelerating technologies) that were riding on the back of Moore's Law. Areas like infinite computing, sensors, networks, artificial intelligence, robotics, digital manufacturing, synthetic biology, digital medicine and nanomaterials. By design and desire, our students would be the world's top entrepreneurs, as well as executives from Fortune 500 companies. Our mission: to help people positively impact the lives of a billion people.

The idea for SU came together at a Founding Conference hosted at NASA's Ames Research Center in Silicon Valley in September 2008. What I remember most clearly from the event was an impromptu speech given by Google co-founder Larry Page near the end of the first day. Standing before about one hundred attendees, Page made an impassioned speech calling for this new university to focus on addressing the world's biggest problems: "I now have a very simple metric I use: Are you working on something that can change the world? Yes or no? The answer for 99.99999 percent of people is 'no.' I think we need to be training people on how to change the world. Obviously, technologies are the way to do that. That's what we've seen in the past; that's what's driven all the change."

One of the individuals in the audience listening to Page was Salim, who had headed up Brickhouse, Yahoo's intrapreneurial incubator. He, too, was taken by that message, and within weeks, he joined Singularity as the university's founding Executive Director. Salim, having run several startups before, navigated the usual crises that come with an early stage company and played a crucial role in making SU the success it is today. But perhaps most important of all, Salim pulled together the diverse thoughts and case studies taught at SU and wove them together into a vision for a new kind of company, one that operated at ten times the price performance of those just a decade ago.

It was my pleasure to help frame the attributes, concepts and practices exhibited by Exponential Organizations, and to join Salim, Yuri van Geest, and Mike Malone in developing this book. Together, we have had the great fortune to study and understand how accelerating technologies are changing the course of nations, industry and all of humanity, and to manifest Salim's "how-to guide" for the Exponential Executive. Some of the work described in the chapters ahead emerged from my own book, *Abundance: The Future Is Better Than You Think* (co-authored with Steven Kotler), as a framing of where we all could end up, but most of it applies to the companies of today and how they need to navigate there.

Salim's co-authors also deserve recognition. First is Yuri van Geest, a Singularity University graduate and one of the world's leading experts in mobile, as well as a keen student of exponential technologies and trends. Yuri has a background in organizational design and has been materially involved since early on in the project. Second is veteran high-technology journalist Mike Malone. Mike is not only a world-class technology reporter, but also the inventor of two influential organizational models that preceded this book: the Virtual Corporation (with Bill Davidow) and the Protean Organization.

Salim's vision of the Exponential Organization is a powerful one. Potent forces are emerging in the world—exponential technologies, the DIY innovator, crowdfunding, crowdsourcing, and the rising billion—that will give us the power to solve many of the world's grandest challenges and the potential to meet the needs of every man, women and child over the next two to three decades. These same forces are now empowering smaller and smaller teams to do what was once only possible via governments and the largest corporations.

Three billion new minds will join the global economy over the next half-dozen years. The relevance of this is twofold. First, these three billion people represent a new population of consumers who have never bought anything before. Consequentially, they represent a long tail of tens-of-trillions of dollars of emerging buying power. If they are not your direct customers, fear not; they are likely your customer's customers. Second, this group—the "rising billion"—is a new entrepreneurial class powered with the latest generation of Internet-delivered technologies—everything from Google and Artificial Intelligence, to 3D printing and synthetic biology. As such, we will see an explosion in the rate of innovation, as millions of new innovators begin to experiment and upload their products and services and launch new businesses. If you think the rate of innovation has been fast in recent years, let me be among the first to tell you: you haven't seen anything yet.

Today the only constant is change, and the rate of change is increasing. Your competition is no longer the multinational corporation overseas, it's now the guy or gal in the Silicon Valley or Bandra (Mumbai) garage using the latest online tools to design and cloud print their latest innovation.

But the question remains: how can you harness all of this creative power? How can you construct an enterprise that is as quick, adept and innovative as the people who will be part of it? How will you compete in this accelerated new world? How will you organize to scale?

The answer is the Exponential Organization.

You won't have much choice, because in many (and soon most) industries, that acceleration is already underway. Lately, I've begun to teach about what I call the 6Ds: Digitized, Deceptive, Disruptive, Dematerialize, Demonetize and Democratize.

Any technology that becomes *Digitized* (our first "D") enters a period of *Deceptive* growth. During the early period of exponentials, the doubling of small numbers (0.01, 0.02, 0.04, 0.08) all basically looks like zero. But once its hits the knee of the curve, you are only ten doublings away from 1,000x, twenty doublings get you to 1,000,000x, and thirty doublings get you a 1,000,000,000x increase.

Such a rapid rise describes the third D, *Disruptive*. And, as you shall see in the pages of this book, once a technology become disruptive it *Dematerializes*—which means that you no longer physically carry around a GPS, video camera or flashlight. All of them have dematerialized as apps onto your smartphone. And once that happens, the product or service *Demonetizes*. Thus, Uber is demonetizing taxi fleets and Craigslist demonetized the classified ads (taking down a flock of newspapers in the process).

The final step to all this is *Democratization*. Thirty years ago if you wanted to reach a billion people, you needed to be Coca-Cola or GE, with employees in one hundred countries. Today you can be a kid in a garage who uploads an app onto a few key platforms. Your ability to touch humanity has been democratized.

What Salim and the team have observed from the front lines—and what you will come to understand as you read this book—is that *no* current commercial, governmental or non-profit enterprise, as currently configured, can keep up with the pace that will be set by these 6Ds. To do so will require something radically new—a new vision of organization that is as technologically smart, adaptive and encompassing (not just of employees but of billions of people in vast social networks) as the new world in which it will operate—and ultimately transform.

That vision is the Exponential Organization.

Peter H. Diamandis
Founder and Chairman, XPRIZE Foundation
Co-Founder and Exec. Chairman, Singularity University
Santa Monica, CA
August 25, 2014

INTRODUCTION

THE IRIDIUM MOMENT

In the late 1980s, in what was generally lauded as a forward-looking move to capture the nascent cell phone industry, Motorola Inc. spun out a company called Iridium. Motorola recognized—before anyone else—that while expensive mobile phone solutions were relatively easy to implement in urban centers thanks to their high population densities, there was no comparable solution for regions outside major cities, much less the countryside. A calculation convinced Motorola that the cost of cell phone towers—about $100,000 each, not including spectrum utilization limits and the not-inconsiderable expense of producing brick-sized handsets—meant that it would too expensive to blanket the vast majority of the landscape.

Soon enough, however, a more radical but also more profitable solution presented itself: a constellation of seventy-seven satellites (Iridium is number seventy-seven on the periodic table) that would cover the globe at low Earth orbit and provide mobile telephony for one price—*no matter the location.* And, Motorola concluded, if just a million people in various developed countries paid $3,000 for a satellite phone, plus a $5-per-minute usage fee, the satellite network would quickly become profitable.

Of course, we now know Iridium failed spectacularly, ultimately costing its investors $5 billion. In fact, the satellite system was doomed before it was even put in place, one of the most dramatic victims of technological innovation.

There were several reasons behind Iridium's failure. Even as the company was launching its satellites, the cost of installing cell phone towers was dropping, network speeds were increasing by orders of magnitude, and handsets were shrinking in both size and price. To be fair, Iridium was hardly alone in its misjudgment. Competitors Odyssey and Globalstar both made the same fundamental mistake. Ultimately, in fact, more than $10 billion in investor money was lost in a misplaced bet that the pace of technological change was too slow to keep up with market demand.

One reason for this debacle, according to Dan Colussy, who drove Iridium's buyout in 2000, was the company's refusal to update business assumptions. "The Iridium business plan was locked in place twelve years before the system became operational," he recalls. That's a long time, long enough that it was almost impossible to predict where the state of the art in digital communications would be by the time the satellite system was at last in place. We thus label this an *Iridium Moment*—using linear tools and the trends of the past to predict an accelerating future.

Another Iridium Moment is the well-documented case of Eastman Kodak, which declared bankruptcy in 2012 after having invented, and then rejected, the digital camera. At around the same time Kodak was closing its doors, the startup Instagram, three years in business and with just thirteen employees, was bought by Facebook for $1 billion. (Ironically, this happened while Kodak still owned the patents for digital photography.)

Iridium's missteps and the epochal industry change from Kodak to Instagram were not isolated events. Competition for many of America's Fortune 500 companies is no longer coming from China and India. As Peter Diamandis has noted, today it's increasingly coming from two guys in a garage with a startup leveraging exponentially growing technologies. YouTube went from a startup funded by Chad Hurley's personal credit cards to being purchased by Google for $1.4 billion, all in less than eighteen months. Groupon leapt from conception to $6 billion in value in less than two years. Uber is valued at almost $17 billion, ten times its value of just two years ago. What we're witnessing is a new breed of organization that is scaling and generating value at a pace never before seen in business. The chart below shows the accelerating metabolism of the economy.

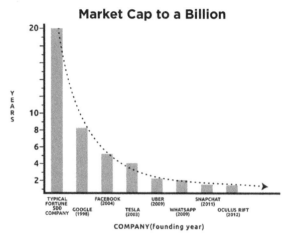

Market Cap to a Billion

Welcome to the new world of the *Exponential Organization*, or ExO. It is a place where, as with Kodak, neither age nor size nor reputation nor even current sales guarantee that you will be around tomorrow. On the other hand, it is also a place where if you can build an organization that is sufficiently scalable, fast moving and smart, you may enjoy success—exponential success—to a degree never before possible. And all with a minimum of resources and time.

We have entered the age of the billion-dollar startup and soon, the trillion-dollar corporation, where the best companies and institutions will be moving at seemingly light speed. If you haven't transitioned into an Exponential Organization as well, it will not only seem as though your competition is racing away from you, but also, like Kodak, that you are sliding backwards at breakneck speed into oblivion.

In 2011, Babson's Olin Graduate School of Business predicted that in ten years, 40 percent of existing Fortune 500 Companies would no longer survive. Richard Foster of Yale University estimates that the average lifespan of an S&P 500 company has decreased from sixty-seven years in the 1920s to fifteen years today. And that lifespan is going to get even shorter in the years to come as these giant corporations aren't just forced to compete with, but are annihilated—seemingly overnight— by a new breed of companies that harnesses the power of exponential technologies, from groupware and data mining to synthetic biology and robotics. And as the rise of Google portents, the founders of those new companies will become the leaders of the world's economy for the foreseeable future.

DOUBLING DOWN

For most of recorded history, a community's productivity was a function of its human power: men and women to hunt, gather and build, and children to assist. Double the number of hands gathering crops or bringing home meat and the community doubled its output.

In time, humanity domesticated beasts of burden, including the horse and ox, and output increased further. But the equation was still linear. Double the beasts, double the output.

As market capitalism came into existence and the industrial age dawned, output took a huge leap. Now a single individual could operate machinery that did the work of 10 horses or 100 laborers. The speed of transport, and thus distribution, doubled, and then, for the first time in human history, tripled.

Increased output brought prosperity to many and, ultimately, a manifold jump in the standard of living. Starting at the end of the eighteenth century and continuing through the present—and largely the result of the intersection of the Industrial Revolution and the modern scientific research laboratory—mankind has witnessed a doubling of the human lifespan and a tripling of inflation-adjusted per capita net worth for every nation on Earth.

During this most recent phase of human productivity, the limiting factor to growth has shifted from the number of bodies (human or animal) to the number of machines and the capital expense deployed. Doubling the number of factories meant twice the output. Companies have grown ever larger, and they now span the globe. With size has come increased global reach, the potential for sector domination and, ultimately, enduring and hugely lucrative success.

But such growth takes time and typically has required enormous capital investment. None of this comes cheap, and the complexity of large-scale hiring efforts and the difficulties of designing, building and delivering new equipment means that implementation timelines are still measured over the better part of a decade. On more than one occasion, CEOs and boards of directors have found themselves (as did Iridium) "betting the company" on a new direction requiring a huge capital investment measured in hundreds of millions or billions of dollars. Pharmaceutical companies, aerospace companies, automotive companies and energy companies routinely find themselves making investments whose returns might not be known for many years.

Although a workable system, it is far from an optimal one. Too much money and valuable talent is locked up in decade-long projects whose likelihood of success can't be measured almost until the moment they fail. All of which adds up to enormous waste, not least in terms of lost potential to pursue other ideas and opportunities that could benefit mankind.

This is neither a tenable nor an acceptable situation, especially when the challenges that face mankind in the twenty-first century will take every bit of the imagination and innovation we can muster.

There must be a better way to organize ourselves. We've learned how to scale technology; now it's time we learned how to scale organizations. This new age calls for a different solution to building new business, to improving rates of success and to solving the challenges that lie ahead.

That solution is the Exponential Organization.

EXPONENTIAL ORGANIZATIONS

Let's begin with a definition:

> An Exponential Organization (ExO) is one whose impact (or output) is disproportionally large—at least 10x larger—compared to its peers because of the use of new organizational techniques that leverage accelerating technologies.

Rather than using armies of people or large physical plants, Exponential Organizations are built upon information technologies that take what was once physical in nature and dematerialize it into the digital, on-demand world.

Everywhere you look you see this digital transformation taking place: In 2012, 93 percent of U.S. transactions were already digital; physical equipment companies like Nikon are seeing their cameras rapidly being supplanted by the cameras on smartphones; map and atlas makers were replaced by Magellan GPS systems, which themselves were replaced by smartphone sensors; and libraries of books and music have been turned into phone and e-reader apps. Similarly, retail stores in China are being replaced by the rise of e-commerce tech giant Alibaba, universities are being threatened by MOOCs such as edX and Coursera, and the Tesla S is more a computer with wheels than it is a car.

The sixty-year history of Moore's Law—basically, that the price/ performance of computation will double about every eighteen months—has been well documented. And we've come a long way since 1971, when the original circuit board held just two hundred chips; today we have teraflops of computing operating within the same physical space.

That steady, extraordinary, and seemingly impossible pace led futurist Ray Kurzweil, who has studied this phenomenon for thirty years, to make four signature observations:

- First, the doubling pattern identified by Gordon Moore in integrated circuits applies to any information technology. Kurzweil calls this the Law of Accelerating Returns (LOAR) and shows that doubling patterns in computation extend all the way back to 1900, far earlier than Moore's original pronouncement.

- Second, the driver fueling this phenomenon is information. Once any domain, discipline, technology or industry becomes information-enabled and powered by information flows, its price/performance begins doubling approximately annually.

- Third, once that doubling pattern starts, it doesn't stop. We use current computers to design faster computers, which then build faster computers, and so on.

- Finally, several key technologies today are now information-enabled and following the same trajectory. Those technologies include artificial intelligence (AI), robotics, biotech and bioinformatics, medicine, neuroscience, data science, 3D printing, nanotechnology and even aspects of energy.

Never in human history have we seen so many technologies moving at such a pace. And now that we are information-enabling everything around us, the effects of the Kurzweil's Law of Accelerating Returns are sure to be profound.

What's more, as these technologies intersect (e.g., using deep-learning AI algorithms to analyze cancer trials), the pace of innovation accelerates even further. Each intersection adds yet another multiplier to the equation.

Archimedes once said, "Give me a lever long enough, and I'll move the world." Simply put, mankind has never had a bigger lever.

Linear vs. Exponential

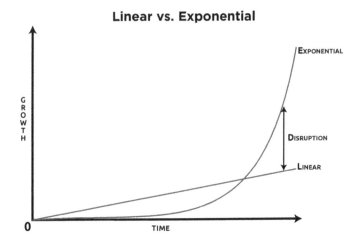

Kurzweil's Law of Accelerating Returns and Moore's Law long ago broke from the confines of semiconductors and have utterly transformed human society over the last fifty years. Now, Exponential Organizations, the latest embodiment of acceleration in human culture and enterprise, are overhauling commerce and other aspects of modern life, and at a scorching pace that will quickly leave the old world of "linear organizations" far behind. Those enterprises that don't jump aboard soon will be left on the ash heap of history, joining Iridium, Kodak, Polaroid, Philco, Blockbuster, Nokia and a host of other once-great, industry-dominant corporations unable to adapt to rapid technological change.

In the pages ahead, we will outline the key internal and external attributes of an Exponential Organization, including its design (or lack thereof), lines of communication, decision-making protocol, information infrastructure, management, philosophy and life cycle. We will explore how an ExO differs in terms of strategy, structure, culture, processes, operations, systems, people and key performance indicators. We will also discuss the crucial importance of a company having what we call a Massive Transformative Purpose (a term we will define in depth). We will then look at how to launch an ExO startup, how to adopt ExO practices in mid-cap companies and how to retrofit them to large organizations.

Our objective is to not make this a book of theory, but rather to present the reader with a how-to guide to the creation and maintenance of an Exponential Organization. We offer a hands-on, prescriptive look at how to organize an enterprise able to compete in the face of today's accelerated pace of change.

Although many of the ideas we will present may seem radically new, they have been around, *sub rosa*, for a decade or more. We first identified the ExO paradigm as a weak signal in 2009, and noticed over a two-year period that several new organizations were following a specific model. In 2011, futurist Paul Saffo suggested to Salim that he write this book, and we have been seriously researching the ExO model for the last three years. To do so, we:

- Reviewed sixty classic innovation management books by such authors as John Hagel, Clayton Christensen, Eric Ries, Gary Hamel, Jim Collins, W. Chan Kim, Reid Hoffman and Michael Cusumano.
- Interviewed C-Level executives from several dozen Fortune 200 companies with our survey and frameworks.
- Interviewed or researched ninety top entrepreneurs and visionaries including Marc Andreessen, Steve Forbes, Chris Anderson, Michael Milken, Paul Saffo, Philip Rosedale, Arianna Huffington, Tim O'Reilly and Steve Jurvetson.
- Investigated the characteristics of the one hundred fastest growing and most successful startups across the world, including those that comprise the Unicorn Club (Aileen Lee's name for the billion-dollar market cap startup group), to tease out commonalities the companies used to scale.

- Reviewed presentations and gleaned key insights from core faculty members at Singularity University regarding the acceleration they are seeing at the edges of their fields and how that acceleration might impact organizational design.

We don't claim to have all the answers. But based upon our own experiences, both good and bad, we believe we can offer management teams critical insight into this era of hyper-accelerated innovation and competition, as well as into the new opportunities (and responsibilities) presented by this new world. If we can't guarantee you success, we can at least put you on the right playing field and show you the new rules of the game. These two advantages, plus your own initiative, offer good odds for being a winner in the new world of Exponential Organizations.

PART ONE

EXPLORING THE EXPONENTIAL ORGANIZATION

In this segment, we'll explore the characteristics, attributes and implications of Exponential Organizations.

CHAPTER ONE
ILLUMINATED BY INFORMATION

While the original Iridium Moment caused enormous embarrassment for the satellite industry, you may be surprised to learn that there have been many similar but less-publicized Iridium moments in the mobile phone industry.

For example, because mobile phones in the early 80s were bulky and expensive to use, renowned consulting firm McKinsey & Company advised AT&T *not* to enter the mobile telephone business, predicting there would be fewer than one million cellular phones in use by 2000. In fact, by 2000, there were one hundred million mobile phones. Not only was McKinsey's prediction off by 99 percent, its recommendation also resulted in AT&T missing out on one of the biggest business opportunities of modern times.

In 2009, yet another major market research firm, the Gartner Group, forecast that by 2012 Symbian would be the top operating system for mobile devices, with a 39 percent market share and two hundred three million units shipped—a leadership position Gartner anticipated the company would hold through 2014. Gartner also predicted in the same report that Android would hold just a 14.5 percent market share.

The reality? Symbian shut its doors at the end of 2012 after shipping only 2.2 million units in Q4. Android, on the other hand, has overtaken even the Apple iPhone OS and today dominates the mobile world, with over one billion Android OS shipments just in 2014.

Venture capitalist Vinod Khosla conducted an insightful piece of research in which he reviewed predictions made by mobile phone industry analysts from 2000 to 2010. He studied major research firms such as Gartner, Forrester, McKinsey and Jupiter to see how they predicted the growth of the mobile phone industry in two-year increments over the course of that decade.

Khosla's research showed that in 2002 experts predicted, on average, 16 percent year-to-year growth. In fact, by 2004, the industry had seen a 100 percent increase. In 2004, their collective predictions called for an increase of 14 percent; by 2006, growth had once again climbed 100 percent. In 2006, the analysts estimated sales would increase just 12 percent—and they doubled again. Despite three previous—and notable—failures, in 2008 these very same experts forecast a measly 10 percent growth, only to see the number double yet again—another 100 percent leap. It is hard to imagine how anyone could be more wrong than to be off by 10x—and yet these were the mobile phone industry experts upon whom corporations and governments worldwide relied for their long-term strategic planning. Nowhere does the phrase "missed by a country mile" seem more appropriate.

What makes this failure valuable for our purposes is that at each point of *exponential* growth in mobile phones over the last decade, the world's top prognosticators predicted largely *linear* change. Again, we would label it Iridium thinking.

Khosla's research proved particularly compelling and valuable when he went on to show that such prediction errors weren't unique just to the mobile phone industry, but also to the oil industry and a host of other sectors. It seemed that, when facing exponential growth, the experts in almost every field *always* projected linearly, despite the evidence before their eyes.

Brough Turner, a noted entrepreneur in VOIP and mobile telephony, has been building companies in that industry since 1990. Having kept close track of industry predictions since the early 90s, he concurs with Khosla's analysis. In a recent interview with Salim, Turner noted that while the initial projections were always aggressive, the experts inevitably expected a tapering after the first eighteen to twenty-four months. Nonetheless, he said, the same rates of growth continued for twenty years. David Frigstad, CEO of research firm Frost & Sullivan, explains at least part of the problem thusly: "Predicting a technology when it's doubling is inherently tricky. If you miss one step, you're off by 50 percent!"

A final example should drive the point home. In 1990, the Human Genome Project was launched with the aim of fully sequencing a single human genome. Estimates called for the project to take fifteen years and cost about $6 billion. In 1997, however, halfway through the estimated time frame, just 1 percent of the human genome had been sequenced. Every expert labeled the project a failure, pointing out that at seven years for just 1 percent, it would take seven hundred years to finish the sequencing. Craig Venter, one of the principal researchers, received calls from friends and colleagues imploring him to stop the project and not embarrass himself further. "Save your career," he recalls them saying. "Return the money."

When Ray Kurzweil was asked his perspective, however, his view of the "impending disaster" was quite different. "1 percent," he said. "That means we're halfway done." What Kurzweil got that no one else did was that the amount sequenced was doubling every year. 1 percent doubling seven times is 100 percent. Kurzweil's math was correct, and in fact the project was completed in 2001, early and under budget. The so-called experts had missed the end point by 696 years.

What is going on here? How can intelligent and well-read analysts, entrepreneurs and investors so consistently get things wrong? And not just a little wrong, but wrong by as much as 99 percent?

If such predictions had been just a little bit off, it would be easy to dismiss them as based on bad data, or even simple incompetence. But no, mistakes this great are almost always due to a complete misinterpretation of the rules defining the nature of the marketplace. They come from relying on a paradigm that performed perfectly up until the moment it didn't, and that is suddenly, often inexplicably, out of date.

But if there is a new paradigm assuming a central role in

the modern economy, one that will define how we live and work, what is it?

The answer lies within the anecdotes cited in the introduction to this book. Consider, for example, the Eastman Kodak story. Was its failure simply a case of a once-great company that had grown complacent and lost its innovative edge, as was suggested by the media at the time? Or was there something larger at work?

Think back, if you are old enough to remember, to the days of film photography. Each photograph cost an incremental amount of money. The cost of the film, the cost of mailing or hand-delivering the film, the cost of processing that film—in the end, it all added up to about a dollar per photograph. Photography was based upon a scarcity model and we carefully conserved and managed our photos and film rolls to ensure no wasted shots.

With the shift to digital photography, something important—indeed something revolutionary—happened. The marginal cost of taking an extra photograph didn't just diminish, as it would with a linear improvement in the technology; instead, it essentially sank to *zero*. It didn't matter if you took five pictures or five hundred. The cost was the same. Eventually, even the storage of the photos themselves became all but free.

And that wasn't the only technological leap. Once you had these digital photographs, you could apply computations to them in the form of image recognition, artificial intelligence, social technologies, filtering, editing, and machine learning. Now anyone with minimal training could become a "darkroom wizard" like Edward Weston or Ansel Adams. You could also manipulate, move and copy a digital photograph infinitely more quickly and easily than a physical one—and as such you became a publisher as well as a print and wire service. And all these things could be done with a camera that was a fraction the cost and size of the traditional analog versions it replaced.

In other words, what happened in the world of photography wasn't just a major improvement. It wasn't even just a single evolutionary leap. Eastman Kodak might have managed to stay competitive had that been the only challenge. But Kodak (and Polaroid, among other giants in the field) was hit by revolutionary technological change coming at it from multiple directions: cameras, film, processing, distribution, retailing, marketing, packaging, storage and, ultimately and most decisively, a radical change in the perceptions of the marketplace.

That is the very definition of a paradigm shift. There's an important and foundational lesson illustrated in each of these anecdotes, which is that an information-based environment delivers *fundamentally disruptive opportunities*.

There are thousands of similar disruptions taking place across the global economy, where just such a profound shift is occurring from a physical substrate to an information substrate. That is, at the heart of every one of these disruptions—these evolutionary leaps—can be found a fundamental change in the role of information: semiconductor chips assuming the role of image capture, display, storage and controller; the Internet transforming supply, distribution and retail channels; and social networks and groupware reorganizing institutions. Together, all indications are that we are shifting to an *information-based paradigm*.

In his book *The Singularity is Near: When Humans Transcend Biology*, Kurzweil identified a hugely important and fundamental property of technology: when you shift to an information-based environment, the pace of development jumps onto an exponential growth path and price/performance doubles every year or two.

As everyone in technology knows, this pace of change was first discovered and described in 1964 by Intel Corporation co-founder Gordon Moore. His discovery, immortalized as Moore's Law, has seen the doubling of price/performance in computing continue uninterrupted for a half-century. As noted in the Introduction, Kurzweil took Moore's Law several steps further, noting that *every* information-based paradigm operates in the same way, something he called the Law of Accelerating Returns (LOAR).

There is a growing recognition that the pace of change formerly seen in computing is now mapping into other technologies with the same effect. For example, the first human genome was sequenced in 2000 at a cost of $2.7 billion. Because of the underlying accelerations in computing, sensors and new measurement techniques, the cost of DNA sequencing has been moving at *five* times the pace of Moore's Law. In 2011, Dr. Moore had his own genome sequenced for $100,000. Today that very same sequencing costs about $1,000, a figure that is expected to drop to $100 by 2015, and to just a penny by 2020, when, in the words of Raymond McCauley, "It will soon be cheaper to sequence your genome...than it will be to flush your toilet."

We've seen a similar movement in robotics. Those twenty dollar toy helicopters all the kids are playing with? Five years ago that capability cost $700. Eight years ago it didn't even exist. As former astronaut Dan Barry says of a toy drone helicopter available on Amazon for seventeen dollars, "It has a gyro in it that space shuttle engineers would have spent $100 million to have thirty years ago."

And that's just biotech and robotics. We are also seeing plummeting costs across a host of other technologies, including the following:

	Cost (averages) for equivalent functionality	Scale
3D printing	$40,000 (2007) to $100 (2014)	400x in 7 years
Industrial robots	$500,000 (2008) to $22,000 (2013)	23x in 5 years
Drones	$100,000 (2007) to $700 (2013)	142x in 6 years
Solar	$30 per kWh (1984) to $0.16 per kWh (2014)	200x in 20 years
Sensors (3D LIDAR sensor)	$20,000 (2009) to $79 (2014)	250x in 5 years

Biotech (DNA sequencing of one whole human DNA profile)	$10 million (2007) to $1,000 (2014)	10,000x in 7 years
Neurotech (BCI devices)	$4,000 (2006) to $90 (2011)	44x in 5 years
Medicine (full body scan)	$10,000 (2000) to $500 (2014)	20x in 14 years

In each of these domains, at least one aspect is being information-enabled, which then catapults it onto the bullet train of Moore's Law as the pace of development accelerates into a doubling pattern.

The physical world is still there, of course, but our relationship to it is changing fundamentally. Note that for many of us, our memories aren't in our heads anymore—they're buried in our smartphones. Via social networks, our relationships are increasingly digital, not analog, and our communication is nearly all-digital. We are rapidly changing the filter through which we deal with the world from a physical, materially-based perspective to an information- and knowledge-based one.

And this is just beginning. Ten years ago we had five hundred million Internet-connected devices. Today there are about eight billion. By 2020 there will be fifty billion and a decade later we'll have a trillion Internet-connected devices as we literally information-enable every aspect of the world in the Internet of Things. The Internet is now the world's nervous system, with our mobile devices serving as edge points and nodes on that network.

Think about that for a second: we'll be jumping from eight billion Internet-connected devices today to fifty billion by 2025, and to a trillion a mere decade later. We like to think that thirty or forty years into the Information Revolution we are well along in terms of its development. But according to this metric, we're just 1 percent of the way down the road. Not only is most of that growth still ahead of us, *all of it is*.

And *everything* is being disrupted in the process.

The magnitude of that disruption, especially in the consumer world, is only now becoming obvious. It started with certain products and industries, such as books (Amazon) and travel (Booking.com). Then classified ads (Craigslist) and auction sites (eBay) decimated the newspaper industry, which has been further disrupted in recent years by Twitter, the *Huffington Post, Vice* and *Medium*. More recently, entire industries—music, for example, thanks initially to Apple's iTunes—have been disrupted.

Now, in 2014, we are hard-pressed to identify *any* industry that hasn't been fundamentally disrupted. And not just businesses, but jobs as well. As David Rose, a leading angel investor and founder of Gust, says, "Every single job function we can identify is being fundamentally transformed." Even "old" industries such as construction are in the throes of disruption. Mike Halsall, a construction company executive, told us that significant disruptions to his industry include:

- Increased collaboration (making an opaque industry more transparent and substantially more efficient)
- Ever-more sophisticated design software and visualization
- 3D printing

Halsall estimates that the sum of these disruptions could reduce the number of people working in construction by more than 25 percent within ten years. (The construction industry, by the way, represents a $4.7 trillion industry annually.) In the corporate travel industry, Russ Howell, EVP of Global Technology at BCD Travel, notes that 50 percent of the transactions at telephone-based call centers moved to the Internet in less than a decade. Furthermore, he expects 50 percent of those to move to mobile smartphones within three years.

As this new information-based paradigm causes the very metabolism of the world to heat up, we're increasingly feeling its macroeconomic impact. For example, the cheapest 3D printers now cost only $100, which means that within five years or so most of us will be able to afford 3D printers to fabricate toys, cutlery, tools and fittings—essentially anything we're able to dream up. The implications of this "printing revolution" are almost unfathomable.

So are the potential repercussions. Consider that, for all of its advances over the past few decades, China's economy is still fundamentally based on the manufacturing and assembly of cheap plastic parts. This means that within a decade, the Chinese economy could be under serious threat from 3D printing technology. And that's just one industry. (Next, consider the ripple effect if an economically distressed China decides to call its overseas debt.)

Historically, disruptive breakthroughs always occur when disparate fields cross. Consider, for example, how combining water power with the textile loom helped launch the Industrial Revolution. Today, we are essentially cross-connecting *all* innovative new fields. And not just new fields: similar collisions are also occurring in age-old disciplines as well, from art and biology to chemistry and economics. It's no wonder that Larry Keeley, founder of Doblin Group, a noted innovation strategy consulting firm, says, "I have never, in thirty-two years, seen anything like the pace of change we're seeing today."

Even industries that were once thought impervious to technology are being affected via second-order impacts of information. For example, in January 2013 Santiago Bilinkis, a renowned entrepreneur in Argentina, noticed that Buenos Aires car wash operators had seen their revenues drop 50 percent over the previous decade. Given Argentina's growing middle class, a steady increase in the sales of luxury cars and a population that takes pride in showcasing clean cars, the fall in revenue made no sense. Bilinkis spent three months researching the situation, checking whether there were more car washes on the market (there weren't) or if new water conservation rules had been introduced (they hadn't). After eliminating all the possibilities, he stumbled upon the answer: Thanks to increased computing power and data, weather forecasters had become 50 percent more accurate in their predictions during that period. When drivers know it's going to rain, they skip the car wash, resulting in fewer visits. Thus have computational improvements in weather forecasting delivered a body blow to an industry as seemingly immune to technology advances as Buenos Aires car wash operators.

To fully comprehend the sheer acceleration we're seeing, recall the $10 billion in investment that was lost on Iridium and other satellite efforts in the 90s. Today, twenty years later, a new breed of satellite companies—Skybox, Planet Labs, Nanosatisfi and Satellogic—are all launching nanosatellites (which are, essentially, the size of a shoebox). The cost per launch is about $100,000 per satellite—a fraction of the $1 billion Iridium incurred per launch for its constellation. More important, by launching a cluster of nanosatellites operating in a coordinated, meshed configuration, the capability of these new satellites blows away what the previous generation could do.

For example, Planet Labs already has thirty-one satellites in orbit and plans to launch another one hundred during 2014. Satellogic, operating out of Argentina, has already launched its first three satellites and will soon be able to provide *real-time video anywhere on earth to a one-meter resolution*. Emiliano Kargieman, the founder of Satellogic, estimates the total cost of launching his fleet will be less than $200 million. All-told, this new breed of satellite companies is operating at one-ten-thousandth the cost and delivering about 100x better performance than twenty years ago—a millionfold increase. Now that's an Iridium Moment.

KEY TAKEAWAYS

- The experts in many fields will project linearly in times of exponential change.
- The explosive transition from film to digital photography is now occurring in several accelerating technologies.
- We are information-enabling everything.
- An information-enabled environment delivers fundamentally disruptive opportunities.
- Even traditional industries are ripe for disruption.

CHAPTER TWO
A TALE OF TWO COMPANIES

In one of the most iconic moments in modern business history, Steve Jobs rocked the world in January 2007 with his announcement of the Apple iPhone, which debuted six months later.

Literally everything in high tech changed that day—indeed, you might even call it a Singularity—as all existing strategies in consumer electronics were instantly rendered obsolete. At that moment, the entire future of the digital world had to be reconsidered.

Two months later, Finnish mobile phone giant Nokia spent a staggering $8.1 billion to buy Navteq, a navigation and road-mapping company. Nokia pursued Navteq because the latter dominated the in-road traffic sensor industry. Nokia concluded that control of those sensors would enable it to dominate mapping and mobile and online local information—assets that would act as a defensive barrier against the increasing market predations of Google and Apple.

The stratospheric price tag represented Navteq's near-monopoly of the road sensor industry. In Europe alone, Navteq's sensors covered approximately a quarter-million miles in thirty-five major cities across thirteen countries. Nokia was convinced that global, Navteq-powered, real-time traffic monitoring would enable it to both compete with Google's growing presence in real-time data and fend off Apple's revolutionary new product.

That was the theory, at least. Unfortunately for Nokia, a small Israeli company called Waze was founded around the same time.

Instead of making a massive capital investment in in-road sensor hardware, the founders of Waze chose instead to crowdsource location information by leveraging the GPS sensors on its users' phones—the new world of smartphones just announced at Apple by Steve Jobs—to capture traffic information. Within two years, Waze was gathering traffic data from as many sources as Navteq had road sensors, and within four years it had ten times as many sources. What's more, the cost of adding each new source was essentially zero, not to mention that Waze's users regularly upgraded their phones—and thus Waze's information base. In contrast, the Navteq system cost a fortune to upgrade.

Nokia made a gigantic defensive bet in acquiring an asset in the hopes of making an end-run around the iPhone. It was the kind of move that is celebrated in business—if it succeeds, that is. But because Nokia didn't understand the larger, exponential implications of Leveraged Assets (see Chapter Three), the effort failed spectacularly. By June 2012, Nokia's market valuation had tumbled from $140 billion to $8.2 billion—pretty much what it spent to acquire Navteq. Not only had the world's largest mobile phone company lost its lead but because it had also lost the capital needed to claw its way back, it also likely lost its role as a leading industry player forever.

In June 2013 Google acquired Waze for $1.1 billion. At that time, the company had no infrastructure, no hardware and no more than one hundred employees. What it did have, however, was fifty million users. More precisely, Waze had fifty million "human traffic sensors," double those of just a year before. That number has probably doubled again since then, to one hundred million location sensors globally.

Nokia followed the old linear rules and bought physical infrastructure (remember Iridium?), hoping it would prove to be a competitive barrier. It was, of course, but only for in-road sensor users, not against information-enabled mobile phone application designers. In contrast, Waze leapfrogged the world of physical sensors simply by piggybacking on its users' smart phones.

In a real-time epilogue to the Nokia/Navteq story, as we write this, Microsoft has acquired Nokia's cell phone device business and patent portfolio for $7.2 billion, or about $1 billion less than Nokia paid for Navteq. Just as Nokia has fallen far from its early lead in the cell phone industry, Microsoft has struggled to gain share for its Windows Phone software.

Microsoft's stated rationale for the Nokia deal is to accelerate its share and profits in phones; to create a first-rate Microsoft phone experience for users; to prevent Google and Apple from foreclosing app innovation, integration, distribution and economics; and to avail itself of an outsized financial opportunity fueled by growth in the smartphone industry. Time will tell how this scenario plays out, and whether Nokia's acquisition is a case of linear, exponential or just an intellectual property land grab.

The story of Waze versus Navteq is important, and relevant to this book, not just because of who won and who lost, but also because of the fundamental difference in the two companies' approaches to *ownership*. Nokia spent enormous resources to purchase and own billions of dollars in physical assets, while Waze simply accessed information already available on user-owned technology.

The former is a classic example of linear thinking, the latter of exponential thinking. While Nokia's linear strategy was dependent on the speed of physical installation, Waze benefited from the exponentially faster speed at which information can be accessed and shared.

From time immemorial, human beings have worked to own "stuff" and then trade access to it. This behavior started in tribes, was adopted by clans, and then later spread to nations, empires, and most recently, global markets, making possible ever-larger human institutions. Value has always been generated by owning more land, more equipment, more machinery, more people. Ownership was the perfect strategy for managing scarce resources and ensuring a relatively predictable, stable environment.

The more you had—that is, the more value you "owned"—the wealthier and more powerful you were. To manage that asset, of course, you needed people. Lots of them. If a plot of land was twice as big, you needed twice as many people to farm or protect it. Luckily, our span of control didn't reach very far across the landscape, so this was a perfectly workable arrangement.

Once we reached a critical mass of people needed to manage or protect our owned assets, we created hierarchies—in every tribe or village, there was an implicit or explicit hierarchical order to the power structure. The bigger the tribe, the bigger the hierarchy. Then, beginning in the Middle Ages but fully taking hold with the Industrial Revolution and rise of the modern corporation, that local, hierarchical thinking was mapped onto companies and into governmental structures, a design that with only limited modification has held ever since.

Today, we still manage and measure ourselves on this linear scale. That is: x amount of work takes y amount of resources, 2x needs 2y, and so on of ever-greater *arithmetic* magnitude.

Automation, mass production, robotics and even virtualization with computers altered the slope of this line, but it still remained linear. If one concrete mixer truck replaces one hundred laborers hand-mixing concrete, two trucks replace two hundred laborers. Similarly, much of society is also measured on this basis: the number of doctors per 100,000 patients, class size per teacher, GDP and energy per capita. Labor is paid hourly, as are legal fees, and housing is priced by the square foot.

In business, the way we build most products and services continues to mirror this linear, incremental, sequential thinking. Thus, the classic way to build a product, be it a giant airliner or a thumbnail-sized microprocessor, is through a template stage-gate process called New Product Development, or NPD, which includes the following steps:

1. Idea generation
2. Idea screening
3. Concept development and testing

4. Business analysis
5. Beta and market testing
6. Technical implementation
7. Commercialization
8. New product pricing

So codified is this process into the DNA of modern business there is even a designated industry association for it, called the Product Development and Management Association (PDMA).

You might think that while this old-fashioned linear approach is still widespread among mature industries, it has long been abandoned in the world of hot new technologies. You would be wrong. The linear process remains pervasive across the world economy, taking on different names in its different iterations. In software, for example, it's been called the *waterfall approach*. And while new development methods, like Agile, have cropped up to short-circuit this approach and parallelize some of the steps, the basic paradigm is still linear and incremental. Whether you are making locomotives or iPhone apps, linear product development remains the predominant name of the game. See the diagram below, noting that this works when both problem and desired solution are precisely known

Traditional Product Development

WATERFALL

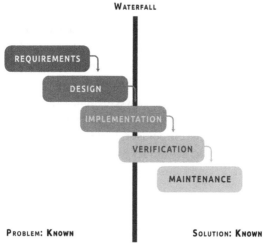

REQUIREMENTS

DESIGN

IMPLEMENTATION

VERIFICATION

MAINTENANCE

PROBLEM: KNOWN   SOLUTION: KNOWN

When you think linearly, when your operations are linear, and when your measures of performance and success are linear, you cannot help but end up with a linear organization, one that sees the world through a linear lens—as did even multi-billion dollar, technologically cutting-edge Nokia. Such an organization cannot help but have many of the following characteristics:

- Top-down and hierarchical in its organization
- Driven by financial outcomes
- Linear, sequential thinking
- Innovation primarily from within
- Strategic planning largely an extrapolation from the past
- Risk intolerance
- Process inflexibility
- Large number of employees
- Controls own assets
- Strongly invested in status quo

As noted business author John Hagel said: "Our organizations are set up to withstand change from the outside," rather than to embrace those changes even when they are useful. Aerospace engineer Burt Rutan's corollary to this is, "Defend and don't question."

Not surprisingly, given all of these characteristics, linear organizations will rarely disrupt their own products or services. They haven't the tools, the attitude or the perspective to do so. What they will do, and what they are built to do, is to keep getting bigger in order to take advantage of economies of scale. *Scale*—but linear scale—is the raison d'être of the linear organization. John Seely Brown calls this "scalable efficiency" and maintains that it is the paradigm that drives most corporate strategy and corporate architectures. Clayton Christensen immortalized this type of thinking in his business classic, *The Innovator's Dilemma: When New Technologies Cause Great Firms to Fall.*

Most large organizations use what is called a *matrix structure.* Product management, marketing and sales are often aligned vertically, and support functions such as legal, HR, finance and

IT are usually horizontal. So the person handling legal for a product has two reporting lines, one to the head of product, who has revenue accountability, and the other to the head of legal, whose job it is to ensure consistency across numerous products. This is great for command and control, but it's terrible for accountability, speed and risk tolerance. Every time you try to do something, you have to get authorization from all the muckety-mucks in HR, legal, accounting and so on, which takes time.

Another major issue Salim has observed with matrix structures is that, over time, power accrues to the horizontals. Often, HR or legal have no incentive to say yes, so their default answer becomes no (which is why HR is often referred to as "inhuman resources"). It's not that HR people are bad people. But, over time, their incentives end up at cross-purposes with those of product managers.

Over the last few decades, the race to capture economies of scale has resulted in an explosion of large globalized corporations. At the same time, the pressure for higher and higher margins has led to offshoring, international expansion and mega-mergers in the name of cutting costs, increasing revenues and improving the bottom line.

But each of these changes comes at great cost, because the flip side of size is flexibility. However hard they try, large companies with extensive facilities filled with tens of thousands of employees scattered around the world are challenged to operate nimbly in a fast-moving world. In his analysis of exponential disruption, Hagel also notes: "One of the key issues in an exponential world…is that whatever understanding you have today is going to rapidly become obsolete, and so you have to continue to refresh your education about the technologies and about the organizational capabilities. That's going to be very challenging." Rapid or disruptive change is something that large, matrixed organizations find extremely difficult. Indeed, those who have attempted it have found that the organization's "immune system" is liable to respond to the perceived threat with an attack. Gabriel Baldinucci, Chief Strategy Officer at

Singularity University and a former principal at Virgin Group's U.S. venture arm, has observed that there are two levels of immune responses. The first is to defend the core business because it's the status quo; the second is to defend yourself as an individual because there's more ROI for you than for the organization.

What makes traditional companies highly efficient at expansion and growth as long as market conditions remain unchanged is also what makes them extremely vulnerable to disruption. As Peter Thiel said, "Globalization is moving from one to N copying existing products. That was the 20th century. Now in the 21st century we move into a world where zero to one and creating new products will increasingly be a priority for companies due to the rise of different exponential technologies."

Whatever else they may be, big companies aren't stupid. They know about this structural weakness and many are striving to fix it. For example, one of Larry Page's first steps upon becoming CEO of Google in April 2011 was to strip management layers and flatten the organization. Similar programs have been implemented at Haier, in China, and other large organizations. While some of these fixes have proven successful, in the longer term, such flattening is merely a stopgap, because the total number of employees—the financial weight and resistance to change—rarely diminishes.

Of course, not all industries are "going lean." One industry headed in the opposite direction is pharmaceuticals—to what we believe will be the industry's regret. Once the low-hanging fruit of blockbuster drugs began winding down around 2012,[1] instead of breaking into smaller, more flexible units, Big Pharma chose to pursue the consolidations and mergers that seemed to make Wall Street happy. We believe that increased size will reduce the flexibility of pharmaceutical companies even further, thus increasing their exposure to disruption.

One exemplar of that pending disruption is teenager Jack Andraka, who at the age of fourteen single-handedly developed

1   www.fool.com/investing/general/2013/02/28/big-pharmas-blockbuster-battle.aspx

an early-stage detection test for pancreatic cancer that costs just three cents. His approach (awaiting peer review) is 26,000 times cheaper, 400 times more sensitive, and 126 times faster than today's diagnostics. Big Pharma has no idea how to deal with Jack, who is one of many wunderkinds emerging globally, all of them with the potential to disrupt great companies and long-established industries. The Jacks of the world bring exponential thinking to our linear world—and nothing is going to stop them.

Getting back to the Navteq versus Waze story, one thing we hope to make clear is that traditional linear thinking doesn't work in an exponential world. Simply put, it cannot compete. Salim saw this firsthand at Yahoo in 2007, which despite its web bona fides, operated within a classic linear matrix organizational structure. Every time a new product was launched or an old one modified, the team behind it had to jump through several clearance hoops—branding, legal, privacy and PR, etc.—each step taking days or weeks, which meant that by the time anything finally landed in the consumer Internet space, it was usually too late; some startup or another had already gotten traction. Salim's conclusion about one root cause of Yahoo's troubles is that its organizational structure is antithetical to the industry.

Yahoo is hardly alone. Even the mighty Google struggles with this. It took two years and enormous effort to get Google+ out the door. Even though the product is brilliantly crafted, by the time of its launch in the summer of 2011, Facebook had an almost insurmountable lead.

As we saw in Chapter One, this pace of change isn't going to slow down anytime soon. In fact, Moore's Law all but guarantees that it will continue to speed up—and speed up exponentially—for at least several decades. And given the cross impact into other technologies, if the last fifteen years has seen enormous disruption in the business world, the next fifteen will make that disruption seem tame by comparison.

Internet companies have changed the way we advertise and market. They have transformed the world of newspapers and publishing. And they have profoundly changed the way we communicate and interact with one another. One reason for that change is that the cost of distributing a product or service, particularly if can be converted almost entirely to information, has dropped almost to zero. It used to require millions of dollars in servers and software to launch a software company. Thanks to Amazon Web Services (AWS), it now costs just a tiny fraction of that amount. Similar stories can be found in every department in every industry of the modern economy.

History and common sense make clear that you cannot radically transform every part of an organization—and accelerate the underlying clock of that enterprise to hyper-speed—without fundamentally changing the nature of that organization. Which is why, over the last few years, a new organizational scheme congruent with these changes has begun to emerge. We call it the Exponential Organization precisely because it represents the structure best suited to address the accelerated, non-linear, web-driven pace of modern life. And while even cutting-edge traditional companies can only achieve arithmetic outputs per input, an ExO achieves geometric outputs per input by riding the doubling-exponential pattern of information-based technologies.

To achieve this scalability, new ExO organizations such as Waze are turning the traditional organization inside out. Rather than owning assets or workforces and incrementally seeing a return on those assets, ExOs leverage external resources to achieve their objectives. For example, they maintain a very small core of employees and facilities, allowing enormous flexibility as margins soar. They enlist their customers and leverage offline and online communities in everything from product design to application development. They float atop the existing and emerging infrastructure rather than trying to own it. And they grow at incredible rates precisely because they aren't dedicated to owning their market, but rather to *enlisting* it to their purposes. A great example is Medium, which is disrupting the magazine business by relying on its users to provide long-form articles.

It is our belief that ExOs will overwhelm traditional linear organizations in most industries because they take better advantage of the information-based externalities inaccessible to older structures, a feat that will empower them to grow faster—shockingly faster—than their linear counterparts, and then accelerate from there.

It's hard to pin down exactly when this new organizational form emerged. Various aspects of ExOs have been around for decades, but it is only over the last few years that they have really started to matter. If we had to pick an official ExO origin date, it would be March 2006, when Amazon launched Amazon Web Services and created the low-cost "Cloud" for medium and small businesses. From that date on, the cost of running a data center moved from a fixed CAPEX (Capital Expenditure) cost to a variable cost. Today, it is almost impossible to find a single startup that doesn't use AWS.

We have even found a simple metric that helps to identify and distinguish emerging Exponential Organizations: *a minimum 10x improvement in output over four to five years.*

The following shows some ExOs and their minimum 10x performance inprovement over their peers:

Airbnb Hotels	90x more listings per employee
GitHub Software	109x more repositories per employee
Local Motors Automotive	1000x cheaper to produce new car model, 5-22x faster process for a car to produce (depending on vehicle)
Quirky Consumer Goods	10x faster product development (29 days vs 300 days)
Google Ventures Investments	2.5x more investments in early stage startups, 10x faster through design process
Valve Gaming	30x more market cap per employee
Tesla Automotive	30x more market cap per employee
Tangerine (formerly ING Direct Canada) Banking	7x more customers per employee, 4x more deposits per customer

Look again at Waze. By harnessing information on its users' phones, Waze currently has one hundred times the traffic movement signals that Navteq/Nokia acquired by buying the physical sensors buried in roads. Even though Waze was just a tiny startup company with just a few dozen employees, it quickly ran down and overtook the linear Nokia, despite its thousands of employees. Nokia thought it dominated the mobile phone world—and while it once had, within the new paradigm it didn't stand a chance.

Two key factors enabled Waze to succeed, and those two factors hold true for all next-generation ExO companies:

- *Access resources you don't own.* In Waze's case, the company made use of the GPS readings already on its users' smartphones.
- *Information is your greatest asset.* More reliably than any other asset, information has the potential to double regularly. Rather than simply assembling assets, the key to success is accessing valuable caches of existing information. Andrew Rasiej, chairman of the New York Tech Meetup, said it best: "I think of Waze as a civics app. It's collecting information about the movement of cars and people in public places. What else could you do with that data?"

Taking Rasiej's observation a step further, the real, fundamental question of our exponential age is: *What else can be information-enabled?*

The key outcome when you access resources and information-enable them is that your marginal costs drop to zero. Quite possibly the granddaddy of information-based ExOs is Google, which doesn't own the web pages it scans. Its revenue model, the butt of many jokes ten years ago, has enabled Google to become a $400 billion company, a milestone it reached by essentially manipulating textual (and now video) information. LinkedIn and Facebook together are worth over $200 billion, and that's just as a result of digitizing our relationships—that is, turning them into information. It is our belief that most great new enterprises in the years to come will either build their businesses off new sources of information or by converting previously analog environments into information. And that environment increasingly includes hardware (sensors, 3D printers/scanners, biotech, etc.): As noted earlier, the Tesla S, which has just seventeen different moving parts in its drivetrain, can be thought of as computer masquerading as a supremely capable luxury car, one that it updates itself every week via a software download.

This search for new sources of information that can underpin new companies and businesses is at the heart of the revolution often labeled Big Data. By combining vast stores of data with powerful new analytical tools, there is an opportunity to see the world in a new way—and to turn the resulting information into new business opportunities.

Sources of this Big Data are emerging everywhere. For example, we mentioned the three separate initiatives for low Earth orbit (LEO) satellite systems that within a few years will deliver real-time video and images anywhere on the planet. Despite the inevitable privacy and security concerns bound to arise with the launch of LEO satellite systems, there is no doubt that scores, even hundreds, of new businesses will emerge from access to this massive new information source.

For instance, what if you could count the number of cars in any or all Sears or Walmart parking lots throughout the country? Or predict natural calamities like tsunamis and typhoons, as well as their impact? Or measure the increasing wattage along the Amazon River at night? Or track every container ship, in real time, around the world? Soon you can—either via nanosatellites or global Internet access initiatives such a Google's Project Loon and Facebook's drones strategies.

Even closer down this road is the Google autonomous automobile. The key navigational technology it uses is light radar, also known as *lidar*. Each car has a spinning lidar unit on its roof that creates a live 3D map of its surroundings to a range of about one hundred meters. As it moves, a Google car collects almost a gigabyte of data per second and creates a 3D image of its surroundings to within a one-centimeter resolution. It can even compare two images to get a perfect before-and-after analysis. If you move a plant off your front porch, if you leave a window open or if your teenager sneaks out of his or her bedroom at night, Google will know.

This is not just static information. It is also *dynamic* information—data that registers the natural world not simply as it is, but as it changes. Mountains (petabytes) of data can be analytically sliced and diced to discover previously unknown truths about the world around us—truths that will result in opportunities currently unimaginable.

As outlined earlier, traditional organizational structures, designed over the last few hundred years to hierarchically manage physical assets or people, are rapidly becoming obsolete. To compete in our rapidly changing world, we need a new kind of organization, one that is not only able manage this change, but also thrives on it.

We opened Chapter One with a discussion of what we refer to as the Iridium Moment. By ironic coincidence, the extinction of the dinosaurs was revealed by an iridium layer in rock formations; this time around, the destructive agent is an Information Comet. What if we are having another, collective Iridium Moment? One that doesn't just involve a single giant corporation that has failed to recognize the revolutionary nature of the technological change taking place around it, but a whole *species*—indeed the dominant species—of large corporations in the modern economy. What if they are all facing the same fate as Iridium?

That question, and the quest for a strategy that both established and new companies can use to survive and thrive in this new world will be the subject of the rest of this book. Exponential Organizations have the capability to adapt to this new world of deep and ubiquitous information and convert it to competitive advantage. The ExO, in fact, is the appropriate commercial response to our new exponential world.

We'll next take a closer look at this remarkable new organizational form: how it works, how it is organized, how it scales its operations and why it will succeed in a transformed marketplace when other, established organizational schemes won't. Most of all, we will explore why, if we are to succeed in business, the Exponential Organization is our destiny.

KEY TAKEAWAYS

- Our organizational structures have evolved to manage scarcity. The concept of ownership works well for scarcity, but accessing or sharing works better in an abundant, information-based world.
- While the information-based world is now moving exponentially, our organizational structures are still very linear (especially large ones).
- We've learned how to scale technology; now it's time to scale the organization.
- Matrix structures don't work in an exponential, information-based world.
- ExOs have learned how to organize around an information-based world.

David S. Rose, author of the bestselling book *Angel Investing: The Gust Guide to Making Money and Having Fun Investing in Startups*, sums it up more dramatically:

> "Any company designed for success in the 20th century is doomed to failure in the 21st."

CHAPTER THREE
THE EXPONENTIAL ORGANIZATION

The modern corporation takes great pride in how fast it can bring products and services to market compared to companies in the past. Annual reports, advertisements and speeches trumpet how companies have virtualized, accelerated supply chains, shortened approval cycles and improved distribution channels.

The result is that it now takes an average of between two hundred fifty and three hundred days for a typical Consumer Packaged Goods (CPG) company to move a new product from invention to retail stores' shelves—and that, believe it or not, is considered a blistering pace.

Consider Quirky, a pioneering Exponential Organization in the same CPG industry. It accomplishes this same cycle in just twenty-nine days. That's twenty-nine days from idea generation to seeing the product on sale at your local Walmart.

A traditional car company spends about $3 billion to bring a new car model to market. Local Motors, an ExO, accomplishes the same thing for just $3 million—a 1,000x improvement, albeit not to the same production scale.

Next, consider Airbnb, a company that leverages users' extra bedrooms. Founded in 2008, Airbnb currently has 1,324 employees and operates 500,000 listings in 33,000 cities. However, Airbnb owns no physical assets and is worth almost $10 billion. That's more than the value of Hyatt Hotels, which has 45,000 employees spread across 549 properties. And while Hyatt's business is comparatively flat, Airbnb's number of room-nights delivered is growing exponentially. At its current pace, Airbnb will be the biggest hotelier in the world by late 2015.

Airbnb

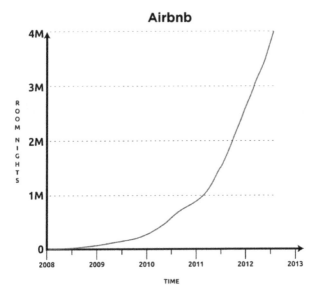

Similarly, Uber, the Airbnb of cars—Uber converts private automobiles into taxis—has been valued at $17 billion. Like Airbnb, Uber has no assets, no workforce (to speak of) and is also growing exponentially.

If you don't find these valuations sufficiently eye-opening, go back and read them again—this time reminding yourself that each of these Exponential Organizations is *fewer than six years old*.

As we saw with Waze in Chapter Two, there are two fundamental drivers that enable ExOs to achieve this level of scalability. The first is that some aspect of the company's product has been information-enabled and thus, following Moore's Law, can take on the doubling characteristics of information growth.

The second is that, thanks to the fact that information is essentially liquid, major business functions can be transferred outside of the organization—to users, fans, partners or the general public. (We'll revisit this concept later.)

Let's now examine the major characteristics of Exponential Organizations. Based on our research—which includes the top one hundred fastest growing startups worldwide over the last six years—we have identified common traits across all ExOs. They include a *Massive Transformative Purpose* (MTP), as well as ten other attributes that reflect the internal mechanisms and externalities they're leveraging to achieve exponential growth. We use the acronym *SCALE* to reflect the five external attributes, and the acronym *IDEAS* for the five internal attributes. Not every ExO has all ten attributes but the more it has, the more scalable it tends to be. Our research indicates that a minimum of four implemented attributes will achieve the ExO label and have you accelerate away from your competition.

In this chapter we will look at the Massive Transformative Purpose and the five external attributes that comprise SCALE. In the next chapter we will investigate the five internal attributes that make up IDEAS. A good metaphor we will use to frame ExO attributes is the two hemispheres of the brain. The right brain manages growth, creativity and uncertainty, while the left brain focuses on order, control and stability.

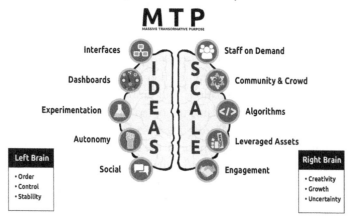

MASSIVE TRANSFORMATIVE PURPOSE (MTP)

Exponential Organizations, almost by definition, think BIG. There's a good reason for that: if a company thinks small, it is unlikely to pursue a business strategy that will achieve rapid growth. Even if the company somehow manages to achieve an impressive level of growth, the scale of its business will quickly outpace its business model and leave the company lost and directionless. Thus, ExOs *must* aim high.

That's why, when we look at the position statements of existing Exponential Organizations, we encounter statements of purpose that might have seemed outrageous in years past:

- **TED:** "Ideas worth spreading."
- **Google:** "Organize the world's information."
- **X Prize Foundation:** "Bring about radical breakthroughs for the benefit of humanity."
- **Quirky:** "Make invention accessible."
- **Singularity University:** "Positively impact one billion people."

At first glance, these statements may seem to align with the trend in recent years to rewrite corporate statements to be shorter, simpler and more generalized. But on closer inspection, you'll note that each of the statements is also very *aspirational*. None states what the organization does, but rather what it aspires to accomplish. The aspirations are neither narrow nor even technology-specific. Rather, they aim to capture the hearts and minds—and imaginations and ambitions—of those both inside and (especially) outside the organization.

This, then, is the *Massive Transformative Purpose*, or MTP— the higher, aspirational purpose of the organization. Every ExO we know has one. Some aim to transform the planet, others just an industry. But radical transformation is the name of the game. And while companies of the past might have felt embarrassed to make such claims, today's ExO declares with sincerity and confidence that it intends to accomplish near-miracles. Even a company in a comparatively small market can "think MTP": Dollar Shave Club, for example, is transforming the shaving industry with the mantra "A dollar a month."

It's important to note that an MTP is *not* a mission statement. Consider Cisco's mission statement, which is neither inspirational nor aspirational: "Shape the future of the Internet by creating unprecedented value and opportunity for our customers, employees, investors, and ecosystem partners." While there's some Purpose there, and it's somewhat Massive, it's certainly not Transformative. Furthermore, it is a statement that could be used by at least a dozen Internet companies. If we were to write Cisco's MTP, it would likely be something along the lines of, "Connecting everyone, everything, everywhere—all the time." Now *that* would be exciting.

The most important outcome of a proper MTP is that it generates a cultural movement—what John Hagel and John Seely Brown call the "Power of Pull." That is, the MTP is so inspirational that a community forms around the ExO and spontaneously begins operating on its own, ultimately creating its own community, tribe and culture. Think of those lines outside the Apple Store or the waiting lists for TED's annual conference. Each has an emergent ecosystem so excited about that product or service that it literally pulls the products and services out from the core organization and assumes its own ownership, complete with marketing, support services, and even design and manufacturing. Consider the Apple iPhone: with a universe of supporting products and a million user-generated applications, who really owns it?

This cultural shift inspired by the MTP has its own secondary effects. For one thing, it moves the focal point of a team from internal politics to external impact. Most contemporary large companies are internally focused and often have lost touch—except through rigid and formalized marketing surveys and focus groups—with their market and customers.

In our increasingly volatile world, this perspective can be fatal. It is critical for a modern enterprise to constantly look outward—not least to spot a rapidly approaching technological or competitive threat. If you're at Google, you are constantly asking yourself (as per the company's statement): "How can I better organize the world's information?" At Singularity University the question we ask ourselves at every turning point is: "Will this positively impact a billion people?"

The biggest imperative of a worthy MTP is its *Purpose*. Building on the seminal work by Simon Sinek, the Purpose must answer two critical "why" questions:

- Why do this work?
- Why does the organization exist?

An MTP as a Competitive Edge

A strong MTP is especially advantageous to "first movers." If the MTP is sufficiently sweeping, there's no place for competitors to go but *beneath it*. After all, it would be very hard for another organization to pop up and announce, "We're *also* going to organize the world's information, but better." Once companies realize this singular advantage we can expect a land grab of genuine MTPs in the near future.

A strong MTP also serves as an excellent recruiter for new talent, as well as a magnet for retaining top talent—both increasingly difficult propositions in today's hypercompetitive talent marketplace. In addition, an MTP serves as a stabilizing force during periods of random growth and enables organizations to scale with less turbulence.

The MTP is not only an effective attractor and retainer for customers and employees but also for the company ecosystem at large (developers, startups, hackers, NGOs, governments, suppliers, partners, etc.). As a result, it lowers the acquisition, transaction and retention costs of these stakeholders.

MTPs don't operate in isolation. Rather, they create a penumbra around them that influences every part of the organization. A prime early indicator is Red Bull, whose MTP is "Giving You Wings."

That's why, over time, we can expect brands to blend into MTPs, along the way becoming increasingly aspirational. Why? Because aspirational brands create positive feedback loops in the ExO's community: customers feel good about the products and are increasingly proud to be part of a larger, virtuous movement. Aspirational branding helps lower costs, improves effectiveness and speeds learning by leveraging intrinsic, rather than external, motivation.

There is also an economic advantage in embracing an MTP. The world is facing many grand challenges, and as Peter Diamandis says, "the world's biggest problems are the world's biggest markets." As a result, over the next decade we expect even shareholders to incorporate MTPs into their stock portfolio strategies.

As an analog to MTPs, we also see a worldwide increase in social enterprises. A study by the G8 in 2013 estimates there are 688,000 social enterprises, generating $270 billion annually.[1] These organizations come in many forms (Benefit or B Corporations, Triple Bottom Line, L3Cs, the Conscious Capital movement, the Slow Money movement) and leverage their MTPs to integrate social and environmental issues—as well as profits—into their business processes. This trend started with the rise of corporate social responsibility (CSR) programs in organizations. In 2012, 57 percent of the Fortune 500 published a CSR report—double the number from the previous year.[2] The difference is that CSR initiatives are add-ons to most companies' core business; for social enterprises, CSR initiatives *are* the core business.

Martin Seligman, a leading expert on positive psychology, differentiates between three states of happiness: the pleasurable life (hedonistic, superficial), the good life (family and friends) and the meaningful life (finding purpose, transcending ego, working toward a higher good). Research shows that Millennials—those born between 1984 and 2002—are showing an orientation towards seeking meaning and purpose in their lives.[3] Worldwide, they are becoming increasingly aspirational and, as such, will be drawn as customers, employees and investors to equally aspirational organizations—that is, to companies that have MTPs

---

1   www.gov.uk/government/publications/g8-factsheet-social-investment-and-social-enterprise/g8-factsheet-social-investment-and-social-enterprise

2   www.sustainablebrands.com/news_and_views/articles/sustain ability-reporting-among-sp-500-companies-increases-dramatically

3   www.bcgperspectives.com/content/articles/consumer_insight_marketing_millennial_consumer/

and live up to their tenets. In fact, we expect to see individuals coming up with their own MTPs, which will juxtapose, overlap and symbiotically exist with the organization's MTP.

According to the United Nations, extreme poverty has decreased 80 percent over the last thirty years, including among a majority of the five billion people who will be online by 2020. We predict they'll all be climbing Maslow's Hierarchy of Needs in search of Self-Actualization. (And isn't that just a complicated way of describing an MTP?)

Why Important?	Dependencies or Prerequisites
• Enables coherent exponential growth • Binds collective aspirations • Attracts top talent across the ecosystem • Supports a cooperative/non-political culture • Enables agility and learning	• Must be unique • Leaders must walk the walk • Must support all three letters in acronym

Now that we understand the meaning and purpose of the Massive Transformative Purpose, it's time to look at the five external characteristics that define an Exponential Organization, for which we use the acronym SCALE:

- **S**taff on Demand
- **C**ommunity & Crowd
- **A**lgorithms
- **L**everaged Assets
- **E**ngagement

STAFF ON DEMAND

In a 2012 white paper for the Aspen Institute, Michael Chui, a partner at the McKinsey Global Institute, described employment theory in the 20th century as follows:

> The best way to harness human talent is through full-time, exclusive employment relationships where people are paid for the amount of time they spend at a common location. They should be organized in stable hierarchies where they are evaluated primarily through the judgment of their superiors, and what and how they do their jobs is prescribed.

Chui then proceeds to dismantle every phrase in that paragraph to show how fundamentally out of date that theory has become in little more than a decade. Literally *none* of it applies today.

For any ExO, having Staff on Demand is a necessary characteristic for speed, functionality and flexibility in a fast-changing world. Leveraging personnel outside the base organization is key to creating and running a successful ExO. The fact is, no matter how talented your employees, chances are that most of them are becoming obsolete and uncompetitive right before your eyes.

As John Seely Brown has noted, the half-life of a learned skill used to be about thirty years. Today it's down to about five years. In his recent book, *The Startup of You*, LinkedIn founder Reid Hoffman notes that individuals will increasingly learn to manage themselves as companies, with brand management (MTP!), and marketing and sales functions all brought down to the individual. Similarly, Ronald Coase, who won the Nobel Prize in Economics in 1991, noted that enterprises are more like families than industries, and that corporations are more of a sociological construct than an economic one.

For any company today, having a permanent, full-time workforce is fraught with growing peril as employees fail to keep their skills up to date, resulting in personnel in need of greater management. In our fast-changing global and Internet-driven marketplace, increasingly desperate organizations are turning to external and temporary workforces to fill their expertise gaps. For example, in an effort to keep the overall skills of the organization fresh, AMP, Australia's largest insurance company, requires that half its 2,600-strong IT department be made up of contractors. According to Annalie Killian, a global executive at AMP, such a requirement is not just helpful; in this day and age, it's mandatory.

While maintaining permanent staff is likely to remain more important in certain equipment- and capital-intensive industries such as shipping, mining or construction, in any information-enabled business a large internal staff seems increasingly unnecessary, counterproductive and expensive. And the old argument that freelancers and contractors only increase the bureaucracy needed to manage them quickly falls away too: thanks to the Internet, the cost of finding and tracking outside staff drops almost to zero. In addition, due to the rapid rise in the number of Internet users, the volume and quality of freelancers has gone up dramatically in the last ten years.

Gigwalk, which relies on half a million smart-phone-enabled workers, offers an example of how this new world of employment works. When Proctor and Gamble needs to know how and where its merchandise is being placed on Walmart shelves around the world, it can use Gigwalk's platform to instantly deploy thousands of people who are paid a few dollars to walk into Walmart and check the shelves. Results come in within an hour.

Staff-on-demand initiatives similar to Gigwalk are springing up everywhere: oDesk, Roamler, Elance, TaskRabbit and Amazon's venerable Mechanical Turk are platforms where all levels of work, including highly skilled labor, can be outsourced. These companies, which represent just the first wave of this new business model, optimize the concept of paying for performance to lower customer risk.

For talented workers, working on and getting paid for multiple projects is a particularly welcome opportunity. But there's another angle as well: an increase in the diversity of ideas. The data science company Kaggle, for example, offers a platform that hosts private and public algorithm contests in which more than 185,000 data scientists around the world vie for prizes and recognition. In 2011, Insurance giant Allstate, with forty of the best actuaries and data scientists money could buy, wanted to see if its claims algorithm could be improved upon, so it ran a contest on Kaggle.

It turned out that the Allstate algorithm, which has been carefully optimized for over six decades, was bested within three days by 107 competing teams. Three months later, when the contest ended, Allstate's original algorithm had been improved 271 percent. And while the prize set the company back $10,000, the resulting cost savings due to better algorithms was estimated to be in the tens of millions annually. Quite an interesting ROI.

In fact, in every one of Kaggle's 150 contests to date, external data scientists have beaten the internal algorithms, often by a wide margin. And in most cases outsiders (non-experts) have beaten the experts in a particular domain, which shows the power of fresh thinking and diverse perspectives.

In years past, having a large workforce differentiated your enterprise and allowed it to accomplish more. Today, that same large workforce can become an anchor that reduces maneuverability and slows you down. Moreover, traditional industries have great difficulty attracting on-demand high-skill workers such as data scientists because the available positions are perceived as being low in terms of opportunity and high in terms of bureaucratic obstacles. A study commissioned by Deloitte found that 98 percent of recent data science graduates went to work for Google, Facebook, LinkedIn or various startups. That doesn't leave much talent left over for everybody else.

That said, even Google's workforce of 50,000 very smart employees pales in comparison to the collective intelligence of the 2.4 billion people online today. We have no doubt that the extraordinary capabilities of this massive collection of intellectual capital will eventually emerge. In the words of Chris Anderson, the former editor-in-chief of *Wired* magazine:

> The reality is that most of the world's smartest people don't have the right credentials. They don't speak the right language. They didn't grow up in the right country. They didn't go to the right university. They don't know about you and you don't know about them. They're not available, and they already have a job.

As we conducted research for this book, it quickly became apparent how easy it is to outsource anything and everything. In fact, Timothy Ferris, author of the bestselling *4-Hour Workweek,* has pioneered many new ideas around this topic.

A firm called Advisory Board Architects (ABA) presents a fascinating example of how to take the Staff-on-Demand concept to a whole new level. ABA noticed two issues with company boards: First, as Jaime Grego-Mayer, a partner at ABA, notes, "95 percent of all boards are simply not managed," since most of a CEO's attention goes to managing the company. Second, removing a non-performing board member can be a delicate and political matter; because it's embarrassing for the CEO, it usually doesn't happen. ABA offers companies a human resources department for boards, allowing CEOs to outsource the management and tracking of the company board to the firm. ABA establishes metrics for each board member (for example, three phone calls per month to open doors) and then tracks those metrics. If a board member is not performing, and a difficult conversation is needed to push that member out, ABA handles it, relieving pressure on the CEO.

In 2010, the world had 1.2 billion people online globally. By 2020, that number will reach five billion. Nearly three billion more people and their brains will be available to work via smartphones, tablets or at Internet cafes. The capabilities that will be unleashed are beyond imagination. Against this onslaught, what traditional organization, bogged down with permanent, full-time employees, can endure?

Why Important?	Dependencies or Prerequisites
• Enables learning (fresh perspectives) • Allows agility • Forms stronger bonds among core team	• Interfaces to manage SoD • Clear task specifications

COMMUNITY & CROWD
Community

Since May 2007, Chris Anderson has been building a community called DIY Drones. Now almost 55,000 members strong, this community has been able to design and build a drone that is very similar to the Predator drone used by the U.S. military (in fact, the DIY drone features 98 percent of the Predator's functionality).

But there's one major difference: A Predator costs $4 million. The DIY drone costs just $300.

Granted, a great deal of that 2 percent difference in performance can be attributed to the weapons systems...but still, how is this possible?

It's possible because Anderson has tapped into a large group of passionate enthusiasts who contribute time and expertise. "If you build communities and you do things in public," he says, "you don't have to find the right people, they find you."

Throughout human history, communities started off as geographically based (tribes), became ideological (e.g., religions) and then transitioned into civic administrations (monarchies and nation-states). Today, however, the Internet is producing *trait-based communities* that share intent, belief, resources, preferences, needs, risks and other characteristics, none of which depend on physical proximity. For an organization or enterprise, its "community" is made up of core team members, alumni

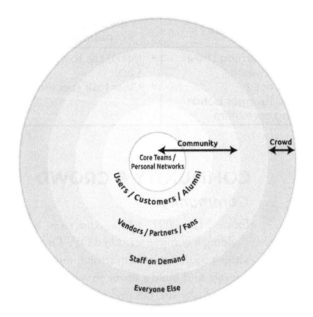

(former team members), partners, vendors, customers, users and fans. The "crowd" can be thought of as everyone outside those core layers.

It is important to note that an Exponential Organization interacting with its community is not simply a transaction. True community occurs when peer-to-peer engagement occurs. The more open the community, though, the more traditional and best-practice-oriented the leadership model has to be. As Anderson states: "At the top of every one of these communities is a benevolent dictator." You need strong leadership to manage the community, because although there are no employees, people still have responsibilities and need to be held accountable for their performances.

Typically, there are three steps to building a community around an ExO:

- *Use the MTP to attract and engage early members.* The MTP serves as a gravitational force that attracts constituents into its orbit. Tesla, Burning Man, TED, Singularity University and GitHub are good examples of communities whose members share common passions.

- *Nurture the community.* Anderson spends three hours every morning attending to the DIY Drones community. Elements of nurturing include listening and giving back. DIY Drones blueprints were open sourced and available from day one, which was fine, but it turned out that the members really wanted DIY Drone Kits. So Anderson provided them. (The same DIY kit demand is occurring in the DIY biotech community). Smart move. "Unlike digital marketing, where ROI is sustained almost as soon as spending happens, communities are a long-term investment that is significantly more strategic," says social business thought leader Dion Hinchcliffe. "Additionally, communities with CxO participation are far more likely to be best-in-class."

- *Create a platform to automate peer-to-peer engagement.* GitHub, for example, has its members rate and review other members' code. Airbnb hosts and users fill out evaluation forms; taxi disrupters Uber, Lyft and Sidecar encourage clients and drivers to rate one another; and the news platform Reddit invites users to vote on stories. In 2013, Reddit, which has just fifty-one employees, most of whom manage the platform, saw 731 million unique visitors cast 6.7 billion votes on 41 million stories. Talk about a platform…(More on this later.)

Tony Hsieh, CEO of Las Vegas-based Zappos, was inspired by the Burning Man community to combine both physical and trait-based communities within his Las Vegas Downtown Project. The project combines work and play in an urban landscape with homes, infrastructure, hacker spaces, shops, cafe/theater and art. In addition to the goal of helping to transform the downtown area into the most community-focused large city in the world, Hsieh aims to create the smartest place on the planet by maximizing the chances of serendipitous learning between Zappos insiders and outsiders. The result is not only a community built around common passions, but also around a common location.

Note that in early stages, many companies find it easier to join an existing community that shares its MTP. The Quantified Self movement, for instance, is drawing together startups engaged in measuring all aspects of the human body. Examples of startups offering wearable technology that have banded together to form a community include Scanadu, Withings and Fitbit. As each startup finds its path, of course, it is free to create its own community, particularly once its user base is more significant.

Crowd

As mentioned earlier, the crowd is made up of concentric rings of people outside the core community. The crowd is harder to reach, but its numbers are much greater—even a million times greater—and that's what makes pursuing it particularly compelling.

While similar, there is a distinct difference between Crowd and Staff on Demand. Staff on Demand is hired for a particular task and usually via a platform like Elance. Staff on Demand is *managed*—you tell workers what it is they have to do. Crowd, on the other hand, is *pull-based*. You open up an idea, funding opportunity or incentive prize…and let people find you.

ExOs can leverage the crowd by harnessing creativity, innovation, validation and even funding:

- *Creativity, innovation* and the overall process of generating, developing, and communicating new ideas can be accomplished through the use of tools and platforms. Some platforms to aid this process include IdeaScale, eYeka, Spigit, InnoCentive, SolutionXchange, Crowdtap and Brightidea.

- *Validation* is achieved by obtaining measurable evidence that an experiment, product or service succeeds in meeting pre-determined specifications. Tools such as UserVoice, Unbounce and Google AdWords can accomplish this.
- *Crowdfunding* is a growing trend to help fund ideas using the web to assemble very large numbers of comparatively small investors—thus not only raising capital, but also reflecting the interest of the market. Two well-known examples of crowdfunding companies are Kickstarter and Indiegogo. In 2012 there was an estimated $2.8 billion raised via crowdfunding campaigns. By 2015 that number is expected to climb to $15 billion. The World Bank predicts crowdfunding to grow to $93 billion by 2025.

In addition to raising enormous amounts of money for causes and startups, such platforms are also democratizing access to working capital. Gustin, a premium designer jeans company, uses crowdfunding for all of its designs. Customers back specific designs, and when a predetermined monetary goal has been reached, the products are created and shipped to all backers. Gustin thus has no product risk or inventory costs.

Already, ExOs are leveraging community and crowd for many functions traditionally handled inside the enterprise, including idea generation, funding, design, distribution, marketing and sales. This shift is powerful and taps into what university professor and social media guru Clay Shirky calls *cognitive surplus*. "The world has over a trillion hours a year of free time to commit to shared projects," he said in a recent TED radio broadcast. And that's just today. By 2020, when three billion additional minds using inexpensive tablets join the two billion currently online, Shirky's trillion hours per year will triple.

As Silicon Valley visionary Bill Joy famously said, "The smartest people in the world don't work for you." For ExOs, their external focus is such that their communities of hundreds and thousands, along with crowds of millions and, ultimately, billions, become extensions of the companies themselves.

As a result of both Staff on Demand and Community & Crowd, the core FTEs of an organization become smaller and its flexible workforce larger. As a result, organizations are not only much more agile, they are also better at learning and unlearning due to the diversity and volume of a flexible workforce. Ideas are also able to circulate much faster.

Why Important?	Dependencies or Prerequisites
• Increase loyalty to ExO • Drives exponential growth • Validates new ideas, and learning • Allows agility and rapid implementation • Amplifies ideation	• MTP • Engagement • Authentic and transparent leadership • Low threshold to participate • P2P value creation

ALGORITHMS

In 2002, Google's revenues were less than a half-billion dollars. Ten years later, its revenues had jumped 125x and the company was generating a half-billion dollars *every three days*. At the heart of this staggering growth was the PageRank algorithm, which ranks the popularity of web pages. (Google doesn't gauge which page is better from a human perspective; its algorithms simply respond to the pages that deliver the most clicks.)

Google isn't alone. Today, the world is pretty much run on algorithms. From automotive anti-lock braking to Amazon's recommendation engine; from dynamic pricing for airlines to predicting the success of upcoming Hollywood blockbusters; from writing news posts to air traffic control; from credit card fraud detection to the 2 percent of posts that Facebook shows a typical user—algorithms are everywhere in modern life. Recently, McKinsey estimated that of the seven hundred end-to-end bank processes (opening an account or getting a car loan, for example), about half can be fully automated. Computers are increasingly performing more and more complex tasks.

There is even a marketplace called Algorithmia, where companies are matched with algorithms that can potentially make sense of their data. Like GitHub (see Chapter Seven), developers can open up their code for others to improve upon.

In particular, there are two types of algorithms that are at the frontier of this new world: Machine Learning and Deep Learning.

Machine Learning is the ability to accurately perform new, unseen tasks, built on known properties learned from training or historic data, and based on prediction. Key open source examples include Hadoop and Cloudera. An illustration of Machine Learning comes via Netflix, which in 2006 set out to improve its movie recommendations. Rather than limit the challenge to its in-house workforce, Netflix launched a $1 million (incentive) competition with a stated goal of improving its movie-rating algorithm by 10 percent. The initial 51,000 contestants, who hailed from 186 countries, received a dataset of one hundred million ratings and had five years to achieve the goal. The contest ended early, in September 2009, when one of the 44,014 valid submissions achieved the goal and was awarded the prize.

Deep Learning is a new and exciting subset of Machine Learning based on neural net technology. It allows a machine to discover new patterns without being exposed to any historical or training data. Leading startups in this space are DeepMind, bought by Google in early 2014 for $500 million, back when DeepMind had just thirteen employees, and Vicarious, funded with investment from Elon Musk, Jeff Bezos and Mark

Zuckerberg. Twitter, Baidu, Microsoft and Facebook are also heavily invested in this area. Deep Learning algorithms rely on discovery and self-indexing, and operate in much the same way that a baby learns first sounds, then words, then sentences and even languages. As an example: In June 2012, a team at Google X built a neural network of 16,000 computer processors with one billion connections. After allowing it to browse ten million randomly selected YouTube video thumbnails for three days, the network began to recognize cats, without actually knowing the concept of "cats." Importantly, this was without any human intervention or input.

In the two years since, the capabilities of Deep Learning have improved considerably. Today, in addition to improving speech recognition, creating a more effective search engine (Ray Kurzweil is working on this within Google) and identifying individual objects, Deep Learning algorithms can also detect particular episodes in videos and even describe them in text, all without human input. Deep Learning algorithms can even play video games by figuring out the rules of the game and then optimizing performance.

Think about the implications of this revolutionary breakthrough. The technology will make most products and services more effective, personalized and efficient. At the same time, many white-collar jobs will be impacted and even disrupted.

Given that the 55,000 trucks in UPS's American fleet make sixteen million deliveries daily, the potential for inefficient routing is enormous. But by applying telematics and algorithms, the company saves its drivers eighty-five million miles a year, resulting in a cost savings of $2.55 billion. Similar applications in healthcare, energy and financial services mean that we're entering a world of Algorithms R Us.

As far back as 2005, writer and publisher Tim O'Reilly stated that, "Data is the new Intel Inside." And that was when there were just a half-billion Internet-connected devices in the world. As we noted in Chapter One, that number is set to grow to a trillion devices as we prepare to embrace the Internet of Things.

In the face of that explosion, the need for algorithms has become mission critical. Consider for a moment that the last two years have seen nine times more data created than in the entire history of humanity. Then consider that the Computer Sciences Corporation believes that by 2020 we'll have created a total 73.5 *zettabytes* of data—in Stephen Hawking's phraseology, that's seventy-three followed by twenty-one zeros.

Remarkably, and often tragically, most companies today are still driven almost solely on the intuitive guesses of their leaders. They may use data to guide their thinking, but they are just as likely to fall prey to a long list of self-delusions—everything from a sunk-cost bias to a confirmation bias (see below for a list of cognitive biases). One reason for Google's success is that it is more ruthlessly data-driven than most other companies, right down to its hiring practices.

In the same way that today we can no longer handle the complexities of air traffic control or supply chain management without algorithms, almost all the business insights and decisions of tomorrow will be data-driven.

An analysis by the American Psychological Association of seventeen studies on hiring practices found that a simple algorithm beat intuitive hiring practices by more than 25 percent in terms of successful hires. Neil Jacobstein, an expert in Artificial Intelligence, notes that we use AI and algorithms to mitigate and compensate for many of the following heuristics in human cognition:

- **Anchoring bias:** Tendency to rely too heavily, or "anchor," on one trait or piece of information when making decisions.
- **Availability bias:** Tendency to overestimate the likelihood of events with greater "availability" in memory, which can be influenced by how recent the memories are or how unusual or emotionally charged they may be.
- **Confirmation bias:** Tendency to search for,

interpret, focus on and remember information in a way that confirms one's preconceptions.

- **Framing bias:** Drawing different conclusions from the same information, depending on how or by whom that information is presented.
- **Optimism bias:** Tendency to be over-optimistic, overestimating favorable and pleasing outcomes.
- **Planning fallacy bias:** Tendency to overestimate benefits and underestimate costs and task-completion times.
- **Sunk-cost or loss-aversion bias:** Disutility of giving up an object is greater than the utility associated with acquiring it.[1]

Jacobstein is fond of pointing out that your neocortex has not had a major upgrade in 50,000 years. It is the size, shape and thickness of a dinner napkin. "What if," he asks, "it was the size of a table cloth? Or California?"

There is an interesting difference of opinion over how much data should be used based on the nature of the market in which the organization operates. While conventional wisdom says to gather as much data as possible (hence the term Big Data), psychologist Gerd Gigerenzer cautions that in uncertain markets, it is better to simplify, use heuristics and rely on fewer variables. In stable and predictable markets, on the other hand, he recommends organizations "complexify" and use algorithms with more variables.

One of the leaders in gleaning insights from massive amounts of data is Palantir. Founded in 2004, Palantir builds government, commercial and health software solutions that empower organizations to make sense of disparate data. By handling technical problems, Palantir liberates its customers to focus on solving human ones. The venture capital industry

---

1   Complete list of all cognitive biases: en.wikipedia.org/wiki/List_of_cognitive_biases

considers Palantir so important that the company has already received an astounding $900 million in total funding, and is valued at 10x that amount.

Michael Chui notes that many successful companies today had Big Data in their DNA. We believe it's just the beginning, and that many more algorithm-focused ExOs will pop up in the coming years, harnessing what Yuri van Geest calls the 5P benefits of big data: *productivity, prevention, participation, personalization* and *prediction.*

To implement algorithms, ExOs need to follow four steps:

1. **Gather:** The algorithmic process starts with harnessing data, which is gathered via sensors or humans, or imported from public datasets.
2. **Organize:** The next step is to organize the data, a process known as ETL (extract, transform and load).
3. **Apply:** Once the data is accessible, machine learning tools such as Hadoop and Pivotal, or even (open source) deep learning algorithms like DeepMind, Vicarious and SkyMind, extract insights, identify trends and tune new algorithms.
4. **Expose:** The final step is exposing the data, as if it were an open platform. Open data and APIs can be used to enable an ExO's community to develop valuable services, new functionalities and innovation layered on top of the platform by remixing the ExO's data with their own. Examples here include the Ford Motor Company, Uber, Rabobank, the Port of Rotterdam, IBM Watson, Wolfram Alpha, Twitter and Facebook.

Needless to say, the impending explosion of data resulting from the billions and trillions of sensors that will soon be deployed makes algorithms a critical future component of *every* business. Given that they are much more objective, scalable and flexible than human beings, algorithms are not only the key to the future of business in general, but they are also critical for organizations committed to driving exponential growth.

Why Important?	Dependencies or Prerequisites
• Allows fully scalable products & services • Leverages connected devices and sensors • Lower error rate stabilizes growth • Easily updated	• Machine or Deep Learning techniques • Cultural acceptance

LEVERAGED ASSETS

The notion of renting, sharing or leveraging assets—as opposed to owning them—has taken many forms throughout history. In the business world, leasing everything from buildings to machinery has been used as a common practice to shift assets from the balance sheet.

And while not owning assets has been standard practice for heavy machinery and non-mission-critical functions (e.g., copiers) for decades, recently there's been an accelerating trend towards outsourcing even mission-critical assets. Apple, for example, leverages the factories and assembly lines of Foxconn, its manufacturing partner, for key product lines. In the case of counterexamples—such as Tesla owning its own factories or Amazon owning its own warehouses and local delivery services—the underlying reason isn't financial; instead, the driving force is the scarcity of mission-critical resources involved, or that it's so new that it's now fully fleshed out.

The information age now enables Apple and other companies to access physical assets anytime and anywhere, rather than requiring that they actually possess them. Technology enables organizations to easily share and scale assets not only locally, but also globally, and without boundaries.

As we noted earlier, the launch of Amazon Web Services in March 2006 was a key inflection point in the rise of ExOs. The ability to lease on-demand computing that would scale on a variable cost basis utterly changed the IT industry.

A new Silicon Valley phenomenon called TechShop is another example of this trend. In the same way that gyms use a membership model to aggregate expensive exercise machinery that few could afford to have at home, TechShop collects expensive *manufacturing* machinery and offers subscribers a small monthly fee (\$125 to \$175, depending on the location) for unlimited access to its assets.

TechShop is neither small-time nor a novelty. The popular Square payment device, for example, was prototyped at TechShop. Square's inventor didn't have to buy expensive machinery to build his prototype—he simply joined TechShop and leveraged the on-demand assets. Square now processes more than \$30 billion annually in transactions and is valued at more than \$5 billion. Established companies such as GE and Ford are also working with TechShop. Ford launched a new TechShop location in Detroit in 2012, and together the two companies created Ford's Employee Patent Incentive Program. Some 2,000 Ford employees joined the program, resulting in a 50 percent increase in patentable ideas. GE, in conjunction with TechShop, Skillshare and Quirky, launched a similar initiative last year in Chicago called GE Garages.

As with Staff on Demand, ExOs retain their flexibility precisely by *not* owning assets, even in strategic areas. This practice optimizes flexibility and allows the enterprise to scale incredibly quickly as it obviates the need for staff to manage those assets. Just as Waze piggybacked off its users' smartphones, Uber, Lyft, BlaBlaCar and Sidecar leverage under-utilized cars. (If you own a car, it sits empty about 93 percent of the time.)

The latest wave of non-asset businesses is something called Collaborative Consumption, a concept evangelized by Rachel Botsman and Roo Rogers in their book, *What's Mine is Yours: The Rise of Collaborative Consumption*. The book pushes the sharing philosophy forward by establishing information-enabled assets of all kinds, from textbooks to gardening tools to housing—assets and resources that are abundant and widely available. Research conducted by Crowd Companies in April 2014 highlights the industries in which seventy-seven of the largest organizations in this new economy operate. As shown in the chart below, retail, transportation and technology are currently the biggest industries.

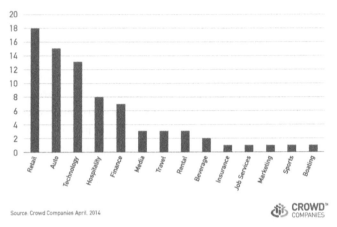

Source: Crowd Companies April 2014

Non-ownership, then, is the key to owning the future—except, of course, when it comes to scarce resources and assets. As noted above, Tesla owns its own factories and Amazon its own warehouses. When the asset in question is rare or extremely scarce, then ownership is a better option. But if your asset is information-based or commoditized at all, then accessing is better than possessing.

Why Important?	Dependencies or Prerequisites
• Allows scalable products • Lowers marginal cost of supply • Removes having to manage assets • Increases agility	• Abundance or easily available assets • Interfaces

ENGAGEMENT

User engagement techniques, such as sweepstakes, quizzes, coupons, airline miles and loyalty cards have been around for a long time. But in the last few years, such techniques have been fully information-enabled, elaborated and socialized. Engagement is comprised of digital reputation systems, games and incentive prizes, and provides the opportunity for virtuous, positive feedback loops—which in turn allows for faster growth due to more innovative ideas and customer and community loyalty. Companies like Google, Airbnb, Uber, eBay, Yelp, GitHub and Twitter all leverage different engagement mechanisms. Nilofer Merchant, author of two books on collaboration and a professor of management at Santa Clara University, references Engagement in her book, *11 Rules for Creating Value in the Social Era*:

> [Engagement] is a way of enabling collaborative human behavior—social behavior—to come into play. The truth is this: connected individuals can now do what once only large centralized organizations could. The effects of which are seen in every Exponential Organizational example. But it's this management truth that requires deeper consideration. Why do people connect together? Based on what kind of purpose? What is it that motivates them to act in common interests, not simply their own? What causes them to trust you enough to want to contribute something of theirs toward a shared goal? So the question for leaders is how do you enable, foster, organize, galvanize and act on that fundamental human capacity to contribute and work with others?

Key attributes of Engagement include:

- Ranking transparency
- Self-efficacy (sense of control, agency and impact)

- Peer pressure (social comparison)
- Eliciting positive rather than negative emotions to drive long-term behavioral change
- Instant feedback (short feedback cycles)
- Clear, authentic rules, goals and rewards (only reward outputs, not inputs)
- Virtual currencies or points

Properly implemented, Engagement creates network effects and positive feedback loops with extraordinary reach. The biggest impact of engagement techniques is on customers and the entire external ecosystem. However, these techniques can also be used internally with employees to boost collaboration, innovation and loyalty.

For the Millennial generation, gaming is a way of life. Today, more than seven hundred million people around the world play online games—159 million in the U.S. alone—and most play for more than an hour each day. The average young person racks up more than 10,000 hours of gaming by the age of twenty-one. That's almost exactly as much time as kids spend in the classroom throughout middle school and high school. Gaming isn't just something that young people *do*, it is a large part of what and who they *are*.

These numbers help explain why AI researchers are using gaming to help them map the human brain. The only problem is that it takes an AI-assisted researcher fifty hours to reconstruct just one neuron in 3D. The brain has 85 billion neurons—which means it would take 4,250 billion hours to completely map the human brain. That's 485.2 million years. Rather linear, wouldn't you say?

To solve this problem and speed up the process, EyeWire—which was spun out of MIT and launched in December 2012—has created a game in which players color 2D pieces to form 3D pieces as they simultaneously reconstruct neurons. This very simple task for a very difficult problem has already resulted in

130,000 people from 145 countries mapping more than one hundred neurons.

EyeWire illustrates how an ExO can apply game elements and mechanics in non-game products and services to create fun and engaging experiences, converting users into loyal players—and in the process accomplish extraordinary things. Other games that use this technique include MalariaSpot (hunt malaria parasites in real images), GalaxyZoo (classify galaxies according to their shapes) and Foldit (help biochemists combat AIDS and other diseases by predicting and producing protein models).

As game designer and author Jane McGonigal sees it, "Human beings are wired to compete."

Engaging gamers, however, requires more than just throwing a game up on a website and letting gamers have at it. "Gamification should empower people, not exploit them. It should feel good at the end of the day because you made progress towards something that mattered to you."

To be successful, every gamification initiative should leverage the following game techniques:

- **Dynamics:** motivate behavior through scenarios, rules and progression
- **Mechanics:** help achieve goals through teams, competitions, rewards and feedback
- **Components:** track progress through quests, points, levels, badges and collections

Gamification is not only used to tackle challenges and problems with the help of a community, it can also be used as a hiring tool. Google is famous for using games to qualify potential hires, and Domino's Pizza created a video game called Pizza Hero in which the goal is to make the perfect pizza neatly and quickly. Customers can create their own pies and then order them, and top pizza makers are encouraged to apply for jobs.

Another use of gamification is to improve a company's internal culture. Karl M. Kapp researched this topic in his book, *The Gamification of Learning and Instruction Fieldbook: Ideas Into Practice.* One example he cites is that of Pep Boys, a large car repair and maintenance retail store that has over seven hundred locations in thirty-five states and generates $2 billion each year. Despite its profit margins, the company found that it suffered from many safety-related incidents and injuries each year, many of them a result of human error. It also found that theft was becoming an increasing problem. To increase awareness of the issues, Pep Boys implemented a platform called Axonify, which used a quiz to educate employees about specific incidents. Correct answers earned the employees prizes; incorrect answers resulted in additional information and testing until the material was fully mastered. The platform achieved a voluntary participation rate of over 95 percent, and even as the number of stores and employees increased over time, safety incidents and claim counts fell more than 45 percent, and theft and human errors dropped 55 percent. As safety became a top focus at Pep Boys, its culture completely shifted.

Gamification initiatives can be created from the ground up (as illustrated by EyeWire), but there are also many startups and companies providing services that an organization can simply adopt and leverage, just as Pep Boys did with Axonify. The Gamification Company provides a list with more than ninety examples, including Badgeville, Bunchball, Dopamine and Comarch. Organizations can also use work.com (a Salesforce company), in which gamification is fully integrated, or Keas, which was specifically created to improve employee wellness.

Incentive competitions are another form of engagement that has been recently popularized by the X Prize Foundation and others. This engagement technique is typically used to find promising people in the crowd and move them into the community. Competitions are also used to challenge, leverage and motivate the community in order to solicit potentially radical breakthrough ideas. For Peter Diamandis, it all started with the Ansari X Prize, which rewarded $10 million to the first non-government organization to launch a reusable manned spacecraft into space twice within two weeks. Twenty-six teams from around the world participated, and contestants included everyone from hobbyists to large-corporation-backed teams. In November 2004, Mojave Aerospace Ventures won the prize with its SpaceShipOne spacecraft. Virgin Galactic is currently using the successors to this design to enable commercial space flight, which will cost $250,000 a ticket and is planned for the end of 2014.

After the success of the Ansari X Prize, more X Prizes were created. One of X Prize's current offerings is the Qualcomm Tricorder X Prize, which will award $10 million to the first team whose handheld medical diagnostic device outperforms ten board-certified physicians. Currently, twenty-one teams are competing for the grand prize. The recently launched X Prize spinoff HeroX takes this model even further, allowing companies to create their own challenges through the HeroX platform to solve local and global challenges.

An incentive prize creates a clear, measurable and objective goal, and offers a cash purse for the first team to reach that objective. The advantage such competitions offers is their ability to deliver huge leverage and efficiency. Incentive prizes are also tools that can be used by individuals, startups, governments, and medium and large corporations, but they are unique in that they allow small teams or lone innovators to launch or transform industries. By tapping into the deep-rooted human desire to compete, these competitions push teams to deliver their very best work. In most cases, incentive competitions have stretch goals embedded within them as well, meaning they require breakthrough thinking and revolutionary products to win.

Perhaps the most important side effect of incentive competition is the peripheral innovation it creates as numerous competitors race towards a common goal. Such innovations can galvanize a company or an entire industry, spurring it forward at an unprecedented pace. From 2008 to 2011, Yuri van Geest and Vodafone Netherlands (later on, Vodafone Group) created and ran the world's largest mobile Internet startup contest, Vodafone Mobile Clicks, with prizes exceeding $300,000. The competition launched in the Netherlands and quickly grew to include a total of seven European countries. Mobile Clicks enabled Vodafone to engage not only with more than 900 mobile Internet startups, but also with the local mobile community in each of those countries. In the process, what began as an external competition funneled into an internal interface that provided Vodafone with opportunities to fund and acquire ideas, identify talent and acquire candidates. Vodafone's "contest" became a form of corporate venture capital, which morphed successfully into the thriving Startupbootcamp (SBC) startup incubator/accelerator program across Europe.

Incentive competitions are hardly new—after all, Charles Lindberg's solo nonstop flight across the Atlantic Ocean in 1927 was in pursuit of just such a prize; in fact, his biography inspired Peter Diamandis to create the X Prize. Another well-known incentive program designed to increase engagement is the longstanding "Employee of the Month" program. Until recently, however, incentive programs have rarely been used to motivate creativity and productivity within communities and crowds.

Another positive side effect of engagement, particularly when it comes to gamification, is *training*. The complexity of some of today's games provides an excellent education in leadership and teamwork skills. In fact, Joi Ito has observed that becoming an effective World of Warcraft guild master is tantamount to a total-immersion course in leadership.

Indeed, what might seem like the least serious tool in a company's user and employee engagement program often proves to be one of its most powerful in terms of finding and training the individuals it needs to reach the next level.

Although a comparatively minor issue as far as traditional enterprises are concerned, engagement proves to be critical for ExOs. It is a key element for scaling the organization into the community and crowd and for creating external network effects. No matter how promising its product or premise, unless an ExO is able to optimize the engagement of its community and crowd, it will wither and fade.

Why Important?	Dependencies or Prerequisites
• Increases loyalty • Amplifies ideation • Converts crowd to community • Leverages marketing • Enables play and learning • Provides digital feedback loop with users	• MTP • Clear, fair and consistent rules without conflicts of interest

Passion and Purpose. We began this chapter by essentially asking two questions: What gives an organization meaning? What compels employees, customers and even members of the general public to devote themselves to the success of that enterprise? These questions become even more vital when discussing Exponential Organizations, given that their extraordinary rates of growth, combined with a heavy dependence on their communities to help them realize their visions, demands a level of unprecedented commitment from a broader set of stakeholders—individuals who traditionally have had only a tenuous connection to the enterprise.

Although such commitment is often found with music groups and sports teams, it is seldom seen in the corporate world. There are, however, a few corporate rock stars, the most famous of which is Apple. Apple's army of millions of true believers, who line up to buy its products, create blogs about the company and products, place Apple stickers in the back windows of cars, and vociferously defend the company against heretics and apostates, is a paradigmatic example of a lively, complex and powerful corporate community.

Obviously, creating such a community requires a great product and a compelling vision. But it also demands a fair amount of time. It took eight years after the introduction of the Macintosh for Apple Computer to become a phenomenon, and another sixteen years for the company to reach its status as a cultural icon.

Exponential Organizations don't have that amount of time. Nor are they likely to have a charismatic leader like Steve Jobs. Instead, they must move quickly and systematically, using proven techniques and tools. In this chapter we've provided both: the MTP to elicit the passionate involvement of all stakeholders in a crusade to achieve a compelling larger vision; and the components of SCALE to build and engage the Community & Crowd, to use Staff on Demand and Leveraged Assets, and to leverage Algorithms.

Are these attributes perfect substitutes for charisma and genius? No. But they are a lot more available and much less subject to chance. They are also much more manageable. Best of all, the combination of MTP and SCALE can be applied to *any* organization, small or large.

Now that we have covered the external attributes of an ExO, in the next chapter we will examine the internal attributes to see how an organization manages the chaos and keeps from breaking apart while running at such a high speed.

KEY TAKEAWAYS

- Exponential Organizations have a Massive Transformative Purpose (MTP)
- Brands will start morphing into MTPs
- ExOs scale outside their organizational boundaries by leveraging or accessing people, assets and platforms to maximize flexibility, speed, agility and learning.
- ExOs leverage five externalities (SCALE) to achieve performance gains:
  - Staff on Demand
  - Community & Crowd
  - Algorithms
  - Leveraged Assets
  - Engagement

CHAPTER FOUR
INSIDE THE EXPONENTIAL ORGANIZATION

The sheer output to be processed when SCALE elements are leveraged requires that the internal control mechanisms of an ExO be managed carefully and efficiently. For example, an X Prize generates hundreds of ideas that need to be evaluated, catalogued, ranked and prioritized. With exponential output, the internal organization needs to be extremely robust, precise and properly tuned to process all the inputs. As a result, Exponential Organizations are far more than how they appear to the outside world, or how they behave with customers, communities and other stakeholders. They also have distinctly different *internal* operations that encompass everything from their business philosophies to how employees interact with one another, how they measure their performance (and what they value in that performance), and even their attitudes toward risk—in fact, *especially* their attitudes toward risk.

And just as the external attributes of the Exponential Organization can be encompassed with the acronym SCALE, so too can an ExO's internal mechanisms be expressed with the acronym IDEAS.

- Interfaces
- Dashboards
- Experimentation

- Autonomy
- Social Technologies

Once again, we will look at each of them in turn.

INTERFACES

Interfaces are filtering and matching processes by which ExOs bridge from SCALE externalities to internal IDEAS control frameworks. They are algorithms and automated workflows that route the output of SCALE externalities to the right people at the right time internally. In many cases, these processes start out manual and gradually become automated around the edges. Eventually, however, they became self-provisioning platforms that enable the ExO to scale. A classic example is Google's AdWords, which is now a multi-billion dollar business within Google. A key to its scalability is self-provisioning—that is, the interface for an AdWords customer has been completely automated such that there is no manual involvement.

In the last chapter we introduced Quirky, a CPG company known for moving a product from idea to store shelves in less than a month. The company leverages a community of more than a million inventors, each eager to get their ideas to market. As a result, Quirky has had to develop special processes and mechanisms to manage, rank, filter and engage that vast community. Interfaces such as the one used by Quirky help ExOs filter and process outputs from external attributes (SCALE) in a systematic and automatic way into the core organization. The use of Interfaces results in more effective and efficient processes, reducing the margin of error. While growing exponentially as a company, Interfaces are critical if an organization is to scale seamlessly, especially on a global level.

The same is true of other firms that coordinate data and oversee everything from prizes to personnel. Kaggle has its own unique mechanisms to manage its 200,000 data scientists. The X Prize Foundation has created mechanisms and dedicated teams for each of its prizes. TED has strict guidelines that help its many "franchised" TEDx events around the world deliver with consistency. And Uber has its own ways of handling its army of drivers.

Most of these Interface processes are unique and proprietary to the organization that developed them, and as such comprise a unique type of intellectual property that can be of considerable market value. ExOs invest considerable attention to Interfaces and a great deal of human-centered design thinking is brought to bear on these processes in order to optimize every instantiation.

As these new processes evolve and become more powerful, they typically feature both heavy instrumentation and the kind of metadata gathering that feeds the company's Dashboards (which we will describe in the next section).

Ultimately, Interfaces tend to become the most distinctive internal characteristics of a fully realized ExO. There's a good reason for this: at peak productivity, Interfaces empower the enterprise's management of its SCALE external attributes—in particular Staff on Demand, Leveraged Assets and Community & Crowd. Without such interfaces the ExO cannot scale, thus making them increasingly mission-critical.

Possibly the most dramatic example today of an Interface is Apple's App Store, which now contains more than 1.2 million apps that have been downloaded a collective seventy-five *billion* times. Apple has about nine million developers within that ecosystem who have earned more than $15 billion.

To manage this unique environment, Apple's Interface is comprised of an internal editorial board that vets new applications and requested changes, as well as recommendations from other employees, who make up an informal network. New products and policies are announced at WWDC conferences, and Apple uses a sophisticated algorithm to help determine which apps are leading their categories and which should be featured on the home page. As might be expected, this process is unique to Apple, as are most interfaces at ExOs. They are not taught at business schools, and there are no pundits talking about how to go about building them. Nonetheless, they are the core levers by which any ExO can manage to scale. The table below shows some ExOs and their interfaces:

	Interface	Description	Internal Usage	SCALE Attribute
Uber	Driver selection	System to allow users to find and choose drivers	Algorithm matches best/closest driver to user location	Algorithm
Kaggle	Leaderboard rankings	Real-time scoreboard that shows the current rankings of a contest	Aggregate and compare results of all users in a contest	Engagement
	User scanning	System to scan for relevant users for private contests	Cherry-pick the best users for special projects	Community & Crowd
Quirky	Ratings/voting	System to vote on each aspect of the production cycle	Priorities in the features and benefits of new products	Engagement
TED	Video translation subtitles	Manage translations created by volunteers (via the vendor dotsub)	Integrate TED Talks translations seamlessly	Community & Crowd
Local Motors	Idea submitter	System to allow users to submit ideas	Algorithm to process only valid or feasible entries	Community & Crowd
	Competition creator	System to create new competitions for the community	Algorithms to streamline all steps in the competition	Community & Crowd
	Ratings/voting	System to vote on each aspect of the production cycle	Priorities in the features and benefits of new products	Engagement

Google Ventures	Employee search	Search relevant and targeted skills/ people in Google's employee database	Match GV startups with targeted Google skills/employees	Algorithms
Waze	Resume search	System to search resumes to find relevant new hires	Match resumes with specific skill sets	Algorithms
	GPS coordinates	Harvests GPS signal from every user	Traffic delays calculated in real time	Leveraged Assets
Google	User gestures while driving	Users spot accidents, police car sightings, etc.	Maps display resulting gestures for all users	Community & Crowd
	AdWords	User picks keywords to advertise against	Google places ads against search results	Algorithms
GitHub	Version control system	Multiple coders updating software sequentially and in parallel	Platform keeps all contributions in sync	Community & Crowd
Zappos	Hiring process	Incentive competitions	Narrows down candidates from large pool	Engagement
Gigwalk	Task availability	Gigwalk workers receive location-based, simple tasks when available	Matches task demand with supply of Gigwalkers	Staff on Demand

One final way to think about Interfaces is that they help manage *abundance*. While most processes are optimized around scarcity and efficiency, SCALE elements generate large result sets, meaning Interfaces are geared towards filtering and matching. As an example, keep in mind that the Netflix prize generated 44,104 entries that needed to be filtered, ranked, prioritized and scored.

Why Important?	Dependencies or Prerequisites
• Filter external abundance into internal value • Bridge between external growth drivers and internal stabilizing factors • Automation allows scalability	• Standardized processes to enable automation • Scalable externalities • Algorithms (in most cases)

DASHBOARDS

Given the huge amounts of data from customers and employees becoming available, ExOs need a new way to measure and manage the organization: a real-time, adaptable dashboard with all essential company and employee metrics, accessible to everyone in the organization.

In the early 1990s, the industry standard for giant retailers such as Sears and Kmart was to batch up point-of-sale transactions on a daily basis across all tills. A regional hub would then tally the results for multiple stores a few days later. Several weeks after that, a buyer at the head office would look over the totals and determine how many boxes of Pampers the company needed to order for its next bulk purchase.

Walmart blew this model apart—and in the process revolutionized retailing—by launching its own geostationary satellite and then tracking inventory and supply chain transfers in real time. It crushed the competition by consistently outperforming other chains by 15 percent—a staggering competitive margin in retail. Sears and Kmart never fully recovered.

There has always been a tension in business created by the need to balance instrumentation and data collection versus running the company and getting things done. Collecting internal progress statistics takes time, effort and expensive IT. That's why results were usually tracked annually or, at best, quarterly.

Today's startups (as well as more mature enterprises) are leveraging wireless broadband, the Internet, sensors and the cloud to track this same data in real time. Will Henshall, founder and CEO of the fascinating startup focus@will, which streams anti-distraction music and sounds to help users focus, has instrumented his business almost completely. Embedded into his operations are the following metrics, which he tracks in real time:

- Total users
- New guests within last day
- Total number of Personal Users
- New Personal User registrations within last day
- Percentage of New Personal Users vs. new Guests within last day
- Total Pro Subscribers
- New Pro Subscribers within last day
- Percentage of New Pro Subscribers vs. new Personal Users within last day
- Total cash receipts
- Cash receipts within last 30 days
- Cash receipts within last day

To a corporate executive from just twenty years ago this would be an astounding list of measurements—almost beyond imagination. But the quality of this list is even more impressive than its quantity. It offers metrics about customer behavior every bit the equal of information stored in the head of an old-time storekeeper about the needs and wants of each of his small-town patrons—but on a *global* scale. And the amount of information stored will only grow each year, even as the Big Data analytics to process it improve over time.

And there's more. Today we are seeing a different *approach* to gathering data than in the past. Traditional vanity metrics (stats such as the number of visitors or mobile app downloads) are being replaced by real value metrics including repeat usage, retention percentage, monetization and Net Promoter Score (NPS). This emergent focus on real value KPIs is being built into the popular new *Lean Startup* movement (see Experimentation).

Even as the instrumenting of businesses accelerates, a similar transformation is also taking place at the level of individual employee and team performance tracking. The dreaded annual performance review is demotivating for most employees, and is especially so for high achievers because of the long delay between accomplishment and recognition. During that interval, top employees are at risk of becoming frustrated, bored, and moving on—costing fast-growth companies the employees they can least afford to lose.

In response, many ExOs are adopting the *Objectives and Key Results* (OKR) method. Invented at Intel by CEO Andy Grove and brought to Google by venture capitalist John Doerr in 1999, OKR tracks individual, team and company goals and outcomes in an open and transparent way. In *High Output Management*, Grove's highly regarded manual, he introduced OKRs as the answer to two simple questions:

1. Where do I want to go? (Objectives)
2. How will I know I'm getting there? (Key Results to ensure progress is made)

In addition to Intel and Google, other fast-growth companies using the system include LinkedIn, Zynga, Oracle, Twitter and Facebook.

In operation, an OKR program, as its name suggests, operates along two tracks. An Objective, for example, might be to "Increase sales by 25 percent," along with "Form two strategic partnerships" and "Run AdWords campaign" as the desired Key Results. OKRs are about focus, simplicity, short(er) feedback cycles, and openness. As a result, insights and improvements are easier to see and implement. In contrast, complexity, secrecy and broad goals tend to impede progress, often leading to unintended consequences. As Larry Keeley, president and co-founder of the innovation strategy firm Doblin Group, says, "The truth is there are about 65 different metrics for innovation. No company needs all 65. You need half a dozen. You need to pick the right half dozen contextually for whatever it is you're trying to achieve strategically."

Some characteristics of OKRs:

- KPIs are determined top-down, while OKRs are determined bottom-up.
- Objectives are the dream; Key Results are the success criteria (i.e., a way to measure incremental progress towards the objective).
- Objectives are qualitative and Key Results are quantitative. OKRs are not the same as employee evaluations. OKRs are about the company's goals and how each employee contributes to those goals. Performance evaluations—which are entirely about evaluating how an employee performed in a given period—are independent of OKRs.
- Objectives are ambitious and should feel uncomfortable.

    [In general, up to five objectives and four key results per initiative are optimal, and key results should see an achievement rate of 60 to 70 percent; if they don't, the bar has been set too low.]

ExOs have more than taken this technique to heart. Many are now implementing *high-frequency* OKRs—that is, a target per week, month or quarter for *each* individual or team within a company.

Scientific results in neuroscience, gamification and behavioral economics have shown the importance of both specificity and frequent feedback in driving behavioral change and, ultimately, having an impact. Specificity and rapid feedback cycles energize, motivate and drive company morale and culture. As a result, a number of services, including OKR Hub, Cascade, Teamly and 7Geese, have been formed to help businesses track these measures.

That said, there is still a long way to go, especially beyond the world of hot startups, and this is true of even the world's high tech centers. Fabio Troiani, managing director of Business Integration Partners, a global consultancy based in Italy, observes that OKRs are still unique even to Silicon Valley. He reports that of the hundred large corporations in Europe and South America with which he's familiar, none use OKRs.

Meanwhile, dashboards of value metrics, used in conjunction with OKRs, are becoming the *de facto* standard for measuring ExOs—everything from the company as a whole to individual teams and employees. At Google, for example, all OKRs are completely transparent and public within the company.

Furthermore, younger-generation employees have experienced different conditioning in terms of measurements and feedback loops than have older generations. For example, embedded within the highly popular game of World of Warcraft are dashboards similar to OKRs and Lean metrics with short feedback cycles.

A good analogy for the benefit of fast-cycle OKRs is mobile phones. Over the last fifteen years, the instant email and always-on connectivity provided by mobile phones has drastically improved decision-making speed and conversation cycle times. OKRs do the same for organizations.

Why are dashboards key for ExOs? Because growing at a rapid pace requires that instrumentation of the business, individual and team assessments be integrated and carried out in real time, not least because small mistakes can grow very big very fast. Without both functions in place, a company is liable to drift back to its earlier focus on "vanity" metrics and lose attention or have misguided KPIs for teams. Or both.

As mentioned at the start of the chapter, tight control frameworks are critical to managing hyper growth. Real-time dashboards and OKRs are key elements of that control framework.

Why Important?	Dependencies or Prerequisites
• Track critical growth drivers in real time • OKRs create control framework to manage fast growth • Minimize exposure from errors because of short feedback loops	• Real-time metrics tracked, gathered and analyzed • OKRs implemented • Cultural acceptance by employees

EXPERIMENTATION

We define Experimentation as the implementation of the Lean Startup methodology of testing assumptions and constantly experimenting with controlled risks. According to Zappos CEO Tony Hsieh, "A great brand or company is a story that never stops unfolding." That is, it is imperative to continuously evolve and experiment. Bill Gates takes Hsieh's insight a step further: "Success is a lousy teacher. It seduces smart people into thinking they can't lose."

In a recent commencement address at Singapore Management University, John Seely Brown made the compelling point that all corporate architectures are set up to *withstand* risk and change. Furthermore, he said, all corporate planning efforts attempt to scale efficiency and predictability, meaning they work to create static—or at least controlled-growth—environments in the belief that they will reduce risk.

But in today's fast-changing world, Seely Brown continued, just the opposite is true. Mark Zuckerberg agrees, noting, "The biggest risk is not taking any risk." Constant experimentation and process iteration are now the *only* ways to reduce risk. Large numbers of bottom-up ideas, properly filtered, *always* trump top-down thinking, no matter the industry or organization. Seely Brown and Hagel call this "scalable learning," and given the growth rates of ExOs, it is their only possible strategy. In the best cases, ExOs feature both—that is, ideas are developed bottom-up and get acceptance/ratification/support from the top. In the end, the best ideas win, regardless of who proposed them.

In an effort to kick-start this kind of thinking, Adobe Systems recently launched the KickStart Innovation Workshop. Participating employees receive a red box containing a step-by-step startup guide and a pre-paid credit card with $1,000 in seed money, and are given forty-five days to experiment with and validate innovative ideas. Although they have access to coaching from some of the company's top innovators, the rest is up to them. In 2013, nine hundred of Adobe's 11,000 employees participated in the workshop. Not only does Adobe's approach stimulate experimentation, but it also establishes a measurable funnel by which promising ideas and concepts can be identified and pursued in a systemic and comparable way.

Many other companies are also exploring experimentation—not just in skunkworks, but also on core processes. It is not, however, a totally new concept. The Japanese have long followed the practice of *kaizen*: constant improvement as a fundamental process management technique. The only difference between scalable learning and *kaizen* is the use of new and more advanced offline and online data-driven tools to test assumptions of customer groups, use cases and solutions.

Apple used a kind of *kaizen* to launch its first retail store, which was considered a highly risky move at the time. After bringing Millard Drexler, CEO of Gap Inc., onto its board, Apple then hired Ron Johnson (who as vice president of merchandising made his name elevating Target's image above that of a high-end Kmart) to manage the new retail operations. With their collective knowledge, the two men prototyped a store, then tested and redesigned it based on customer data and feedback. Apple kept iterating until it had enough validation to roll out its first Apple Store in northern Virginia on May 15, 2001. Once the concept became successful, Apple scaled it aggressively; the company currently has 425 retail stores in sixteen countries.

This technique is popularly known as the Lean Startup movement, which was created by Eric Ries and Steve Blank and is based on Ries's book of the same name. The Lean Startup philosophy (also known as the Lean Launchpad) is in turn based upon Toyota's "lean manufacturing" principles, first established a half-century ago, in which the elimination of wasteful processes is paramount. (Sample principle: "Eliminate all expenses with any goal other than the creation of value for the end customer.")

Lean Approach

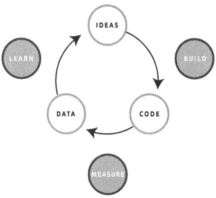

The Lean Startup concept was also given impetus by Steve Blank's book, *The Four Steps to the Epiphany*, which focuses on customer development. (Sample concept: "We don't know what the customer wants until assumptions are validated.") The most important message of the Lean Startup movement is to *"Fail fast and fail often, while eliminating waste."* Its approach can be summarized as a new, scientific, data-driven, iterative, and highly customer-driven approach to practical innovation that is used by startups, mid-market companies, corporations and even governments. To illustrate how this credo can have such a positive impact on a company, compare it to the traditional method of product development, also known as the waterfall model.

As mentioned in Chapter Two, the traditional waterfall approach to product development is a linear process (most often referred to as NPD, for New Product Development) that uses sequential steps such as idea generation, screening, product design, development and commercialization. This process not only burns up a great deal of precious time but, more importantly, increasingly results in new products that don't fit—or, because the market is changing so quickly, no longer fit—the needs of the customer, culminating in a product no one wants. Inevitably, even more time and money is spent adapting the product to fit the customer, a process that once again takes too long as the market moves on.

In the end, of course, the product fails. In sum, NPD has become a process in which thinking and doing are separated for a long time period and where data-driven and behavioral customer feedback is delivered too late in the development process. As Nassim Taleb explains, "Knowledge gives you a little bit of an edge, but tinkering (trial and error) is the equivalent of 1,000 IQ points. It is tinkering that allowed the Industrial Revolution."

By comparison, consider the same scenario using the Lean Startup method:

The company first researches the needs of the customer, then conducts an *experiment* to see if a proposed product matches those needs. By relying on quantitative and qualitative data, a company forms a *conclusion* based on a series of well-considered questions:

- Does a product fit the need of the customer?
- How did a customer solve a problem or need in the past?
- What are the current costs created by the customer problem?
- Should we adapt or change our course?

- Are we ready to scale?

This process of constant learning can be accomplished in just a couple of weeks or months, at minimal cost. Best of all, it usually becomes clear early on if a product is doomed to failure. A good way of looking at this is that when you move from point A to point B, you can then see point C. But you can't see point C from point A. Iteration/experimentation is the only way.

As Eric Ries explains, "The modern rule of competition is whoever learns fastest, wins." Most digital markets are winner-takes-all markets due to network effects. This makes a culture of continuous experimentation even more important.

The Martin Trust Center for MIT Entrepreneurship uses a Lean Startup process for corporate innovation that is similar to the one used at Adobe. It's called the *5x5x5x5 method* (54). Five corporate teams with five complementary team members compete for five weeks (one to two days a week), spending no more than $5,000 to produce one innovation. The budget is ideal for testing assumptions with real customers related to the customer group, customer problem (use case), and solution (innovation concept) using different offline and online methods.

After five weeks, each team presents its output, which is a combination of concept, competitive analysis, business model canvas and validated learning based on different experiments or Minimal Viable Products (MVPs). In short, it is a data-driven, scientific, problem-solution fit and product-market fit for the innovative idea that maximizes learning and speeds up the product development process—both key requirements for a rapidly changing world. Not bad for little more than one month's work.

Maria Mujica, who heads up the two-year-old innovation unit Fly Garage for Mondelez International, a confectionery company, uses Experimentation to run several-day "Garages" to create new brand engagements. Groups of free thinkers from inside and outside the organization are invited to participate in a no-boundary environment. The following steps constitute a "Garage" experience:

- Detox by disconnecting and unplugging from everything
- Empathize and immerse so as to connect with the opportunity
- Boil ideas down to a creative brief (brief then transcribed onto a T-shirt that's worn)
- Agitate to drive ideation and mix/shake up solutions
- Prototype rapidly to enable a fast user experience

Fascinating outcomes have resulted from Garages, including the "Traffic Karaoke in Bogota" and a vending machine where users pay with hunger (which is measured by a swallowed sensor). Fly Garage is successfully balancing corporate procedural repeatability with highly creative outcomes—a holy grail for any organization. Mujica has also mastered another traditionally difficult balance: top-down direction with bottom-up creativity and little or no cultural tension.

A final and critical pre-requisite for experimentation is a willingness to fail. Thirty years ago, Regis McKenna, a Silicon Valley marketing pioneer, was the first to note that whatever its reputation for success, the Valley was in fact built on failure— or more precisely, a willingness to accept and even reward "good" failure.

Unfortunately, within the traditional corporate environment, failure more often than not still results in career-level consequences due to long lead times and large investments. This, of course, reduces risk appetite. At the same time, sunk-cost bias (the momentum that attaches to projects solely because of the money already invested) also kicks in. Before long, a company can find itself spending even more money launching a doomed product despite clear data that it will fail. Remember the Iridium mobile phones case? The Navteq–Waze case? In addition, consider the well-known NASA motto: "'Failure is not an option." Although noble and inspiring, it was ultimately a death knell for exploration. When failure is not an option, you end up with safe, incremental innovation, with no radical breakthroughs or disruptive innovations.

By integrating experimentation as a core value and adopting approaches like Lean Startup, enterprise failures—while still accepted as an inevitable part of risk—can be quick, relatively painless and insightful. Google, for example, is particularly good at experimentation: If a product is not meeting its goals, and resources could be better leveraged elsewhere, the product is shut down. Recriminations are limited, the company quickly moves on and the employees involved never experience career-limiting consequences.

Some corporations have even taken to celebrating failure in order to counteract what they see as a cultural resistance among their employees to the very idea of failure. For example, the Procter & Gamble Heroic Failure award honors the employee or team with the biggest failure that delivered the greatest insight. Similarly, Tata offers an annual Dare To Try award, which recognizes managers who took the biggest risk. In 2013 alone, the award attracted more than 240 entries.

This doesn't mean, of course, that just any failure or mistake is encouraged or celebrated. But if a team is operating within strategic, commercial, ethical and legal frameworks and avoids recreating old mistakes, a failure can and should be celebrated for the learning such experimentation offers. A well-known Silicon Valley credo holds that it is crucial to distinguish a "good" failure, one done for all of the right reasons and that produces useful results, from a "bad" one—and even from a "bad" success, where success is more luck than accomplishment—and then to reward accordingly.

Not only does failure free people, ideas and capital for future learning and breakthroughs, it's also worth noting that, though rarely recognized, a corporate culture that accepts failure benefits from diminished internal politics and much less in the way of pointing fingers and "blame games" thanks to trust, transparency and openness.

There are some limitations to the Lean Startup approach, including lack of competitor analysis or considerations in design thinking. Also, it is important to note that the ability to fail is much easier in software and information-based environments because iteration is so much easier. For a hardware company, it's much harder to iterate. Apple launches hardware only when it's perfect. You wouldn't want to iterate and fail fast when building a nuclear reactor.

As Nathan Furr and Jeff Dyer state in their new book, *The Innovator's Method: Bringing the Lean Start-up into Your Organization*: "Don't try to scale it until you nail it."

Why Important?	Dependencies or Prerequisites
• Keeps processes aligned with rapidly changing externalities • Maximizes value capture • Faster to market (MVP) • Risk taking provides an edge and faster learning	• Measurement and tracking of experiments • Cultural acceptance (failure=experience)

AUTONOMY

We describe Autonomy as self-organizing, multi-disciplinary teams operating with decentralized authority. Valve Software, a game company, is a most unusual enterprise. It has 330 staffers but no classic management structure, reporting lines, job descriptions or regular meetings. Instead, the company hires talented, innovative self-starters, who decide which projects they wish to join. They are also encouraged to start new projects, so long as they fit the company's MTP. Autonomy is a prerequisite for *permissionless innovation*.

Extreme autonomy—relying on small, independent, multi-disciplined teams—has worked well for Valve. It has a higher revenue-per-employee number than any other gaming company, and its approach enables changing roles and activities for all workers. This organizational style also creates a sociable, open and trusting culture featuring a highly satisfied staff. In fact, the company is confident enough in its way of doing business that its employee manual is open sourced and available to anyone, including competitors.

Valve isn't alone in pioneering new organizational models in order to amp performance. Its approach to autonomy is similar to the MIT Media Lab: both are passion-driven organizations in which employees and students are self-starters who launch their own projects or pick from a collection of ongoing projects. Some projects are even begun with external partners for the sole purpose of collaborating on innovative ideas.

In perhaps the most extreme case of Autonomy, Philip Rosedale, founder and former CEO of Second Life and founder and CEO of High Fidelity, has made it a practice at High Fidelity to have his employees vote each quarter on whether or not to keep him on as CEO. In addition, instead of relying on employee reviews, share options are allocated on an anonymous peer-to-peer basis.

From teleworking to outsourcing to flattened, virtual organizations, there has been a clear and steady trend toward increased autonomy in the workplace. As a result, we predict the lightweight OKR approach will gradually replace traditional top-down managerial oversight. Furthermore, many Exponential Organizations are organizing internally—though not in traditional departments with layers of middle management, but rather by self-organized, interdisciplinary teams and with radically decentralized authority. The Millennial generation, armed with Internet and gaming skills, which cultivate a self-starter and entrepreneurial mindset, is increasingly at odds with classic hierarchical structures that are optimized for efficiency over adaptability.

Ed Catmull, co-founder of Pixar Animation Studios and president of Pixar Animation and Walt Disney Animation, expands on this idea in his *New York Times* bestselling book, *Creativity, Inc.: Overcoming the Unseen Forces That Stand in the Way of True Inspiration*: "We start from the presumption that our people are talented and want to contribute. We accept that, without meaning to, our company is stifling that talent in myriad unseen ways. Finally, we try to identify those impediments and try to fix them."

The need for autonomy and decentralization is further driven by increasingly critical and knowledgeable consumers who expect zero latency service and delivery, and are quick to complain on review sites if their ever-climbing expectations are not met. One survey by McKinsey found that after experiencing poor customer experience, 89 percent of consumers switched their business to a competing company. On the flip side, 86 percent said they were willing to pay more for better customer experience. These hypercritical and demanding consumers can only be satisfied with companies placing their most empowered and proactive employees on the front line.

A good example of this trend towards Autonomy is a company called Holacracy, which has taken Agile techniques from the software world and the Lean Startup approach and extended them to all aspects of the organization. Holacracy (a concept as well as the company's name) is defined as a social technology or system of organizational governance,[1] in which authority and decision-making are distributed via fractal, self-organizing teams rather than being vested at the top of a hierarchy. The system combines Experimentation, OKRs, openness, transparency and Autonomy.

The following table compares traditional organizational characteristics with autonomous organizations like those advocated by Holacracy:

---

1   en.wikipedia.org/wiki/Governance

Without Holacracy	With Holacracy
Central control and authority	Distributed control and authority
Predict and plan for long term	Dynamic and flexible: changes can and are constantly occurring
Hierarchic structure OR flat, based on consensus	Neither, as everyone is the 'highest authority' in their own role and 'follower' of other roles
Interest oriented	Core goal oriented
Tension as a problem	Tension as fuel
Reorganization and change management	Natural development, evolution and movement
Job titles	Dynamic roles
Heroic leaders, employees and process supervisors	Vital people who fulfill their role
Organizing people	Organizing work
Instrumental use of human relationships to serve Organizational goals	Clear separation between people, relationships and roles

Holacracy is said to increase agility, efficiency, transparency, innovation and accountability within an organization. The approach encourages individual team members to take initiative and gives them a process by which their concerns or ideas can be addressed. The system of distributed authority also reduces the burden on leaders to make every decision alone.

Importantly, Autonomy does not imply a lack of accountability. As organizational design expert Steve Denning explains it: "There are still hierarchies in a network, but the hierarchies tend to be competence-based hierarchies, relying more on peer accountability than on authority-based accountability—that is, accountability to someone who knows something, rather than to someone simply because they occupy a position, regardless of competence. It is a change in the role of the manager, not an abolition of the function."

The following shows some enterprises at the cutting edge of organizational autonomy:

Medium (2012) – 40 employees

Market: Content platform. Medium is a new Internet site where people can share ideas and stories in more than 140 characters. Not just for friends.

How is the company organized? Medium has no people managers and emphasizes maximum autonomy. Key components at Medium are:

- Tension resolution (identify issues and resolve them systematically).
- Organic expansion (employees can hire personnel if a job demands it).
- Decision-making power distributed and consensus seeking discouraged.

What is the financial impact? Recent investment in 2014, valuing the company at $250 million.

Zappos.com (1999) – 4,000 employees

Market: Online retail market for shoes and clothing

How is the company organized?

- Company places great emphasis on company culture and core values.
- Zappos pays people to leave if they don't fit into the company culture.
- Employees encouraged to go beyond traditional customer service.
- Representatives encouraged to make decisions on their own.
- No job standards available.

What is the financial impact? In November 2009, Zappos.com was acquired by Amazon.com in a deal valued at $1.2 billion on the day of closing. Gross sales exceeded $1 billion in 2008 (20 percent better than the year before) and 75 percent of its customers are repeat buyers. Company profitable since 2006.

Valve Corp (1996) – 400 employees

Market: Game development

How is the company organized?

- Company has no managers.
- Every employee has the freedom to create without having to worry about the consequences of failure.
- Employees are encouraged to select and work on their own projects.
- Employees are responsible for go/no go of projects and for hiring personnel.

What is the financial impact? Over 75 million active users on the social entertainment platform. $2.5 billion equity in 2012.

Morning Star Company (1970) – 400 to 2,400 employees (more during harvest)

Market: Agribusiness and food processing (tomato)

How is the company organized?

- No supervisory management.
- Employees are encouraged to innovate independently, define job responsibilities themselves, make equipment purchasing decisions.
- Employees negotiate and set individual responsibilities with fellow workers.
- Compensation is peer-based. Each employee crafts a Colleague Letter of Understanding (CLOU), which outlines how worker will meet the personal mission statement. Associates most affected by this person's work must accept the CLOU before it goes into effect.

What is the financial impact? The company has funded virtually all its growth from internal sources, which suggests it is robustly profitable. On the basis of its own benchmarking data, Morning Star believes it is the world's most efficient tomato processor.

FAVI (1960) – 440 employees

Market: Designer and manufacturer of copper alloy automotive components

How is the company organized? FAVI has no hierarchy or personnel department, and there is no middle management or formal procedures. Teams are organized around customers. Each team is responsible not only for the customer, but for its own human resources, purchasing and product development.

What is the financial impact? In 2010 FAVI generated a turnover of €75 million, 80 percent of it automotive. 38 percent of personnel have been with the company for over 15 years. Workforce grew from 140 to 440.

Other companies that have implemented autonomous structures include W. L. Gore & Associates, Southwest Airlines, Patagonia, Semler, AES, Buurtzorg and Springer.

University of Michigan economist Scott Page found that diverse teams are more successful at answering complex questions than are homogenous groups or individuals, *even if* the homogenous groups and individuals are more talented. His conclusion, however, shouldn't be all that surprising. Charles Darwin discovered that evolution progressed fastest wherever small groups of a species isolated from the main population adapted to stressful conditions. By the same token, small, independent and interdisciplinary teams are critical to future organizations, especially at the edges.

A final note: Approaches towards employee autonomy, like those found at Holacracy, are not just for small companies. Large organizations, including Zappos and Semler, have also adopted this structure across much bigger operations.

Harvard professor Rosabeth Moss Kanter puts it best: "When dealing with a rapidly changing environment and the fluid boundaries of business units that come and go, more work will be done by crosscutting project teams, and there will be more bottom-up self-organizing."

Why Important?	Dependencies or Prerequisites
• Increased agility • More accountability at customer face • Faster reaction and learning times • Better morale	• MTP (as a gravity well) • Self-starting employees • Dashboards

SOCIAL TECHNOLOGIES

Social technology is an overused industry buzz phrase that has been giving CIOs heartburn for the last decade. Regardless, however, it has had the effect of pushing old analog business environments to become more digital, low-latency environments. Social technologies—whose analog counterpart, of course, is the so-called water cooler effect—create horizontal interactions in vertically organized companies.

Social technology is finding fertile ground because the workplace has become increasingly digitized. It started with email, which provided asynchronous connectivity; next came wikis and intranets that provided synchronous information sharing; today we have activity streams that provide real-time updates throughout organizations. As Marc Andreessen said, "Communication is the basis for civilization and will be a catalyst and platform in the future for more innovations in many industries." The reason we think this is important is the frame that social business expert Theo Priestley puts around it when he says, "Transparency is the new currency. Trust is the bill we'll just be paying for." Priestley's equation for social business is: CONNECTION + ENGAGEMENT + TRUST + TRANSPARENCY.[1]

When it comes to advancing your business, J.P. Rangaswami, chief scientist at Salesforce, views social technology as having

---

1   bpmredux.wordpress.com/2012/09/20/the-social-business-equation-connection-engagement-trust-transparency/

three key objectives:

1. Reduce the distance between obtaining (and processing) information and decision-making.
2. Migrate from having to look up information to having it flow through your perception.
3. Leverage community to build out ideas.

From our perspective, Social Technologies are comprised of seven key elements: Social objects, Activity streams, Task management, File sharing, Telepresence, Virtual worlds and Emotional sensing.

When implemented, these elements create transparency and connectedness and, most importantly, lower an organization's information latency. The ultimate objective is what the Gartner Group calls a *zero latency enterprise*—that is, a company in which the time between idea, acceptance and implementation all but disappears—and implementing one can provide significant return on investment.

Just how significant? Forrester Research studied one implementation of Microsoft's Yammer enterprise social network within a 21,000-employee organization. During a payback period of just 4.3 months, and with only one third of the workforce using the product, the company saw an ROI of 365 percent.

Given such results, it's not surprising that Yammer now has 8 million installations. Similarly, Salesforce's Chatter product grew from 20,000 active networks in February 2011 to 150,000 in less than eighteen months. Further, Salesforce's data indicates that employee engagement among companies that adopt its platform increases by 36 percent and access to information speeds up 43 percent.

Employee relationship management is just one type of **social object** that is being information-enabled. Also in the mix are location, physical objects, ideas and knowledge—including updates to pricing data, inventory levels, meeting room occupancy and even coffee refills. All are now being broadcast company-wide and are the basis of **activity streams** to which anyone in the organization can subscribe.

Task management is also becoming increasingly social. In the past, it was mostly used as a to-do list, but it is now shifting towards a more Agile approach. Teams are continuously measuring themselves by pushing codes and closing tickets, living by the metrics that task management software provides. Asana, a software company founded by Dustin Moskovitz (a co-founder of Facebook) and Justin Rosenstein improves work productivity, and is based on the principle that "your to-do list should be just as addicting as your Facebook wall."

File sharing, the fourth leg of the social stool, has recently enjoyed widespread adoption. Tools, from Google Drive, Box, Dropbox and Microsoft's OneDrive, are vital to sharing information and providing updates to a single instantiation of customer information. For example, Citibank once had more than three hundred different customer databases, each consuming valuable overhead and costing enormous sums in duplication and redundancy. Such drag on costs and operations is simply not acceptable in an Exponential Organization—or, indeed, for any company trying to compete in the 21st century.

Telepresence has been around for many years in the form of videoconferencing. Although videoconferencing was quite a hassle in the past, an organization can now leverage services such as Skype and Google Hangout, which are fast, easy to use and available on every device. Telepresence enables employees to work proactively from any location and interact on a global scale, reducing travel costs and improving well-being. Even greater improvement comes from Telepresence robots such as Beam, from Suitable Technologies, and Double Robotics, which leverage the user's tablet. These robots even allow the user to be on multiple locations at once, which can greatly impact how to conduct business.

While Telepresence lets people interact in a real environment, virtual reality allows interaction, collaboration, coordination and even prototyping in a **virtual world**. Philip Rosedale's Second Life is one of the best-known examples: "One of the things about Second Life was that it enabled somebody like IBM to basically set up a big get-together with a thousand people from around the world," he says. Although Second Life didn't fully meet customer (or investor) expectations and stopped growing after a few years, it has remained consistent, with one million people online every month and an economy of $600 million in transactions.

To enable a fully immersive virtual world, Rosedale's new High Fidelity platform is leveraging hardware such as Oculus Rift, the PrimeSense depth camera and the Leap Motion gesture controller. The High Fidelity environment has reduced the time lag between gesture and system response to almost the speed of human perception, resulting in a truly real-time experience.

Emotional sensing, the last key element of social technology, makes use of sensors—such as health sensors and neurotechnology—within a team or group to create Quantified Employees and a Quantified Workforce. Employees will be able to measure everything about themselves and their work, preventing illness, burnout and irritation, and also improving team flow, collaboration and performance. While work in the past was mostly focused on the importance of the Intelligence Quotient (IQ), the Emotional Quotient (EQ) and Spiritual Quotient (SQ) are now becoming increasingly important metrics as well.

The entire social paradigm presents several critical implications for ExOs. Organizational intimacy is increased, decision latency is reduced, knowledge improves and is more widely spread, and serendipity increases. In short, social technologies enable the real-time enterprise.

Finally, the social paradigm also serves as a gravity force, keeping the organization tightly connected to its MTP and ensuring that its diverse parts don't drift away in pursuit of conflicting, even opposing, goals.

Why Important?	Dependencies or Prerequisites
• Faster conversations • Faster decision cycles • Faster learning • Stabilizes team during rapid growth	• MTP • Cloud social tools • Cooperative culture

If you remember our list of linear attributes of traditional organizations from way back in Chapter Two, we can now juxtapose linear versus exponential characteristics:

Linear Organization Characteristics	ExO Characteristics
Top-down and hierarchical in its organization	Autonomy, Social Technologies
Driven by financial outcomes	MTP, Dashboards
Linear, sequential thinking	Experimentation, Autonomy
Innovation primarily from within	Community & Crowd, Staff on Demand, Leveraged Assets, Interfaces (innovation at the edges)
Strategic planning largely an extrapolation from the past	MTP, Experimentation
Risk intolerance	Experimentation
Process inflexibility	Autonomy, Experimentation
Large number of FTEs	Algorithms, Community & Crowd, Staff on Demand
Controls/owns its own assets	Leveraged Assets
Strongly invested in status quo	MTP, Dashboards, Experimentation

Let's now look back at our definition of an ExO: **"An Exponential Organization is one whose impact (or output) is disproportionally large—at least 10x larger—compared to its peers because of the use of new organizational techniques that leverage accelerating technologies."**

As we have researched the paradigm, we have uncovered over sixty organizations with scores over our ExO threshold, each achieving at least a 10x performance improvement over others in its space. The following are our top 10 (in alphabetical order): **Airbnb, GitHub, Google, Netflix, Quirky, Tesla, Uber, Waze, Valve, Xiaomi**.

It may seem odd to look back four centuries to capture the essence of the most modern of company organizations. Nevertheless, Isaac Newton's second law precisely summarizes the overall concept of an Exponential Organization. The law, $F = MA$, states that force causes acceleration in inverse proportion to mass. A small mass allows dramatic acceleration and quick changes in direction—precisely what we're seeing with many ExOs today. With very little internal inertia (that is, number of employees, assets or organizational structures), they demonstrate extraordinary flexibility, which is a critical quality in today's volatile world.

This remarkable characteristic has been well demonstrated by Netflix. As mentioned earlier, the company offered a $1 million prize (Engagement) to anyone who could improve its rental recommendation program. What is less well known is that Netflix *never implemented the winning algorithm.*

Why? Because, tellingly, the market had already moved on. By the conclusion of the contest the industry had shifted away from rental DVDs; meanwhile Netflix's streaming video business was exploding and, unfortunately, the winning algorithm didn't apply to streaming recommendations. (Streaming was much less a matter of gathering the family together on a Friday night with popcorn than of having forty-five minutes at an airport to watch an episode of *Mad Men.*)

Now, imagine that Netflix had invested the 2,000 hours the winning team spent on the project to develop that very same, now-obsolete algorithm. With prevalent sunk-cost biases and institutional insistence to see a return on that investment (plus the egos involved), there would have been enormous internal pressure within the company to implement the algorithm, regardless of market realities. As a result, Netflix might have not have altered course to become, primarily, a streaming business—which, as we now know, would have been a devastating mistake. But because the algorithm was developed externally, there was much less corporate emotional attachment (i.e., mass) and inertia (force) to its implementation. Netflix was free to focus elsewhere, ultimately allowing it to evolve into the streaming content giant it has become.

The key question for any organization is not whether you "look" like an Exponential Organization, but "How exponential are you?" That is, how much have you internalized the philosophy of being an ExO? How does it inform your daily operations in terms of autonomy and social technology? How efficiently do you use the right tools, from dashboards to interfacing? And how open are you to risk, to experimentation and even to failure?

These are questions you need to ask yourself—not just once but every month or even week. That's what it takes to be become, and remain, an Exponential Organization.

KEY TAKEAWAYS

- ExOs manage the abundant output of SCALE externalities with guidance from their MTP and the control framework of five internal IDEAS elements:
  - Interfaces
  - Dashboards
  - Experimentation
  - Autonomy
  - Social Technologies
- The more assets and workforce you have, the harder it is to switch strategies and business models. The more information-enabled you are, the more strategic flexibility you have.
- A diagnostic survey (Appendix A or **www. exponentialorgs.com/survey**) will help measure the Exponential Quotient of your organization.
- Interfaces create frictionless migration from external to internal attributes.
- SCALE and IDEAS elements are self-reinforcing and integrative.

CHAPTER FIVE
IMPLICATIONS OF EXPONENTIAL ORGANIZATIONS

While the notion of an Exponential Organization may seem revolutionary, in fact many of its characteristics have long shown up in certain corners of the business world—most notably, Hollywood.

Why did Hollywood, 3,000 miles away from both the acting world of Broadway and the banking center of New York City, become the world capital of the film industry by the end of the 1920s? Initially, it was due to little more than an abundance of natural lighting. But soon there was a second reason. The West Coast was far removed from the traditional culture of the East, and with its almost unlimited cheap real estate and pliant local government, the early film barons were free to do almost anything they wanted, including writing their own rules.

The result was the *studio system*, in which early filmmakers set out to own the entirety of their assets and their workforces, from the sets to the studios to the employees. Even actors were contracted to single studios, and distribution was exclusive to the theaters owned by that studio.

This strategy quickly built one of the most valuable industries on the planet. But as the decades passed, inefficiencies and antitrust issues crept in, and by the 1960s, the studio system was all but dismantled. What replaced it was a system that was almost the exact opposite of what came before.

Today, Hollywood operates in exactly the same loosely

coupled, networked environment of an ExO ecosystem. Each participant, from the writer and actor, to the director and camera grip, manages his or her own career. Meanwhile, agents at every level help find and connect scripts with talent, production companies and equipment. These days, when a film is created, a swarm of independent entities come together for the duration of the production, operating on 24/7 schedules and in close collaboration. Once the film is finished, sets are broken down for re-use, equipment is reassigned and all the actors, grips and production assistants disband and scatter to pursue their next projects, which often start the very next day.

Hollywood didn't plan this metamorphosis; rather, it evolved into an ExO-like ecosystem because it is the nature of film to be a series of discrete projects. The filmmaking process itself has always been characterized by a singular combination of high density, close proximity and loosely coupled constituents. These factors made Hollywood a pioneer in the virtualization of enterprises and now, combined with new social and communications technologies, puts it in the vanguard of the rise of the Exponential Organization.

The high-tech startup ecosystem of Silicon Valley is another example of this model: entrepreneurs, employees, scientists, marketers, patent lawyers, angel investors, venture capitalists and even customers—all operate within a small geographic region of the San Francisco Bay Area. Another (more dysfunctional) example is Wall Street.

Leveraged by new generations of technology that, thanks to Moore's Law, have emerged every few years, the infrastructure is now in place for many industries to move to this framework— and they will, not only because it confers enormous competitive advantage, but also because it rewards first movers.

In this chapter, we'll examine in depth some of the characteristics of an ExO ecosystem. In particular, we've identified nine key dynamics at play:

1. INFORMATION ACCELERATES EVERYTHING

Everywhere you look, the new information paradigm, created as a result of Moore's Law and other fundamental forces that bear upon the digital world, is accelerating the metabolism of products, companies and industries. In industry after industry, the development cycle for products and services grows ever shorter. And like the shift from film photography to digital photography, once you change the substrate from a material, mechanical basis to a digital and informational one, the match is lit for an inevitable explosion.

In 1995, 710 million rolls of film were developed at thousands of processing centers. By 2005, nearly 200 billion digital photographs, equaling about eight *billion* rolls, had been taken and edited, stored and displayed in ways that were unimaginable just a few years before. Today, web users upload almost one billion photographs *per day* to sites like Snapchat, Facebook and Instagram.

As we saw in Chapter One, the shift from analog to digital is occurring in multiple core technologies that feature multiplier effects at their intersections. This process of "virtualizing" one industry after another is not just advancing exponentially, but at multiples of even that as data about the many different components of a single item or process is systematically analyzed and automated by software (data analytics). And that's just the beginning: as we add trillions of sensors on every device, process and person, the process will accelerate even faster to an almost unimaginable pace (Big Data). Finally, according to Ericsson Research, within the next eight years we will see the next generation of mobile networks (5G) sporting speeds of five gigabits per second. Just imagine what that will make possible.

When Marc Andreessen proclaimed in a 2011 *Wall Street Journal* article that "software is eating the world," he was addressing this very phenomenon. Andreessen, who helped invent the Internet browser and is now one of Silicon Valley's most powerful venture capitalists, argued that in every industry, and at every level, software is automating and accelerating the world. Cloud computing and the app store ecosystems are clear testaments to this trend, with the Apple and Android platforms each hosting more than 1.2 million applications programs, most of them crowdsourced from customers.

Nowhere is this staggering pace of change more apparent than with the consumer Internet. Many products are now launched early—unfinished and in perpetual beta—for the sole purpose of gathering data from users as early as possible to determine how to "finish" the product. Data collected from these early users is quickly analyzed for insights on bugs that need fixing and the features users most want to see. Once the changes are implemented, the product is rereleased and analyzed…and the process continues.

As LinkedIn founder Reid Hoffman has said, "If you're not embarrassed by the product when you launch, you've launched too late."

These days, product development cycles are measured not in months or quarters, but in hours or days. The Lean Startup movement, with its paradigm of constant iteration/experimentation, began on the Toyota car production line in the 1970s, moved to the Internet in the 1990s, and is today showing that it is applicable to almost any type of business.

A great example of this new approach is Wercker, a delivery software development platform based in Holland. Wercker helps developers reduce risk and eliminate waste by continuously testing and deploying code using advanced testing and debugging techniques. Wercker's goal is to free the individual developer to focus on the code and the application, where such attention is most valuable, rather than on tedious install processes or systems management.

The open source movement has further accelerated this trend. A single developer working on, say, a printer driver, can now benefit from the transparency of a hundred other developers who've worked on similar projects. And that's just the beginning: when network effects kick in, the overall community begins learning at a much-accelerated pace. We can see this happening in web-hosted developer communities such as GitHub and Bitbucket.

This information acceleration isn't just confined to software development. It is also happening in the hardware world. Consider Illumina, a biotech company that pioneered the development of high-speed genome sequencing machines. In 2008, Illumina's products sold for $500,000 each, plus as much as an additional $200,000 a year in consumable supplies to keep the machines running. Meanwhile, the product development cycle for new models was eighteen months.

That eighteen-month product development cycle was particularly bad news. Why? Because the pace of change (driven by the new information basis of the genome) in the industry was so fast that the shelf life of any new design was just nine months. Which meant that even while Illumina's sales team was selling one version of the company's gene sequencer, two future versions of the same machine were at different points in the development cycles.

The cost of having three generations of technology either in inventory or development was enormous for everyone involved. Then, a new open source community appeared on the scene. Called OpenPCR, it was dedicated to building a DNA-copying machine for just $599. This was analogous to the Home Brew club hobbyists creating the first PCs that then revolutionized computing. The result has been an industry-wide transformation, allowing new entrants and hobbyists into the field, which has benefitted all players in the business, including Illumina.

Though few industries have experienced such a stunning transformation as biotech, similar trends can also be seen in many other hardware arenas. Thus, while a basic 3D printer in 2007 cost nearly $40,000, the new Peachy Printer—recently funded on Kickstarter—is now available for just $100. And that's only the start: Avi Reichental, CEO of market leader 3D Systems, sees no obstacles to bringing his company's high-end 3D printers to market for just $399 within the next five years.

Another example of this trend includes single-board computers for robotics and education, where the open sourced

Raspberry Pi platform has proved transformative. The same is true of single-board controllers, where Arduino has assumed dominance. No surprise, then, that one of the most popular new memes in the computer business is that "hardware is the new software." Dan Barry, a former astronaut who now builds robots, notes that whenever he gets stuck on a robot configuration or sensor problem, he posts a question online before he goes to bed, waking the next morning to finds answers from tens of thousands of robot enthusiasts.

This "going digital" is fundamentally shifting the competitive landscape in many sectors, allowing new entrants from unexpected places. In some countries, banks are getting into the travel business. We're also seeing travel agents moving into insurance and retailers into media (Amazon, Netflix). As a result, whatever business you are in, chances are your competitors are not what they used to be.

A final outcome of this trend is that we seem to be entering an era of "winner-takes-all" markets. There's really only one search engine (Google), one auction site (eBay) and one e-commerce site (Amazon). Network effects and customer experience lock-in seem to be at the root of this fundamental change in the nature of competition.

2. DRIVE TO DEMONETIZATION

One of the most important—and least celebrated—achievements of the Internet during the last decade was that it cut the marginal cost of marketing and sales to nearly *zero*.

By this we mean that with the web, it is possible to promote an online product worldwide for a tiny fraction of what it cost just twenty-five years ago. And, in concert with a viral referral loop, customer acquisition costs can also be cut to what was once deemed impossible: zero. It is precisely this advantage that allowed businesses such as Craigslist, eBay and Amazon to scale with extraordinary speed to become some the world's biggest companies.

The virtual advantage of these companies devastated their competitors—in particular, the traditional print classified advertising business. Presented with the option of free online classified ads as opposed to paid newspaper ads, consumers flocked to sites like Craigslist and eBay. As a result, in 2012, newspaper revenue fell to $18.9 billion, its lowest annual level since the Newspaper Association of America began tracking the data in 1950. Unable to compete with free, many newspapers have gone out of business, while others have faded to a shadow of their former selves.

This revolution is still underway. Recently, the French startup Free has begun offering mobile service supported by a large and active digital community of brand advocates. The company cultivates highly connected opinion leaders who interact with the rest of the base via blogs, social networks and other Internet channels, thus building a wave of buzz that quickly spreads across the digital landscape. Although Free's marketing budget is relatively low, the company has gained substantial market share and achieved high levels of customer satisfaction.

What's important to understand is that in the age of the Exponential Organization, the new information-enabled technologies will power exponential cost drops not just in sales and marketing, but also across *every* business function.

In a 2003 *Harvard Business Review* article entitled "One Number You Need to Grow," Fred Reichheld introduced the concept of a Net Promoter Score (NPS), which measures the loyalty that exists between a provider and a consumer. An NPS can be as low as -100 (everybody is a detractor) or as high as +100 (everybody is a promoter). An NPS that is positive (i.e., higher than zero) is considered good, and an NPS of +50 is excellent.

The NPS is largely based on a single, direct question: *How likely is it that you would recommend our company/product/service to a friend or colleague?* If you have a high NPS, then your sales function is free. If you are using peer-to-peer models, your service costs can also essentially be free. Using crowdsourcing and community ideation (such as Quirky or Gustin), your R&D

and product development costs can also approach zero.

And it doesn't stop there. What we're now seeing with ExOs—and this is tremendously important—is that **the marginal cost of supply goes to zero**.

A case in point: it costs Uber essentially zero to add an additional car and driver to its fleet. By the same token, Quirky can find its next consumer product for essentially zero. ExOs are able to scale their businesses with near 100 percent variable costs, even in traditionally capital-expenditure-heavy industries.

This advantage seems obvious when it comes to information-based or information-enabled sectors. But remember: *every* industry is becoming information-based, either by being digitized or by using information to identify under-utilized assets (e.g., collaborative consumptions). With Airbnb, for example, the marginal cost of a new room to rent is essentially zero. Not so for Hyatt or Hilton. A key reason for this drop in marginal cost is that there is (relative) abundance of supply. As shown in their book *Abundance*, Peter Diamandis and Steven Kotler argue that as technology brings us a world of abundance, access will triumph over ownership. By comparison, scarcity of supply or resources tends to keep costs high and stimulates ownership over access.

Today, a trend known as Collaborative Consumption leverages the Internet and social networks to create a more efficient utilization of physical assets. The following shows just some of the vertical markets affected by the phenomenon of moving from "possess" to "access": bartering, bike sharing, boat sharing, carpooling, ride sharing, car sharing, collaborative workspace, co-housing, co-working, crowdfunding, garden sharing, fractional ownership, peer-to-peer renting, product service systtem, seed swaps, taxi shares, time banks, virtual currency (Source: Wikipedia).

Note that in traditional industries that can be fully information-enabled, new competition has produced a staggering drop in revenues for old companies. The business models for music, newspapers, and book publishing have all suffered through this transformation, and today look almost nothing like they did ten years ago. Thus, the newspapers that have survived have largely shifted their revenue efforts to their web pages; the albums and CDs of the music industry have atomized to the selectable singles world of MP3 files; and many of today's bestsellers enjoy most of their profits from e-book sales.

Note that today there is a whole category of the media industry—named for the underlying physical media it's been trying to sell—which is actually made up of information businesses that have now been digitized. We believe the television industry will be the next to fall to the information ax.

3. DISRUPTION IS THE NEW NORM

In his influential bestseller *The Innovator's Dilemma*, Clayton Christensen points out that disruptive innovation rarely comes from the status quo. That is, established industry players are rarely structured or prepared to counter disruption when eventually it appears. The newspaper industry is a perfect example: it sat by for a decade as Craigslist systematically disrupted the classified advertising model.

Today, the outsider has all the advantages. With no legacy systems to worry about, as well as the ability to enjoy low overhead and take advantage of the democratization of information and—more important—technology, the newcomer can move quickly and with a minimum of expense. Thus, new actors and entrants are well equipped to attack almost any market, including yours—along with your company's profit margins.

Indeed, the rate of change is so high everywhere these days that you now must *assume* that someone will disrupt you, and often from a direction you least expect. As Steve Forbes sees it, "You have to disrupt yourself or others will do it for you." This applies to every market, geography and industry.

A century ago, competition was mainly driven by production. Forty years ago, marketing became dominant. And now, in the Internet era, as production and marketing have been commoditized and democratized, it is all about ideas and ideals.

Marketing has increasingly become product innovation—i.e., a good product sells itself. As young people and startups have plenty of ideals and ideas, the competitive advantage—as well as the field of competition—migrates towards their game and strong points. This is one of the key reasons why disruption today is more likely to come from startups than from existing direct competitors.

This pattern will take longer to impact older, capital-intensive industries such as oil and gas, mining and construction. But have no doubt: disruption is coming. Consider that solar energy, which is powered by information technology, has been doubling in its price-performance every three years. In fact, in another four years, it's estimated to reach grid parity in the U.S., when it will change the energy equation forever.

Meanwhile, other traditional industries, including real estate and automotive, are already succumbing to this new zeitgeist. The automobile industry in particular has had its cage rattled by the emergence of the all-electric Tesla. While the Tesla is a high-performance luxury car, it's much more than just that. In fact, in Silicon Valley, it is common to describe it is as a computer that happens to move—and move very well. Who would ever have predicted that in just three years a Silicon Valley team of (mostly) electrical engineers would have created the safest car ever built? For one thing, they weren't dragging 120 years of Iron-Age automotive history behind them like an anchor, as Chevrolet was when it designed the Volt, a plug-in that relies on a traditional gas engine to power a generator that charges the battery. The result is indeed no-range anxiety, but the Volt power train is very complex—and expensive.

We see a consistent set of steps around disruptive innovation comprising the following:

- Domain (or technology) becomes information-enabled

- Costs drop exponentially and access is democratized
- Hobbyists come together to form an open source community
- New combinations of technologies and convergences are introduced
- New products and services appear that are orders of magnitude better and cheaper
- The status quo is disrupted (and the domain gets information-enabled)

We are seeing this evolution occur in drones, DNA sequencing, 3D printing, sensors, robotics and, certainly, Bitcoin. In each domain, an open source, networked community has sprung up, delivering an accelerated stream of innovation exactly in line with the steps listed above.

The reason "Disruption is the New Norm" is that democratized, accelerating technologies, combined with the power of community, can now extend Christensen's Innovator's Dilemma to an unstoppable force.

4. BEWARE THE "EXPERT"

The old saw that an expert is "somebody who tells you why something can*not* be done" is truer than ever before. History has shown that the best inventions or solutions rarely come from experts; they almost always come from outsiders. That is, from people who aren't domain experts but who offer a fresh perspective.

When Kaggle runs a competition, it has found that the first responders are experts in a particular domain who say, "We know this industry, we've done this before and we'll figure it out." And just as inevitably, within two weeks, complete newcomers to the field trounce their best results. For example, the Hewlett Foundation sponsored a 2012 competition to develop an automated scoring algorithm for student-written essays. Of the

155 teams competing, three were awarded a total of $100,000 in prize money. What was particularly interesting was the fact that none of the winners had prior experience with natural language processing (NLP). Nonetheless, they beat the experts, many of them with decades of experience in NLP under their belts.

This can't help but impact the current status quo. Raymond McCauley, Biotechnology & Bioinformatics Chair at Singularity University, has noticed that "When people want a biotech job in Silicon Valley, they hide their PhDs to avoid being seen as a narrow specialist."

So, if experts are suspect, where should we turn instead? As we've already noted, everything is measurable. And the newest profession making those measurements is the data scientist. Andrew McAfee calls this new breed of data experts "geeks." He also sees the HiPPO, or "highest paid person's opinion" as the natural enemy of geeks because HiPPOs still base their opinions largely on intuition or gut feeling. We don't believe that this is a contest that should be won completely by one side or the other. Instead, we think that when it comes to ExOs, both groups will co-exist—but with a proviso: the role of HiPPOs (or experts) will change. They will continue as the best people to answer questions and identify key challenges, but the geeks will then mine the data to provide the solutions for those challenges.

5. DEATH TO THE FIVE-YEAR PLAN

One of the hallmarks of large companies is the presence of corporate strategy departments that formulate and publish five-year plans. These are multi-year strategies that are supposed to outline a company's long-term vision and goals. In fact, the primary function of many corporate development departments is simply to fill in the details of that vision and provide specifics on planning, purchasing, HR and operations.

Five-year plans used to be secret internal documents.

In recent years, however, after recognizing the need to enlist suppliers and customers in their crusades, there has been a trend among even old-line corporations—such as Amtrak, the United States Postal Service and Chrysler—to publicize their five-year plans.

Many established companies still consider transparency to be the height of progressive business thinking. But the truth is that the five-year strategic plan is itself an obsolete instrument. In fact, rather than offering a competitive advantage, it is often a drag on operations, as has been well documented in the seminal book by Henry Mintzberg, *Rise and Fall of Strategic Planning*.

A few decades ago, it was feasible (and important) to plan out that far. Companies made strategic investments by looking ahead a decade or more, and the five-year plan served as the central document outlining the implementation details of those long-term strategic bets. However, in an exponential world, the five-year plan is not only unworkable, it is seriously counterproductive—and the advent of ExOs signals its death.

All of this may seem counterintuitive. After all, as companies accelerate faster and faster shouldn't they need *more* forward surveillance as an early warning system? Theoretically, yes. But the reality is that the future is changing so quickly that any forward look is likely to produce false scenarios, so much so that today's five-year plans have a high probability of offering the *wrong* advice. Consider TED and its launch of TEDx events. Imagine that Chris Anderson had stood up in early 2009 and said, "Okay, folks, let's do this TEDx thing. We want to have several thousand such events in five years." He would have instantly lost the buy-in of his team because that many events would have sounded both insane and impossible.

Now, imagine if Anderson had asked Lara Stein, the guiding light for the TEDx brand, to actually develop a five-year plan for TEDx. A very aggressive plan by Stein might have looked like this:

Number of events per quarter						
Year	Q1	Q2	Q3	Q4	Total	Comment
2009	2	8	20	40	70	Start slowly to test and learn
2010	60	30*	80	100	270	* Slower in the summer
2011	120	100	140	160	520	Steady improvement
2012	180	150	190	200	720	Starting to reach saturation
2013	200	180	220	250	850	Some variations drive increase
					2,430	Total TEDx events over five years

Even that sounds crazy: almost 2,500 events in five years? No way. In linear thinking, that goal is clearly a stretch, what Jim Collins and Jerry Porras termed a BHAG (Big Hairy Audacious Goal) in their 1994 classic, *Built to Last: Successful Habits of Visionary Companies*. (As an aside, consider that an MTP is a BHAG with purpose.)

Yet as we now know, over 12,000 TEDx events have been held within five years, a figure that would have been inconceivable at the outset. Had Anderson and Stein presented even the 2,500-event goal, they would have either likely triggered a mutiny among the team or they'd have left a lot on the table. Instead, they simply plunged in and let the community set the pace for TEDx. Indeed, Anderson, Stein and the team had no idea they could maintain such a torrid pace until they actually did so.

In short, a five-year plan is a suicidal practice for an ExO. If it doesn't send the company racing off in the wrong direction, it can present an inaccurate picture of what lies ahead, even in the right direction. The only solution is to establish a big vision (i.e., an MTP), set an ExO structure into place, implement a one-year plan (at most) and watch it all scale while course-correcting in real time. That's exactly what TED did, and that's what the winning companies of the future will do as well.

Now, we can't talk about operating plans and decision making without addressing the bane of departmental or company strategy meetings. In their fascinating new book, *Moments of Impact: How to Design Strategic Conversations That Accelerate Change*, Chris Ertel and Lisa Kay Solomon outline the elements of successful planning and strategic meetings and decision-making within organizations to address a widespread problem: most planning and strategic meetings are a failure. Ertel and Solomon boil it down to five distinct phases for any team planning session or strategic decision:

1. Define your purpose
2. Engage Multiple Perspectives
3. Frame the Issues
4. Set the Scene
5. Make it an Experience

Moments of Impact is an important guide for anyone interested in reducing the rash of mind-numbing, unproductive meetings and optimizing the time that management spends together.

Thus, the near future, certainly for ExOs, sees five-year plans being replaced with the following elements:

- MTPs for overall guidance and emotional enrollment.
- Dashboards to provide real-time information on how a business is progressing.
- Leveraging "Moments of Impact" for clean, productive decision-making.
- A one-year (at most) operating plan that is connected to the Dashboard.

In an ExO world, purpose trumps strategy and execution overrides planning. Replacing five-year plans with these new, real-time elements can be scary but it's also liberating, and the rewards for those willing to stay on the ride will be both decisive and astonishing. Besides, being eaten alive by an upstart competitor is anything but relaxing.

This shift will, of course, be quite challenging for large organizations, which rely on drawn-out projections and tracking for planning and control purposes.

6. SMALLER BEATS BIGGER (AKA SIZE DOES MATTER, JUST NOT THE WAY YOU THINK)

Ronald Coase won the 1991 Nobel Prize in Economics for his theory that larger companies do better because they aggregate assets under one roof and, as a result, enjoy lower transaction costs. Two decades later, the reach delivered by the information revolution has negated the need to aggregate assets in the first place.

For decades, scale and size have been desirable traits in an enterprise. A bigger company could do more, the argument went, because it could leverage economies of scale and negotiate from strength. That's one reason why, for generations, business schools and consulting firms have focused on the management and organization of extremely large companies. And Wall Street has gotten rich trading the stock of giant companies, which often merge to create even more gigantic organizations.

All that is changing. In *The Start-up of You*, Reid Hoffman shows that transaction costs are no longer an advantage and that each individual can (and should) manage himself or herself as a business. Why? One reason is the unparalleled and unprecedented ability of a small team today to do big things—an ability that grows ever greater if the exponential technologies described in Chapter One are put to use. Both now and in the coming years, adaptability and agility will increasingly eclipse size and scale.

A telling example is how Netflix, with its centralized DVD rentals and small footprint, easily outmaneuvered and eventually destroyed Blockbuster, despite its 9,000 stores and distributed geographical assets. In the software world, Salesforce.com, which operates 100 percent in the cloud, can adapt to changing market conditions much faster than can competitor SAP, given that the latter requires customized installations onsite.

We've already discussed Airbnb, which by leveraging its users' existing assets, is now valued at more than the Hyatt Hotels chain worldwide. While Hyatt has 45,000 employees spread out across its 549 properties, Airbnb has just 1,324, all located in a single office. Similarly, Lending Club, Bitcoin, Clinkle and Kickstarter are forcing a radical rethinking of the banking and venture capital industries, respectively. (No retail outlets are involved in these new financial tech startups.)

Richard Branson's Virgin Group is structured to maximize the benefits of a small-form factor. Its global research center is home to the company's R&D department and a unit that spins out new businesses under the umbrella brand. The Branson group now consists of more than four hundred companies, all operating independently. Collectively, they are worth $24 billion.

As Peter Diamandis has often noted, one key advantage of a small team is that it can take on much bigger risks than a large one can. This can be seen clearly in the graphs opposite— courtesy of Joi Ito, director of the MIT Media Lab—which shows how startups are characterized by high upside potential and low downside, while large organizations are characterized by just the opposite.

In healthcare, we currently have no solution for the new strains of antibiotic-resistant superbugs showing up in hospitals, which the World Health Organization considers an existential threat as we enter the post-antibiotic era. Neither do we have a way to block the onset of allergies and autoimmune diseases, which afflict more than a billion people worldwide. Quotient Pharmaceuticals, however, aims to change that by building on the pioneering work of Dr. William Pollack, who in the early 1960s developed the first blocking human antibody solution, which has

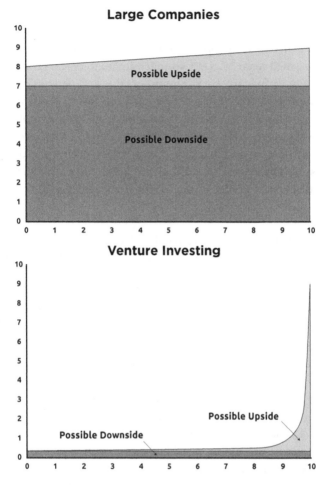

protected over sixty million mothers and their babies from the dreaded Rh disease. The vaccine resolved mother-fetus blood incompatibility, which was responsible for tens of thousands of infant deaths per year in the U.S. alone. By leveraging the body's own ability to fight, the Anaheim-based company already has a working product that stops most superbugs in their drug-resistant tracks—and this just four years after it decided to take on the challenge. A mind-boggling side effect is that their products can also cure most allergies; Quotient's blocking antibodies control the immune cascade response, which is responsible for allergies like hay fever and asthma. Incredibly, Quotient's team consists of only ten people. Significant reasons for the capability of this small team to cover so much immunological ground is the multidisciplinary backgrounds of the key personnel and the vastly decreased cost of developing products. Quotient has high containment laboratories and pilot fractionation facilities, which allows it to separate antibodies, develop products and test them in days rather than years, all in-house. The company is bypassing decades of effort and the hundreds of millions in capital normally needed in the bio/pharmaceutical industry.

A fundamental question we regularly hear is: How big can an ExO get? We think the more important question is: *What happens to an ExO after it grows up?*

While this new paradigm is still in its early days, preliminary indications are that when successful, ExOs will build on the leverage created by their externalities and become *platforms*.

But that answer creates its own set of questions, the most germane of which right now is: How can ExOs leverage the benefits of SCALE elements like crowdsourcing, community management, gamification, incentive competitions, data science, leveraged assets and staff on demand to *become* platforms?

We believe the answer is that they will wire themselves into the infrastructure and start enabling other ExOs to emerge from and operate off of those platforms.

Perhaps the earliest example of this platform model was Google. Its search prowess allowed it to scale quickly, and once the company hit critical mass, the AdWords platform enabled self-provisioning advertising platforms from which other companies could grow. Google in turn took its share by taxing that growth. Facebook was also successful at becoming a platform, relying on its extraordinary market penetration and knowledge about its users to spawn such ExOs as Zynga and its recent mobile efforts. Amazon is another success story, as is Apple's App Store ecosystem, which is probably the clearest example of an ExO product becoming a platform. MySpace and Friendster, on the other hand, failed to become platforms.

So, the answer to the question of how big an Exponential Organization can get yields yet another, more precise, question: How quickly can you convert exponential growth into the critical mass needed to become a platform? Once that happens there is no practical limit. It's one big coral reef.

For example, as Uber scales, it is helping its drivers buy cars. Its pre-purchase of 2,500 Google cars will provide an enormous data surge it can turn into new services. Uber today already is a platform with a critical mass of drivers, which allows it to move horizontally and offer new services: postal, gift and grocery delivery, as well as limousine and even medical services. All leverage Uber's key retail and demand-driven positioning, resulting in nearly instant gratification using a smartphone, combined with an outstanding customer experience.

Importantly, the platform must be symbiotic and serve the feeders as well. We're all familiar with the dramatic success of Rovio's Angry Birds. What's less known is that for Rovio, Angry Birds was its 53rd game—the company has been at it since the early 1990s. But when creating a game twenty years ago, companies had to create bilateral agreements with 150 different mobile phone companies, each of which wanted 75 percent of the revenues. All focus, time and energy went into the hell of negotiating with mobile telcos. Once on the Apple platform, however, Rovio only had to contend with a single point of negotiations, freeing it up to focus on its games—a scenario we strongly suspect the company prefers.

Now that the asteroid of digitized information has hit, the global economy has changed forever. The era of traditional, hierarchical market domination by dinosaur companies is coming to an end. The world now belongs to smarter, smaller and faster-moving enterprises. This is certainly true now for information-based industries, and it will soon be true for more traditional industries as well.

7. RENT, DON'T OWN

An important mechanism empowering individuals and small teams everywhere is low-cost access to technology and tools.

Emblematic of this new reality is cloud computing, which offers the ability to store and manage massive amounts of information with unlimited processing, all on a cost-per-use basis requiring no upfront costs or capital investments. In practice, this makes memory almost free. The cloud also puts small companies on the same footing as—or even gives them an advantage over—big companies, which are burdened by expensive internal IT operations. In addition, the growing body of innovative Big Data analytical tools will give all companies, big and small, unprecedented understanding of their markets and customers.

We're seeing that same access to other tools elsewhere as well. As first profiled in Chapter Three, TechShop makes expensive equipment, previously available only to government agencies and large corporate laboratories, accessible to anyone.

An example: Richard Hatfield, CEO and founder of Lightning Motorcycles, wanted to set a motorcycle speed record. The motorcycle he needed to do so, however, wasn't on the market, so he built it himself at TechShop. To date, according to TechShop CEO and co-founder Mark Hatch, about $6 billion worth of new products have been created at TechShop labs.

It is estimated there are now hundreds of "fablabs" operating around the world. Soon, every town and neighborhood will have one, meaning that any individual or small team will be able to rent equipment and be as capital-empowered as an established corporation.

A comparable transformation is taking place with biotech equipment. BioCurious, another Silicon Valley invention, is an open wetlab where enthusiasts take courses, use centrifuges and test tubes, and synthesize DNA. Genspace offers a similar resource in New York City.

This rent-not-own philosophy further extends the current craze of collaborative consumption and the sharing economy.

There's less and less need to own a factory, a laboratory or even a scientific tool. Instead, why not rent those assets, reducing up-front investment and leaving the ownership and maintenance of state-of-the-art facilities to someone else? Further, given that the control mechanisms offered by software and the Internet allow the management of these capabilities at a distance, why build your own? Even Apple essentially rents capabilities from Foxconn to manufacture its products. And Alibaba, the Chinese e-commerce giant, allows you to outsource your entire manufacturing cycle.

First computing, then tools and manufacturing. Today, that same rent-not-own philosophy even encompasses employees. Individual "temps" are nothing new, of course, but the concept now includes groups of temporary workers. Organizations can rent staff on demand from Gigwalk and other companies when a large amount of work needs to be done quickly, relieving them of the traditional, nightmarish practice of serial hiring and firing. In this instance, there is no distinction between "rented" staff and the ExO attribute, Staff on Demand.

Be it facilities, equipment, computing or people, the concept of renting rather than owning is a major factor contributing to an ExO's agility and flexibility, and thus its success. This too can be seen as the culmination of a long-term trend. Over the decades business owners have steadily moved from viewing business through the lens of a balance sheet to instead focusing on P&L—that is, emphasizing the primacy of profits over ownership. Much of this movement has grown out of the realization that the ownership of assets, even if mission-critical, is better handled by experts. So, in that sense, the rise of ExOs is a deepening of the specialization trend that started 10,000 years ago: only focus on those areas in which you are really outperforming. This not only maximizes profits, but in a world with pervasive digital reputational systems, also sets your image at the highest possible level, as author Tyler Cowen says in the title of his book: *Average is Over.*

Airline operators used to build their own engines, an intricate and high-risk operation. Then GE and Rolls Royce, both experts in manufacturing engines, began offering leasing programs. Today, airlines pay for engines by the number of hours flown. In other words, something as expensive and complex as an aircraft engine has now become a rented, pay-as-you-go asset, rather than an expensive internal business unit.

Rolls Royce has even taken the process a step further. By installing hundreds of sensors in each of its engines, the company is now able to gather and analyze immense quantities of information about its engines *while they are in use*. In the process, of course, it is transforming itself into a Big Data company—and thus into an ExO. This trajectory, from ownership to access to data analytics, can also be seen in numerous other vertical markets such as automobiles and real estate.

8. TRUST BEATS CONTROL AND OPEN BEATS CLOSED

As we saw with Valve software, autonomy can be a powerful motivator in the age of the Exponential Organization. The Millennial generation is naturally independent, digitally native and resistant to top-down control and hierarchies. To take full advantage of this new workforce and hang on to top talent, companies must embrace an open environment.

Google has done just that. As we outlined in Chapter Four, its Objectives and Key Results (OKR) system is fully transparent across the company. Any Googler can look up the OKRs of other colleagues and teams to see what they're trying to achieve and how successful they've been in the past. Such transparency takes a considerable amount of cultural and organizational courage, but Google has found that the openness it engenders is worth any discomfort.

Tony Hsieh built Zappos into a billion dollar company using this very same philosophy. Everything at Zappos is about customer service and openness. Its publicly available and annually updated 500-page Culture Book defines who and what the company is. According to David Vik, Zappos' "company coach," there are five key precepts to Zappos that drive culture across the organization:

- **Vision:** What you're doing
- **Purpose:** Why you do it
- **Business model:** What will fuel you as you're doing it
- **Wow and uniqueness factors:** What sets you apart from others
- **Values:** What matters to you

The control frameworks used by traditional organizations were devised because the longer (and slower) feedback loops between management and teams often required considerable oversight and intervention. Over the last few years, however, a new wave of collaborative tools has emerged to allow an organization to monitor each of its teams with little oversight and maximum autonomy. ExOs are learning to harness these capabilities and deliver self-management—often with extraordinary outcomes—by tracking data on a real-time basis. An excellent example is Teamly, which combines project management, OKRs and performance reviews with the power of an internal social network.

Another key reason that ExOs are implementing trust frameworks is that in an increasingly volatile world, predictable processes and steady, stable environments are now all but extinct. Anything predictable has been or will be automated by AI or robots, leaving the human worker to handle exceptional situations. As a result, the very nature of work is changing and requires more initiative and creativity from every team member. At the same time, team members often wish their organizations had more trust in them. According to a 2010 survey conducted for The Conference Board, a global business membership and research association, only 51 percent of Americans said they were satisfied with their bosses.

It is important to understand that open trust frameworks cannot be implemented in isolation or simply by fiat. They are an important consequence of implementing Autonomy, Dashboards and/or Experimentation.

One of the reasons Facebook has been so successful is the inherent trust that the company has placed in its people. At most software companies (and certainly the larger ones), a new software release goes through layers upon layers of unit testing, system testing and integration testing, usually administered by separate quality assurance departments. At Facebook, however, development teams enjoy the full trust of management. Any team can release new code onto the live site without oversight. As a management style, it seems counterintuitive, but with individual reputations at stake—and no one else to catch shoddy coding—Facebook teams end up working that much harder to ensure there are no errors. The result is that Facebook has been able to release code of unimaginable complexity faster than any other company in Silicon Valley history. In the process, it has seriously raised the bar.

9. EVERYTHING IS MEASURABLE AND ANYTHING IS KNOWABLE

The first accelerometers (devices used to measure new motion in three dimensions) were the size of a shoebox and weighed about two pounds. Today's model is now just four millimeters across and is found in every smartphone on the planet.

Welcome to the sensor revolution, one of the most important and least celebrated technological revolutions taking place today. A BMW automobile today has more than two thousand sensors tracking everything from tire pressure and fuel levels to transmission performance and sudden stops. An aircraft engine has as many as three thousand sensors measuring billions of data points per voyage. And as we mentioned in Chapter One, a Google car, with its lidar (light radar) scanning the surrounding environment with sixty-four lasers, collects almost a gigabyte of data per second per car.

This revolution is also impacting our human bodies. In 2007, *Wired* magazine editors Gary Wolf and Kevin Kelly created the Quantified Self (QS) movement, which focuses on self-tracking tools. The first Quantified Self conference was held in May 2011, and today the QS community has more than 32,000 members in thirty-eight countries.

Many new devices have been spun out of this movement. One of them is Spire, a QS device that measures respiration. Singularity University alumnus Francesco Mosconi is the chief data officer of Spire. The analytics and software he has written are all about real-time feedback regarding breath and how it relates to stress and focus—not unlike the way sensor feedback in a BMW's traction control system reduces wheel slip.

With more than seven billion mobile phones in use globally, many equipped with a high-resolution camera, anything and everything can be recorded in real time, from a baby's first words to the events of the Arab Spring. Like it or not, we are hurtling towards a world of radical transparency—and being driven off the privacy cliff by trillions of sensors recording our every move. Beyond Verbal, an Israeli company, can analyze the tonal variations of a 10-second clip of your voice to determine mood and underlying attitude with an 85 percent certainty.

Now, toss into this mix Google Glass, the smart eyewear that enables video or images to be recorded or transmitted in real time anywhere as people move throughout their day. Next, add drones, which cost less than $100 and can be flown at a variety of altitudes, their 5-gigapixel cameras capturing everything in the landscape below. And, finally, consider the several nanosatellite companies which are launching mesh configurations of hundreds of satellites into low Earth orbit, and which will provide real-time video and images anywhere on the planet. Given the staggering pace of technological innovation, the possibilities are endless.

On a much more intimate level, the human body has approximately ten trillion cells operating as an ecosystem of unimaginable complexity. For all that intricacy, however, we usually track our health using just three basic metrics: temperature, blood pressure and pulse rate. Now, imagine if we could measure *each one* of those ten trillion cells—and not with just three metrics, but with a hundred. What would happen if we could track the enzyme levels in our bloodstream, kidneys and liver and correlate those levels in real time with other metrics? What larger meta-factors that we never knew even existed will emerge from these mountains of data?

Laser spectroscopy, for example, is currently being used to analyze food and drink for allergens, toxins, vitamins, minerals and calories. Companies already exploring this technology's capabilities include Apple, SCiO by Consumer Physics, TellSpec, Vessyl and Airo Health. Before long, laser spectroscopy will be used as a medical and wellness indicator, as well as to measure and track everything in our bodies, including biomarkers, diseases, viruses and bacteria. For example, Yonatan Adiri, founder of OwnHealth, uses the cloud to analyze photographs of urine test strips in order to diagnose many medical conditions.[1]

Meanwhile, as mentioned in Chapter Three, the Qualcomm Tricorder X Prize will award $10 million to the first team that develops a handheld medical device that not only diagnoses and monitors health conditions quickly and accurately, but is also capable of outperforming ten board-certified doctors. Three hundred teams from around the world, including Scanadu—a company created for the sole purpose of winning the prize—are competing, and the prize is likely to be awarded within a year. (At least this aspect of *Star Trek* won't take one hundred fifty years to be realized.)

ExOs are taking advantage of this accelerating trend in one of two ways: by creating new business models on existing data streams or by adding new data streams to old paradigms. As an example of the former, consider PASSUR Aerospace. Since the early or late arrival of a flight can cost as much as $70 per minute, the company has set up refrigerator-sized ADS-B (automatic dependent surveillance-broadcast) tracking stations across the U.S. These stations monitor every plane in the sky and can accurately predict *to the minute* when an aircraft will arrive at its gate. In addition to offering enormous cost savings, the system is also being used in reverse by both the FAA and airlines

---

1   en.wikipedia.org/wiki/Urine_test_strip

to determine exactly when a given flight should take off.

As these and hundreds more examples suggest, we are moving toward a world in which everything will be measured and anything can be knowable, both in the world around us and within our bodies. Only enterprises that plan for this new reality will have a chance at long-term success.

Now that we have finished describing the characteristics of ExOs and their implications, we can look at the how an ExO maps onto other constructs. The following table compares ExO Attributes with Joi Ito's MIT Media Lab Principles and the heuristics in Nassim Taleb's Anti-Fragile theory.

Joi Ito (MIT Medialab)	Nassim Taleb (Anti-Fragile Theory)
MTP	
Pull over push; Compasses over maps	Focus on the long term, not just the financials and short term
Staff on Demand	
Resilience over strength	Stay small and flexible
Community & Crowd	
Systems (ecosystems) over objects; Resilience over strength	Build in options; Stay small and flexible
Algorithms	
-	Build in stressors > Simplify and Automate; Heuristics (skin in the game, orthogonal)
Leased Assets	
Resilience over strength	Reduce dependency and IT; stay small and flexible; Invest in R&D; Invest in data and social infrastructure

Engagement (IC, gamify)	
Pull over push	Build in options; Heuristics: skin in the game
Interfaces	
-	Simplify and Automate; Overcome cognitive biases
Dashboard	
Learning over financial	Simplify and Automate; Short feedback loops; Rewards only after project completion
Experimentation	
Practice over theory; Risk over safety; Learning over education	Diversify; Build in hacking and stressors by yourself (fail fast and often; Netflix case w/ Chaos Monkey), especially in good times; Build in options; Risk over safety (not risk insensitivity); Avoid too much focus on efficiency, control and optimization
Autonomy	
Emergence over authority; Disobedience over compliance	Decentralization; Do not overregulate; Challenge senior management; Compartmentalize; Share ownership within ExO on the edges (skin in the game)
Social Technologies	
Emergence (peer-to-peer learning) over authority	Build in stressors

HOW EXPONENTIAL IS YOUR ORGANIZATION?

In Chapters Three and Four, we described the singular characteristics of ExOs. In this chapter we turned outward to discuss the broader implications of ExOs and the brave new world in which they will operate. We suspect that the key questions many readers are now asking include:

- How exponential is my organization?
- How prepared are we to compete in this new reality?
- What do we need to change to become an Exponential Organization?

Not surprisingly, we have discovered that not all ExOs have all of the characteristics of paradigmatic ExO. In fact, our studies suggest that for an ExO to achieve the 10x baseline threshold and earn the ExO title, it often needs only four (or more) of the eleven attributes to succeed. That is a sufficient number to dominate a new market with information services or to drop the denominator (costs) into an existing one.

Furthermore, some of the attributes, while pointing the way, may not apply (at least not today) to certain industries. Thus, if you are working in the Secret Service or your company runs oil rigs in the North Sea, the Staff on Demand attribute may not apply. (Having said that, it probably does!)

The only way to know where your company stands on the path to becoming an Exponential Organization is to conduct an *ExO audit*. To help you do just that, we have created a diagnostic test (see Appendix A). You may find it comforting—or you may find it disconcerting. Either way, we are sure you will find it illuminating.

KEY TAKEAWAYS

- Information accelerates everything.
- Marginal cost of supply is dropping exponentially for the first time ever. Everything is being disrupted.
- In a disruptive world, smaller is better.
- "Experts" tell you how something can*not* be done.
- Rent, don't own, assets.
- Everything is being turned into information—and is thus measurable and knowable.
- An ExO Diagnostic can help you score and analyze your organization.
- Implementing four or more ExO attributes can yield the 10x performance improvement.

PART TWO

BUILDING THE EXPONENTIAL ORGANIZATION

Now that we have examined the attributes and implications of ExOs, we turn for the remainder of this book to the practical aspects of their implementation, as well as to the likely future of these organizations. From the start, we have been committed to making this book not just an intellectual exercise in documenting this new phenomenon, but also a prescriptive guide to implementing the ExO model within your own enterprise.

The next few chapters will answer the following questions:

- How do you start an ExO, either as a pure startup or from within an existing organization?
- How do you apply these ideas to a mid-market company?
- How do you retrofit ExO principles into a large organization?
- Which organizations are implementing ExO thinking?

By the time you have finished Part Two, you should be able to see how the ExO framework can be applied to an organization of any size, be it a startup, a mid-market company or a large organization. In addition, you'll learn how to become an Exponential Executive, as well as how to identify the problems and issues to track now so they don't surprise you a few years down the line.

CHAPTER SIX
STARTING AN EXO

From the dawn of the Internet, we've seen fundamental changes in how businesses are built and grown. In particular, the earliest playbook for building a hyper-growth company emerged during the dot-com boom of 1998 to 2000. That narrative gained a new chapter in 2005 with the rise of social media, and 2008 saw yet another chapter thanks to the widespread availability of low-cost cloud computing.

Today, we are seeing the addition of the most important text yet with the rise of the Exponential Organization. Driven by accelerating technologies, ExOs allow us to organize ourselves in new ways to tap into this information-enabled world.

Local Motors is a good example of an ExO startup. Founded by Jeff Jones and Jay Rogers in 2007, and based in Phoenix, Arizona, it is a global co-creation platform that empowers its community to design, build and sell custom-built vehicles. While serving as a Marine in Iraq in 2004, Rogers read Amory Lovins' book *Winning the Oil Endgame* and was inspired to create a new type of car company. His goal (and MTP) was to bring exciting cars to market in an efficient way.

Rogers visited several car companies, including Ferrari, GM and Tesla, and set himself three goals:

1. Build the first-ever open source community for car body design
2. Build a vehicle
3. Build a channel to market

To attract community, Local Motors started by approaching

design schools and soliciting ideas from students. This strategy failed, largely due to legal issues about ownership and licensing costs, although another problem was that the students lacked a sense of purpose and commitment insofar as the company was concerned, which resulted in almost no contribution to the platform [Experimentation]. Undaunted, Jones and Rogers took another shot at attracting community, this time via crowdsourcing. They were successful this time around, and in March 2008, Local Motors debuted as the first community to completely crowdsource a car. (The company currently has eighty-three employees and three micro-factories for manufacturing.) The Local Motors staff then turned its attention to evangelizing, sharing its passion for the product on numerous designer sites, which acted as magnets for a like-minded community [Community & Crowd].

Next, implementing Engagement, Local Motors undertook its first competition for a car design. At that time, the company had only four employees, who were in charge of managing *a thousand* community members (talk about abundance). Ultimately, a hundred contest entries poured in, kicking off the platform's formation. Today, the Local Motors community consists of 43,100 members collaborating on 6,000 designs and 2,000 ideas across thirty-one projects. Members average 200 to 400 hours per project.

The Local Motors community consists of enthusiasts, hobbyist innovators and professionals. They are designers, engineers and makers who participate in each component of the design (interior, exterior, name, logo, etc.), which is then open sourced with a Creative Commons license. The platform can be thought of as a combination of Quirky (product development) and Kaggle (incentive competitions), but for cars and other vehicles.

Once the initial community was established, Rogers moved on to his next goal: to build the first crowdsourced automobile. In 2009, Local Motors achieved that goal with the production of the Rally Fighter, a car whose ultimate design was a culmination of 35,000 designs contributed by 2,900 community members from more than 100 countries. Produced in just a year and a half, about five times faster than conventional processes, the Rally Fighter cost just $3 million to develop. Buyers don't receive an assembled car; instead, $99,900 buys them a kit, complete with manuals, wikis and videos. They also have access to Local Motors experts at one of three U.S.-based micro-factories (one hundred more are slated to open worldwide in the next ten years). There are currently twenty-three Rally Fighters in operation around the world, and its designer, Sangho Kim, landed a job at General Motors in South Korea as a result of his work on the car.

Local Motors also encourages other organizations to access its community. In conjunction with the Shell Oil Company, Local Motors created a competition in 2012 called the Shell GameChanger DRIVEN (Design of Relevant and Innovative Vehicles for Energy Needs). Contestants were tasked with designing a vehicle that could be produced in the next five to ten years at one of five locations (Amsterdam, Bangalore, Basra, Houston and Sao Paolo), using locally sourced energy and materials. The design also required contestants to address social challenges specific to each location. One winner in each location received $2,000, and the Grand Prize winner (of a total of 214 entries) received an additional $5,000, as well as a quarter-scale model of his design that was to be shown around the world.

Together with BMW, Local Motors launched the Urban Driving Experience Challenge, in which contestants were required to address the likely needs of an urban BMW driver in 2025. There were 414 entrants, and the top ten received a total of $15,000 [Engagement]. Other challenges the Local Motors community contributed to include designing the best delivery vehicle for Domino's Pizza and inventing driving shoes for Reebok. Local Motors' next two goals are to create the world's first 3D-printed car and to design a highly customizable car with fewer than twenty parts.

IGNITION

With Local Motors pointing the way, it is now time, at long last, to discuss how to launch an Exponential Organization. One caveat, however: This is *not* meant to be an exhaustive startup manual—that book remains to be written. Rather, we'll discuss the elements relevant to building an ExO that is leveraged by information and is highly scalable, either as a pure startup or from within an existing enterprise.

A quick but relevant side note here: We strongly recommend reading *The Lean Startup* by Eric Ries as an accompaniment to this chapter, since we'll be referring to it frequently. In fact, the best definition we've found for a startup comes from Ries: "*A startup is a human institution designed to deliver a new product or service under conditions of extreme uncertainty.*" A second book we recommend is Peter Thiel and Blake Masters' recent publication, *Zero to One: Notes on Startups or How to Build the Future.*

This is perhaps the best time in the history of business to build a new enterprise. The confluence of breakthrough technologies, acceptance (and even celebration) of entrepreneurship, different crowdsourcing options, crowdfunding opportunities and legacy markets ripe for disruption—all create a compelling (and unprecedented) scenario for new company creation. Furthermore, traditional risk areas have been mitigated like never before. Continuing our earlier comet/dinosaur analogy: the comet has struck, the dinosaurs are teetering and the conditions are ripe for a new category of small, nimble organisms to thrive. A new Cambrian Explosion, if you will.

When assessing a startup for funding, investors typically categorize three major risk areas:

- **Technology risk:** Will it work?
- **Market risk:** Will people buy the product?
- **Execution risk:** Is the team able to function and pivot as needed?

The challenge facing every startup lies in discovering how to de-risk each of these areas and, in the process, find a business model in the chosen problem space. Nothing is more important.

Let's look at each of these three risk areas in turn:

Technology Risk

In 1995, it cost about $15 million to build a software startup based in Silicon Valley. That money mostly went to build server stacks, purchase software and hire staff to configure and manage all that technology, as well as to write new code. By 2005, the cost had dropped to about $4 million. Servers were cheaper, and software, now often open sourced, was easier to develop and configure. Most hard costs were focused on marketing and sales.

Today, with now-established capabilities such as cloud computing and social media, that same effort costs less than $100,000. The technology risk that was once enormous (particularly software) has been reduced over the last twenty years by 150x. Most of the remaining risk concerns mere scalability issues. A case in point: the rise of standardized web services allows complex software functionality to be integrated into a startup at the press of a button. Examples include Google's Prediction API for predictive analytics and AlchemyAPI for deep learning software for pattern recognition.

To illustrate the sheer extent of this reduced technology risk, consider hardware startups. A new wave of large companies in Shenzhen, China (e.g., Foxconn, Flextronics, PCH International), as well as open source hardware platforms such as Arduino, Raspberry Pi and 3D printers, allow anyone to design a hardware product and quickly prototype and build it. Liam Casey, the CEO of PCH, has aggressively turned his company into a platform on which anyone can launch a hardware startup, to the extent that individual wants to create the equivalent of an App Store for hardware startups. Brady Forrest, head of Highway1, a PCH incubator, puts it simply: "We want hardware to be as easy as software." Indeed, hardware is increasingly dissolving into software.

According to entrepreneur Chris Dixon, the most

important change for entrepreneurs versus a decade ago is the ratio of reach to capital. Today, the reach of a startup is 100x larger, while the capital needed is one tenth that of a decade ago—a *thousandfold* improvement in just ten years. The result is that technology risk, particularly for largely information-based or information-enabled businesses, has all but evaporated. (Needless to say, if you want to build a supertanker, you still need some capital.)

Market Risk

As to whether or not anyone will buy the product, we turn once again to Steve Blank, who famously said, "No business plan survives first contact with a customer." Historically, one had to first commission classic market research, fully build the product or service, hire an expensive sales force, and then spend time and money marketing the idea—all before ever really knowing the answer to that question.

The Internet took one giant bite out of that paradigm and the emergence of social media took another. Starting in the 2000s, startups could test the market like never before by leveraging A/B testing, Google AdWords campaigns, social media and landing pages. Now an idea could be partially validated before product engineering even began.

The epitome of market validation, of course, is crowd-funding. Fundraising sites such as Kickstarter and Indiegogo allow users to pre-purchase a product. If enough people pre-purchase, the website releases money to the developer. While there's a great deal of understandable excitement about the democratization of the fundraising process, we think the far more interesting consequence is that, for the first time in history, entrepreneurs can validate market demand *before* building the product.

Execution Risk

So, of the three major risk areas, execution risk remains the only real issue in building a company. How will the enterprise organize itself to maximize performance from its founders and management team? How will it leverage technology and information to create a unique and sustainable advantage and business model? Answering these questions correctly is the key to building a successful Exponential Organization. For this reason, we need to look more closely at each of the steps in building a powerful and effective team.

In 2013, Aileen Lee published an extensive overview in *TechCrunch* of U.S.-based software startups with a market value of more than $1 billion over the previous ten years, a group of companies she called *Unicorns*. As every company increasingly becomes a software company, her findings are ever more relevant for classic vertical markets and sectors as well. While we recommend reading the entire article,[1] Lee's key findings as they pertain to ExOs are as follows:

- It takes more than seven years, on average, before a "liquidity event."
- Inexperienced twenty-something founders are outliers. Companies with well-educated thirty-something co-founders who have history together tend to be most successful.
- The idea of a "big pivot" to a different product after startup is an outlier. Most Unicorns stick to their original vision (i.e., their founding MTP).

We have found that there is a strong correlation between ExOs and Lee's Unicorns. In fact, in our diagnostic, most of Lee's Unicorns score well above the ExO threshold score. Their relatively young age means these Unicorn companies have been leveraging new information streams, have a low cost of supply and embrace community—and can thus scale. Most have gotten to their current heights by following some combination of the steps below.

---

1 techcrunch.com/2013/11/02/welcome-to-the-unicorn-club/

STEP 1: SELECT AN MTP (MASSIVE TRANSFORMATIVE PURPOSE)

This is the most elemental and foundational aspect of a startup. Feeding on Simon Sinek's "Why?" question, it is critical that you are excited and utterly passionate about the problem space you plan to attack. So, begin by asking the question: *What is the biggest problem I'd like to see solved?* Identify that problem space and then come up with an MTP for it. Even as a child, Elon Musk, perhaps the world's most celebrated entrepreneur today, had a burning desire to address energy, transportation and space travel at a global level. His three companies (SolarCity, Tesla and SpaceX) are each addressing those spaces. Each has a Massive Transformative Purpose.

Keep in mind, however, that an MTP is *not* a business decision. Finding your passion is a personal journey. As Travis Kalanick, CEO of Uber, said at the 2013 LeWeb conference in Paris, "You have to be self-aware and look for that startup idea and purpose that is a perfect fit with you—with you as a person, not as a business[person]." Howard Thurman, the American author and philosopher, summarizes the same idea as follows: "Don't just ask what the world needs. Ask what makes you come alive and go do it. What the world needs is people who have come alive."

Drew Houston, founder of Dropbox, agrees: "The most successful people are obsessed with solving an important problem, something that matters to them. They remind me of a dog chasing a tennis ball. To increase your own chances of happiness and success, you must find your tennis ball—the thing that pulls you."

Finding an MTP can be seen as a novel and perhaps more interesting way of asking yourself the following questions:

- What do I really care about?
- What am I meant to do?

Two more questions that can help speed the process of discovering your passion:

- What would I do if I could never fail?
- What would I do if I received a billion dollars today?

It is not only about you as an entrepreneur, however. It is also about your employees. PayPal co-founder Peter Thiel poses the following question as an effective way to test if a startup has an MTP that will attract not only friends, but also employees beyond your personal network who share your motivation: "Why would the 20th employee join your startup without the perks, [such as] a co-founder title or stock [options]?"

Accordingly, you should gauge your MTP against each of the acronym's letters. Is it Massive? Is it Transformative? Is it Purposeful? A profit motive alone is insufficient to build an ExO—or, frankly, *any* startup. Rather, it's the burning passion to solve an obsessive, complex problem that keeps an entrepreneur pushing along the rollercoaster ride of ebullience and despair that is the story of every startup. Chip Conley, an expert at building purpose-driven companies such as Airbnb, frequently references Kahlil Gibran: "Work is love made visible. The goal is not to live forever; the goal is to create something that will."

STEP 2: JOIN OR CREATE RELEVANT MTP COMMUNITIES

The collaborative power of communities is critical to any ExO. Whatever your passion (let's say you dream of curing cancer), there are communities out there filled with other passionate, purpose-driven people devoted to the same crusade.

The recent rise of the Quantified Self (QS) movement, first introduced in Chapter Five, is a great example of a community with an MTP. Operating in 120 cities and in forty countries, approximately 1,000 companies and 40,000 members currently participate in the QS ecosystem. Anyone interested in setting up a medical device company or addressing a major area such as cancer or heart disease can find and join a rich community of interested fellow participants. For example, some of the many communities devoted to cancer or heart disease research include TED MED, Health Foo, DIYbio, GET (Genes/Environment/Traits), WIRED Health, Sensored, Stream Health and Exponential Medicine.

If you think your problem space doesn't have community support, take a look at **www.meetup.com**. Meetup's mission is both to revitalize local communities and to help people around the world organize. The company believes that people can change the world by organizing themselves into groups that are powerful enough to make a difference. Founded by Scott Heiferman in January 2002, Meetup helps convene more than 150,000 interest-based groups—made up of about ten million members—in 197 countries around the world. Given those numbers, the odds are pretty good that a passionate and purpose-driven community concerned with your problem space already exists in your own country.

However, in any community-driven startup, there's a tension between the good of the community and the good of the company. For Chris Anderson the choice is an easy one:

> There is a fundamental DNA path dependency here. Are you primarily a community or are you primarily a company? The reason you have to ask yourself this is because sooner or later the two will come in conflict. We [DIY Drones] are primarily a community. Every day, we make decisions that disadvantage the company to bring advantage to the community.

Anderson said the advice to opt for the good of the community came from Matt Mullenweg, the CEO of WordPress, the world's most widely used blogging platform. According to Mullenweg, "Whenever this moment comes up, always bet on the community, because that's the difference between long-term thinking and short-term thinking."

Basically, if you get the community right, opportunities will arise. If you get community wrong, the engine of innovation dissolves and you won't have a company anymore.

STEP 3: COMPOSE A TEAM

While the founding team in any startup is important, given the rapid scaling of an ExO company with a very small footprint in terms of resources, the careful composition of its founding team is especially critical.

In his book *The Advantage: Why Organizational Health Trumps Everything Else In Business*, Patrick Lencioni argues that the single best way to determine the health of an organization is by "observing the leadership team during a meeting." Leadership interaction proves to be an accurate barometer of team dynamics, clarity, decisiveness and cognitive biases. Furthermore, the key to putting together a successful ExO founding team is that everyone shares a passion for the MTP. Ben Horowitz, co-founder of Andreessen-Horowitz, one of the world's most successful VCs, noted the importance of shared passion in his recent book, *The Hard Thing About Hard Things: Building a Business When There Are No Easy Answers*: "If founders are in a startup for the wrong reasons (money, ego), it often degenerates into a nasty situation."

Similarly, it's worth revisiting one of the main points of Aileen Lee's Unicorn study: companies composed of well-educated thirty-something co-founders with a shared work or school history have the highest success rate. Her research shows that the average age of a Unicorn founder is thirty-four, and the average number of co-founders is three. In addition, most successful founder CEOs have technical backgrounds.

One caveat is that for a community-driven company, diversity is an important part of the package. While building out his DIY Drones community, for example, Chris Anderson came across Jordi Munoz of Mexico, who was just nineteen years old at the time. Anderson found that along with a mutual passion for drones, Munoz's skills were both fundamentally different from and complementary to his own. Impressed by the young man's capabilities, enthusiasm and ability to learn, Anderson brought him on as a co-founder. Today, though young and without the "right" background, Munoz is thriving in his role as CEO of a multi-million dollar company.

The following roles are critical if founding ExO teams are to deliver diverse backgrounds, independent thought and complementary skills:

- **Visionary/Dreamer:** The primary role in the company's story. The founder with the strongest vision for the company comes up with the MTP and holds the organization to it.
- **User Experience Design:** Role focuses on users' needs and ensures that every contact with users is as intuitive, simple and clear as possible.
- **Programming/Engineering:** Role responsible for bringing together the various technologies required to build the product or service.
- **Finance/Business:** The business function assesses the viability and profitability of the organization, is the cornerstone of interactions with investors and manages the all-important burn rate.

In *The Innovator's DNA: Mastering the Five Skills of Disruptive Innovators*, co-author Clayton Christensen approaches the skill portfolio question slightly differently, identifying two distinct sets of skills:

- **Discovery skills:** The ability to generate ideas—to associate, question, observe, network and experiment.
- **Delivery skills:** The ability to execute ideas—to analyze, plan, implement, follow through and be detail-oriented.

These are just two of many ways of looking at how to put a founding team together. Whatever the approach, however, founders must be intrinsically motivated self-starters. Most of all, in the face of rapid growth and change, they must have complete trust in one another's judgment.

Think about the PayPal story. Peter Thiel told his co-founders (Elon Musk, Reid Hoffman, Luke Nosek, Max

Levchin and Chad Hurley) and employees that they all should work together as friends rather than more formally as employees. Looking back, perhaps friendship was PayPal's MTP. Not only was PayPal very successful as a company—it was sold to eBay for $1.2 billion—but the friendships that grew out of it were equally successful. The original team is now known as the "PayPal Mafia," and its members have helped one another on subsequent startups, including Tesla, YouTube, SpaceX, LinkedIn, Yelp, Yammer and Palantir—companies that today have a total market cap of more than $60 billion.

The pace of growth of an ExO requires an extra emphasis on a fully synergistic core team. As Arianna Huffington says, "I would rather have somebody much less brilliant and who's a team player, who's straightforward, than somebody who is very brilliant and toxic to the organization."

STEP 4: BREAKTHROUGH IDEA

We don't have to tell you that this next step is a big one. It is essential to leverage technology or information in some way to *transform* the status quo. And when we say transform, we really do mean it. ExOs are not about incremental improvement in a marketplace. They are about radical change. According to Marc Andreessen, "Most entrepreneurs prefer failing conventionally rather than succeeding unconventionally."

Remember, the three key success factors for an ExO idea are:

- First, a minimum 10x improvement over the status quo.
- Second, leveraging information to radically cut the cost of marginal supply (i.e., the cost to expand the supply side of the business should be minimal).
- Third, the idea should pass the "toothbrush test" originated by Larry Page: Does the idea solve a real customer problem or use case on a frequent basis? Is it something so useful that a user would go back to it several times a day?

It is also possible to leverage a community or crowd to discover breakthrough ideas or new patterns of implementation. Elon Musk set an MTP for transforming transportation with his Hyperloop high-speed transportation idea. At the same time, he opened up the design and implementation of that idea to whoever wanted to take a crack at it.

It may seem counterintuitive to delay the breakthrough idea several steps into the process. After all, legend holds that most startups begin with an explosive new idea that's then applied to a problem space. We believe, however, that it's better to start with a passion to solve a particular *problem*, rather than to start with an idea or a technology.

There are two reasons for this. First, by focusing on the problem space, you are not tied to one particular idea or solution, and thus don't end up shoehorning a technology into a problem space where it might not be a good fit. Silicon Valley is littered with the carcasses of companies with great technologies searching for a problem to solve. Second, there is no shortage of either ideas or new technologies. After all, *everybody* in a place like Silicon Valley has an idea for a new tech business. Instead, the key to success is relentless execution, hence the need for passion and the MTP. To demonstrate, consider the number of times the founders of the following companies pitched investors before finally succeeding:

Company	Number of Investor Pitches
Skype	40
Cisco	76
Pandora	300
Google	350

What if Larry Page and Sergey Brin had stopped pitching after 340 attempts? The world would be a very different place today. Just as intriguing: what magical technologies and businesses don't exist today because the founders gave up one investor pitch too soon?

We've said this already, but it can't be emphasized enough:

Entrepreneurial success rarely comes from the idea. Instead, it comes from the founding team's never-say-die attitude and relentless execution. Those who *really* want something will find options. Those who just kind of want it will find reasons and excuses. This has been the case since Hewlett and Packard started their business in that now-famous Palo Alto dirt-floor garage—where, don't forget, they began with a passion and not a product. In the end, only raw, unbridled passion can solve an important problem and overcome the endless hurdles that present themselves. As investor Fred Wilson says, "Startups should be hunch-driven early on, and data-driven as they scale."

PayPal co-founder Peter Thiel builds on this with a profound question for startup founders: "Tell me something you believe is true but [that] you have a hard time trying to convince others [of]." This is about conviction and passion on the one hand, and radical, unconventional, breakthrough ideas on the other. As Peter Diamandis is fond of saying, "The day before a major breakthrough, it is just a crazy idea."

To illustrate: In a recent conversation with Elon Musk, Salim asked Musk about his Hyperloop concept: "Elon, I have a background in physics and it seems impossible to accelerate humans to 1,000 kilometers an hour and then decelerate them to zero in such a short space of time. Have you thought about that?"

Musk's answer? "Yes, it's an issue."

To a true entrepreneur, there are no impossibilities, just barriers to overcome. (And yes, it turned out there is a solution to that particular physics problem—quite an easy one, in fact—via fluid dynamics).

As mentioned earlier, Chris Anderson's DIY Drones product ArduCopter replicates 98 percent of the functionality of a military-grade Predator drone at one-thousandth the cost. That's a drone for less than $1,000. It's also transformational. Note the sudden appearance of drones in the planning agendas of companies as diverse as Amazon, QuiQui and UPS. This is not a coincidence.

Such breakthrough thinking also inspires. At Singularity

University, students form teams in major problem spaces such as healthcare, education, clean water and so on. They are then given the challenge of coming up with a product or service that could positively impact a billion people within a decade [MTP]. One team, which called itself Matternet, chose poverty as its problem space after reading that 85 percent of all roads in Africa are regularly washed out during the wet season.

But how do you alleviate poverty if you can't easily transport people or items? That question led Matternet to home in on "Transportation in Developing Countries" as its MTP. When Anderson described his DIY Drones idea in a lecture, the team had an epiphany: In the same way that Africa leapfrogged the entire copper wire telephony generation by going straight to wireless, why not use drones to do the same thing with transportation, and avoid building roads altogether?

The most exciting trend in drones today is that they're doubling their price/performance ratio every nine months. That's twice as fast as Moore's Law. A drone today can carry a four kilogram package up to a distance of twenty kilometers. In nine months, that drone's capacity will double to eight kilograms per twenty kilometers, and nine months after that things will get really interesting at sixteen kilograms over twenty kilometers. By leveraging this doubling capability by building drones to deliver food and medicine in developing countries, Matternet is revolutionizing transportation as we know it.

Matternet, which has completed trials in Haiti and is now launching in Bhutan, is a great example of an ExO because it harnesses information technologies, has an exponentially dropping cost of supply, and can either transform the problem space or inspire the startups that will do so. Amazon's recent announcement that it wants to deliver packages via drones has added blue-chip legitimacy to this effort.

STEP 5: BUILD A BUSINESS MODEL CANVAS

Once a core idea or breakthrough has been identified, the next step is to elaborate how to get it to market. Our suggested tool for this is the Business Model Canvas (BMC), which was created by Alexander Osterwalder and has been popularized by the Lean Startup model. As shown below, you begin the process by diagramming the various components of the model (value propositions, customer segments, etc.). A warning: At this stage, it is important that the BMC be simple and not overthought. Experimentation will navigate you to the best path and provide the next level of fidelity.

Key Partners	Key Activities	Value Proposition	Customer Relationships	Customer Segments
	Key Resources		Channels	
Cost Structure		Revenue Streams		

Credit: Alexander Osterwalder. For more on how to create effective value propositions, we recommend reading Osterwalder's new book, *Value Proposition Design: How to Create Products and Services Customers Want.*

STEP 6: FIND A BUSINESS MODEL

It is also important to understand that if you're going to achieve a 10x improvement, there's a strong likelihood that your company will require a completely new business model. As Clayton Christensen illustrated in *The Innovators Dilemma,* which was published in 1997, disruption is mostly achieved by a startup offering a less expensive product using emerging technologies and meeting a future or unmet customer need or niche. Christensen emphasized that it is not so much about disruptive products, but more about new business models threatening incumbents.

For example, Southwest Airlines treated its planes like buses and created an entire niche for itself. Google created the AdWords business model, which never existed before the advent of web pages. In the near future, micro-transactions, enabled by crypto-currencies like Bitcoin, will create entirely new financial business models that have never existed before.

In his 2005 book, *Free: The Future of a Radical Price*, Chris Anderson built on the lower cost positioning of the disruptor, noting that pretty much all business models, and certainly those that are information-based, will soon be offered to consumers for free. The popular "freemium" model is just such a case: many websites offer a basic level of service at no cost, while also enabling users to pay a fee to upgrade to more storage, statistics or extra features. Advertising, cross-subsidies and subscription business models are other ways of layering profit-generating operations on top of what is essentially free baseline information.

Kevin Kelly expanded further on this idea in a seminal post entitled "Better than Free," which appeared on his Technium blog in 2008.[1] In digital networks *anything* can be copied and is thus "abundant." So how do you add or extract value? What is valuable for customers? What is the new scarcity? What are the new value drivers? Kelly identified the following eight ways to build a business model when the underlying information is free:

1. **Immediacy:** Immediacy is the reason people order in advance on Amazon or attend the theater on opening night. Being the first to know about or experience something has intrinsic cultural, social and even commercial value. In short: time confers privilege.

---

1   kk.org/thetechnium/2008/01/better-than-fre/

2. **Personalization:** Having a product or service customized just for you not only gives added value in terms of quality of experience and ease-of-use or functionality, it also creates "stickiness," as both parties are invested in the process.

3. **Interpretation:** Even if the product or service is free, there is still considerable added value to any service that can help shorten the learning curve to using it—or using it better. Kelly often jokes: "Software: free; the manual: $10,000."

4. **Authenticity:** Added value comes from a guarantee that the product or service is *real and safe*—that it is, in Kelly's words, "bug-free, reliable and warranted."

5. **Accessibility:** Ownership requires management and maintenance. In an era where we own hundreds of apps on several platforms, any service that helps us organize everything and improve our ability to find what we need quickly is of particular value.

6. **Embodiment:** Digital information has no "body," no physical form, until we give it one—high definition, 3D, a movie screen, a smartphone. We willingly pay more to have free software delivered to us in the physical format we prefer.

7. **Patronage:** "It is my belief that audiences WANT to pay creators," Kelly wrote. "Fans like to reward artists, musicians, authors and the like with tokens of their appreciation, because it allows them to connect. But they will only pay if it is very easy to do, the amount is reasonable, and they feel certain the money will directly benefit the creators." He adds that another benefit of a simple payment process is that it capitalizes on users' impulsiveness. Examples include iTunes songs and Spotify, as well as Netflix subscriptions. Customers choose to pay for each of these services even though the same content can be acquired through piracy.

8. **Findability:** A creative work has no value unless its potential audience can find it. Such "findability" only

exists at the aggregator level, as individual creators typically get lost in the noise. Thus, attaching yourself to effective channels and digital platforms like app stores, social media sites or online marketplaces where potential users can find you has considerable value to creators (and, ultimately, to users).

We believe the above list offers a set of working business models for an information age. The chart below shows how budding ExOs are leveraging one or more of these models:

	Authenticity	Personalization	Interpretation	Embodiment	Findability	Accessibility	Patronage	Immediacy
Uber					✓	✓		
Airbnb					✓	✓		
Topcoder					✓	✓		
GitHub		✓					✓	✓
Quirky	✓			✓			✓	
Local Motors	✓			✓			✓	
Xiaomi							✓	✓
Valve					✓	✓		
Zappos		✓			✓			
Amazon		✓	✓					
Google		✓	✓		✓			
Waze		✓			✓			
Netflix		✓				✓		

Let's return to the Business Model Canvas—and in particular to partnering, which is one of its features.

Fred Wilson, of Union Square Ventures, has pointed out that many incumbents in different industries are currently being disrupted—and not by just one startup, but by many different startups, all attacking one individual service within an industry. He sees major disruption in business models as either unbundling or rebundling.

For example, let's look at the financial services industry. A classic bank offers many services such as payment infrastructure, trust, mobile and social wallets, e-commerce and m-commerce solutions, lending, investments, stocks, etc. It is a consolidated or aggregated offering of different individual financial services. Those banks are now being disrupted by a variety of financial startups, including Square, Clinkle, Stripe, Lending Club, Kickstarter, eToro and Estimize. We consider this fragmentation of individual financial services a form of *unbundling*.

Now, what if all these startups decided to cooperate or merge within the next five years? What if they agreed to create alliances via open APIs? What if they partnered and *rebundled?* You'd end up with a completely new bank with at least 10x less overhead than that of its predecessors, as the new entity would require less real estate and fewer employees.

In sum, Step 6 is about creating new business models, which increasingly tend towards free and freemium models. These new business models have, potentially, eight new value drivers to generate revenues, differentiate them from competitors, and allow for a long-term strategy to align with adjacent ExOs in a particular industry to fully disrupt incumbents, rather than just one individual good or service offered. Talk about a powerful double-disruption scenario.

STEP 7: BUILD THE MVP

A key output of the Business Model Canvas is what's called the *Minimum Viable Product*, or MVP. The MVP is a kind of applied experiment to determine the simplest product that will allow the team to go to market and see how users respond (as well as help find investors for the next round of development). Feedback loops can then rapidly iterate the product to optimize it and drive the feature roadmap of its development. Learning, testing assumptions, pivoting and iterating are key in this step.

Note the transformation: while Step 1 is about the MTP, or Purpose, Step 7 is about Experimentation. However, this is not the whole story when it comes to most successful startups. As Peter Thiel explains: "Not all startups thrive by experimentation and purpose only." LinkedIn, Palantir and SpaceX were fundamentally successful due to a strong vision of the future. Similarly, Thiel's observation is further substantiated by Aileen Lee's Unicorns research (which we addressed earlier in the chapter).

The early websites of LinkedIn, Facebook, Twitter and Foursquare are all examples of MVPs in action. Their early sites were clunky and inelegant with difficult navigation paths. However, they were able to quickly ratify core assumptions, understood key user requirements and implemented rapid feedback loops to fix problems.

STEP 8: VALIDATE MARKETING AND SALES

Once the product is being used in its chosen market(s), a customer acquisition funnel will need to be established to help drive new visitors to the product. Its role is to qualify potential customers and convert them into users and paying customers. A good starting point for this is Dave McClure's AARRR, an onomatopoeically titled "Pirate" model for startup metrics. The model tracks the following layers and key metrics:

- **Acquisition:** How do users locate you? (Growth metric)
- **Activation:** Do users have a great first experience? (Value metric)
- **Retention:** Do users come back? (Value metric)
- **Revenue:** How do you make money? (Value metric)
- **Referral:** Do users tell others? (Growth metric)

The AARRR model is not easy to forget once you use it

(and neither is McClure sporting an eye patch and waving a fake sword).

STEP 9: IMPLEMENT SCALE AND IDEAS

As already noted, becoming an ExO does not mean implementing all 11 SCALE and IDEAS attributes. A great MTP and three or four other attributes are usually sufficient for success. The key, of course, is determining *which* attributes are the right ones to execute. The following is a guide to implementing ExO attributes into a startup:

MTP: Formulate an MTP in a particular problem space, one that all founders feel passionate about.

Staff on Demand: Use contractors, SoD platforms wherever possible; keep FTEs to a minimum.

Community & Crowd: Validate idea in MTP communities.

Get product feedback.

Find co-founders, contractors and experts.

Use crowdfunding and crowdsourcing to validate market demand and as a marketing technique.

Algorithms: Identify data streams that can be automated and help with product development. Implement cloud-based and open source machine and deep learning to increase insights.

Leveraged Assets: Do NOT acquire assets.

Use cloud computing, TechShop for product development.

Use incubators like Y Combinator and Techstars for office, funding, mentoring and peer input. Starbucks as office.

Engagement: Design product with engagement in mind.

Gather all user interactions.

Gamify where possible.

Create a digital reputational system of users and suppliers to build trust and community.

Use incentive prizes to engage crowd and create buzz.

Interfaces: Design custom processes for managing SCALE; do not automate until you're ready to scale.

Dashboards: Set up OKR and value, serendipity, and growth metrics dashboards; do not implement value metrics until product finalized (see Step 10).

Experimentation: Establish culture of experimentation and constant iteration. Be willing to fail and pivot as needed.

Autonomy: Implement lite version of Holacracy. Start with the General Company Circle as a first step; then move onto governance meetings.

Implement the GitHub technical and organizational model with radical openness, transparency and permission.

Social Technologies: Implement file sharing, cloud-based document management.

Collaboration and activity streams both internally and within your community.

Make a plan to test and implement telepresence, virtual worlds and emotional sensing.

The table opposite shows our assessment of leading ExOs and the attributes they've most leveraged, showing a good distribution and usage of both SCALE and IDEAS elements.

STEP 10: ESTABLISH THE CULTURE

Perhaps the most critical step in building an ExO involves establishing its culture. Think again about PayPal's culture of close friendship rather than formal work relationships. In a fast-scaling organization, culture—along with the MTP and Social Technologies—is the glue that keeps a team together through the quantum leaps of an ExO's growth. Needless to say, given that even *defining* the term culture has proven enduringly difficult,

	MTP	S	C	A	L	E	I	D	E	A	S
GitHub	✓		✓			✓				✓	✓
Airbnb	✓		✓		✓	✓	✓				
Quirky	✓	✓	✓		✓				✓		
Uber	✓		✓		✓	✓	✓				
Topcoder	✓	✓		✓			✓				
Waze	✓		✓			✓	✓				
Local Motors	✓	✓	✓		✓		✓				
Supercell	✓							✓	✓	✓	✓
Google Ventures	✓			✓			✓	✓	✓		
Valve	✓							✓		✓	✓
BlaBlaCar	✓		✓		✓	✓	✓				

this is a particularly challenging step.

According to noted hotelier Chip Conley, "Culture is what happens when the boss leaves." We think that pretty much sums it up, and would only add that culture is a company's greatest intangible asset. (As many have observed, including Joi Ito, head of the MIT Media Lab, "Culture eats strategy for breakfast.") From the "HP Way" and IBM's "Think" to Google's playrooms and Twitter's warehouse, it is hard to overstate culture's added value. Very few people would argue that a big part of Zappos' success (and its billion-dollar valuation) is not due to its company culture.

Establishing a corporate culture starts with learning how to effectively track, manage and reward performance. And that begins with designing the OKR system we outlined in Chapter Four, and then continues through the process of getting the team habituated to transparency, accountability, execution and high performance.

STEP 11: ASK KEY QUESTIONS PERIODICALLY

There are eight key questions to think about—not once, but repeatedly—as you build out your startup. Successfully answering each one gives you a passing grade in terms of this chapter:

1. Who is your customer?
2. Which customer problem are you solving?
3. What is your solution and does it improve the status quo by at least 10x?
4. How will you market the product or service?
5. How are you selling the product or service?
6. How do you turn customers into advocates using viral effects and Net Promoter Scores to drive down the marginal cost of demand?
7. How will you scale your customer segment?
8. How will you drive the marginal cost of supply towards zero?

As mentioned earlier, that final question is the most critical for an ExO. To be truly disruptive to the status quo and achieve the 10x scalability that is the hallmark of ExOs, some combination of IDEAS and SCALE must drive down the cost of supply exponentially.

A final word on timing: For any startup to be successful, it must combine requisite skills, hard work and great market timing (especially when it comes to technology).

As Ray Kurzweil says: "*An invention needs to make sense in the world in which it is finished, not the world in which it is started.*" This is a profound point, one often missed by founders. It is about understanding the evolutionary trajectory of technology. That is, which functionalities and capacities will become feasible in two or three years given the pace of Moore's Law? When you develop a product with the near future in mind instead of the present, it greatly increases your chances of success.

Futurist Paul Saffo has said that most transformative (technological) inventions fail the first few times when launched, and generally take fifteen years to be fully realized. Why? Various reasons: too early, bad timing, unproven business models, integration issues—all result in a poor customer experience in an even poorer marketplace. Michiel Muller adds: "It takes a 9x improvement to move people from incumbent products to new products from startups." There is a certain threshold value, which is why we've set a minimum 10x requirement for starting Exponential Organizations.

STEP 12: BUILDING AND MAINTAINING A PLATFORM

Leading platform expert Sangeet Paul Choudary identified the four steps needed to build a successful platform (as opposed to a successful product):

1. Identify a *pain point* or use case for a consumer.
2. Identify a *core value* unit or social object in any interaction between a producer and consumer. This could be anything. Pictures, jokes, advice, reviews, information about sharing rooms, tools and car-rides are examples of things that have led to successful platforms. Remember that many people will be both producers and consumers, and use this to your advantage.
3. Design a way to *facilitate* that interaction. Then see if you can build it as a small prototype that you can curate yourself. If it works at that level, it will be worth taking to the next level and scaling.
4. Determine how to build a *network* around your interaction. Find a way to turn your platform user into an ambassador. Before you know it, you'll be on a roll.

To implement platforms, ExOs follow four steps in terms of data and APIs:

- **Gather:** The algorithmic process starts with harnessing data, which is gathered via sensors, people, or imported from public datasets.

- **Organize:** The next step is to organize the data. This is known as ETL (extract, transform and load).
- **Apply:** Once the data is accessible, algorithms such as machine or deep learning extract insights, identify trends and tune new algorithms. These are realized via tools such as Hadoop and Pivotal, or even (open source) deep learning algorithms like DeepMind or Skymind.
- **Expose:** The final step is exposing the data in the form of an open platform. Open data and APIs can be used such that an ExO's community develops valuable services, new functionalities and innovations layered on top of the platform by remixing published data with their own. Examples of companies that have successfully exposed their data this way are the Ford Company, Uber, IBM Watson, Twitter and Facebook.

We can't emphasize the following strongly enough: the world that is emerging is very different from the one we've known. Power is becoming easier to acquire but harder to keep. Thanks to strong viral and social network effects that allow startups to scale rapidly, it is now easier than ever before to start new companies and disrupt industries. But when it comes to social networks, the reverse is also true. Facebook, for example, is an incumbent, and its network effects and lock-in make it hard to usurp—underscoring the great advantage a platform has over a product or service.

In her book, *The End of Competitive Advantage: How to Keep Your Strategy Moving as Fast as Your Business*, Rita Gunther McGrath illustrates that we can only obtain what she calls Transient Competitive Advantages via platforms and purpose, community, and culture.

IN CONCERT

When it all comes together—when a great MTP is devised and the right attributes are implemented—the results can be stunning. France's BlaBlaCar is a case in point.

Founded in 2004 by Frédéric Mazzella, Nicolas Brusson and Francis Nappez, BlaBlaCar (formerly known as covoiturage. fr) is a peer-to-peer marketplace that connects drivers with empty seats with passengers looking for rides. The service is active in twelve countries and has over eight million members. One million people currently use the service each month (a total that is expected to climb), more than the number of passengers who ride Eurostar, Europe's leading train company, which carries 833,000 customers a month. BlaBlaCar uses the same business model as Airbnb—drivers are paid for every ride—with BlaBlaCar taking 10 percent. While Uber currently faces many legal issues like commercial and liability insurance, BlaBlaCar won't face those same problems, since the model it follows is comparable to asking friends to pay for fuel when they hitch a ride. Essentially, BlaBlaCar offers carpooling over longer distances—city to city, for example, rather than within individual cities—making it a great deal, since it is much cheaper to share a ride than to take a train or plane. An average 200-mile ride, for example, costs only $25. To enable its platform, BlaBlaCar—which was named runner-up for Best International Startup at the 2013 Crunchies Awards, and was bested only by Waze—utilizes algorithms to match drivers and riders [Algorithms]. (Clearly 2013 was a bad traffic year.)

BlaBlaCar has achieved success by creating an entirely new transport network (its MTP is People-Powered Transport) comprised of a trusted community of drivers and passengers. The result is a more social and efficient form of transport, allowing drivers to save an estimated $345 million each year. The business also prevents the release of 700,000 tons of carbon dioxide into the atmosphere each year, offering a clear social and ecological benefit.

Like Tony Hsieh of Zappos, Mazzella wants BlaBlaCar

to be considered among the best companies to work for. To keep morale high, he initiated the BlaBlaSwap program, which offers all employees (the company currently has a staff of 115) the opportunity to work in any of the company's international offices for one week a year. In addition, the company gathers all employees together for weekly "BlaBlaTalk" sessions—international employees join via videoconferencing—which provide staff the opportunity to share their achievements from the previous six weeks and their plans for the next six [Social Technologies].

The company also takes a Lean approach in terms of software development, enabling multiple small teams to develop its software through iteration. It is also important to note that BlaBlaCar stalled (pun intended) several times on its journey over the past ten years, transforming from B2B to C2C and pivoting through three different business models [Experimentation and Autonomy].

To engage the community, BlaBlaCar relies on its own digital reputation system, a framework it refers to as D.R.E.A.M.S. (Declared, Rated, Engaged, Activity-Based, Moderated and Social) [Engagement], which is outlined below:

- **Declared:** Trusted online profile, providing more information about users.
- **Ratings:** Collaborative services ask users to rate one another after having met "In Real Life," enabling people to build good online reputations.
- **Engagement:** If members are to feel completely comfortable transacting with one another, they must believe other parties will honor financial commitments.
- **Activity-based:** Offer contextually relevant and real-time information to both buyer and supplier, ensuring that the transaction progresses smoothly, from initial interest through to payment.
- **Moderation:** All payment information transferred by users of a sharing service must be third-

party verified.

- **Social:** Allow users to connect their online identity with their real world identity, be it socially, via Facebook, or professionally, via LinkedIn.

Finally, to expand its reach throughout Europe, BlaBlaCar acquires local competitors before they become too big. Clearly, the company is doing everything right; in July 2014, it raised a staggering $100 million in equity funding.

LESSONS FOR ENTERPRISE ExOs (EExOs)

Much of what we have covered in this chapter applies to pure startups, as well as to startups growing out of existing enterprises. However, there are some special considerations for Enterprise ExOs (EExOs). According to Salim, the greatest danger when building an Enterprise ExO is that the "immune system" of the parent company will come and attack it.

- Only go after new markets (to avoid the immune system response). If you want to transform an existing cash cow or leapfrog a current business unit, you need a stand-alone unit with a small team that is isolated and fully autonomous.
- Establish direct support from—and a direct formal link to—the CEO. Whatever you do, do not settle for any other reporting line below the CEO, and that goes triple for the CFO.
- Spin out versus spin in. If you are successful, spin everything out and create a new company; don't try to wedge the emerging business back into the mother ship. A new enterprise won't fit neatly anywhere and internal politics will ensue, especially if you are cannibalizing an existing revenue stream. The only exception we've found is when individual EExOs are part of a larger platform play like

Apple's products, which start out at the edge and are brought into the center.

- Invite the most disruptive change-makers from within your existing organization to work on your EExO. Management expert Gary Hamel has said that young people, dissidents and those working on the geographic and mental peripheries of your organization are the most interesting, free and open thinkers. Look for rebels. The good news is that they won't be difficult to find.

- Build your ExO completely independent of existing systems and policies. That includes actual physical separation. Try hard not to use existing premises or infrastructure unless they deliver a huge strategic advantage. As with any new startup, it's critical for a new ExO to operate as a greenfield operation, relying on stealth and confidentiality.

As Steve Jobs said, "We run Apple like a startup. We always let ideas win arguments, not hierarchies. Otherwise, your best employees won't stay. Collaboration, discipline and trust are critical."

For those interested in a more thorough treatment of starting an ExO, Peter Diamandis and Steven Kotler's second book, *BOLD* (Simon & Schuster, Feb 2015), is written for the entrepreneur interested in going from an idea to running a billion-dollar company in record time.

CHAPTER SEVEN

EXOS AND MID-MARKET COMPANIES

In the last chapter, we discussed how to start an Exponential Organization. But the ExO model is not exclusive to entrepreneurship and startup companies. In fact, it is possible to take an established mid-market company and supercharge it to exponential growth.

In this chapter, we'll look at mid-market enterprises and show how they can take advantage of the ExO philosophy. Unlike startups (where you can build all of the internal operations from scratch around exponential growth), with established companies, the solution is inevitably customized: you must start with what already exists and build from there. In other words, there is no universal template for "going exponential."

For that reason, we will look at case studies of five very different companies that became Exponential Organizations, illustrating how to take an established organization whose growth has plateaued in a stable business environment... and then *transform* it into an ExO and achieve the desired 10x performance improvements promised by the model.

EXAMPLE 1: TED

In 1984, Richard Saul Wurman created the TED (Technology, Entertainment, Design) Conference. By curating the talks with extreme care and pioneering the now-famous eighteen-minute format, TED thrived, becoming an annual pilgrimage for many of the world's movers and shakers. Eighteen years after its creation, TED had reached middle age. It was profitable and respected, hosting about a thousand people every year in Monterey, California, but had leveled off in terms of annual growth (albeit deliberately). In short, TED had achieved a comfortable stasis.

Then, in 2001, Chris Anderson, who built Business 2.0 and IGN via his entity the Imagine Media Group, acquired TED. Anderson had a vision for taking TED to the next level by expanding its scale of operations to a global operation and its base of participants from power brokers to the educated masses.

To do so, he made two game-changing alterations. First, he offered both new and past TED talks for free over the Internet. Second, as noted in Chapter Five, working with Lara Stein, he created a toolkit for any TED member to create a TEDx franchise event in his or her own locale. The results were astounding: Today, more than thirty-six thousand TED and TEDx talks are available on the web and have been viewed almost two billion times. Along the way, TED has gone from an annual gathering of dilettantes to one of the world's most popular and influential forums for the exchange of ideas.

Now, let's look at this program from an ExO perspective. From the beginning, as first elucidated by Wurman, TED had both an appealing and scalable MTP: "Ideas Worth Spreading." When Anderson turned the TED talks into free online content, he created Engagement and quickly built the critical mass needed to turn Crowd into Community. The TED talks also leveraged the exponential nature of cloud services (Leveraged Assets). At the same time, the franchise format of TEDx, supported by the toolkit, created a scalable set of optimized processes that allowed this newly created Community to build the organization outside the traditional, formal boundaries of its reporting lines. At the same time, TED was now free to grow much faster than Anderson and his team could have ever have accomplished than if its growth depended solely on their management.

The lesson here is that it is possible to take an established, medium-sized organization and transform it into an ExO by thoughtfully applying ExO attributes.

For TED, the results have been phenomenal. In just a few short years, Anderson turned a localized program into a global media brand. Despite its rapid growth, however, TED never compromised on the excellence of content or the quality of the attendee experience that made it so great in the first place.

Let's look at how the ExO attributes were implemented:

MTP: "Ideas Worth Spreading"

Community & Crowd: Leverage the TED community for TEDx events. TED talks have turned millions of casual members into community.

Algorithms: Used to gauge which TED talks to promote on main site.

Interfaces: Fixed rules about how to create a TEDx event.

Dashboards: Live statistics on TEDx events globally.

Experimentation: Different formats tried and evaluated (e.g., within corporations).

EXAMPLE 2: GITHUB

Ever since Linus Torvalds created Linux in 1991 and first established the "open source" paradigm, a vast global community has been steadily creating new software for millions of applications. One such initiative, the website SourceForge (**www.sourceforge.net**), has more than 430,000 open source projects on it, some of which have achieved remarkable success.

Aside from Linux itself, perhaps the best-known open source project is the Apache Web Server, a free piece of software created in 1996 by a team led by open source guru Brian Behlendorf, which competed with and subsequently humbled mighty Microsoft. Today, Apache runs the majority of the websites around the world—a fact that remains little known. In an illuminating exercise conducted in 1998, IBM asked a hundred blue-chip company chief information officers if they used open source software in their companies. 95 percent said no. Yet when interviewers asked the same question of those companies' systems administrators, 95 percent answered yes, an outcome that led IBM to make a major strategic shift into open source. Celebrated—even recognized—or not, open source software runs the Internet (and thus the world) today.

After that extraordinary initial success, the open source movement settled into a stable, stratified environment over much the last decade, with the community producing little in the way of new innovation. Everything changed in 2008, however, when Chris Wanstrath, P.J. Hyett and Tom Preston-Werner (all out of Paul Graham's Y Combinator entrepreneurial incubator program) founded a company called GitHub.

An open source coding and collaboration tool and platform, GitHub has utterly transformed the open source environment. It is a social network for programmers in which people and their collaborations are central, rather than just the code itself. When a developer submits code to a GitHub project, that code is reviewed and commented upon by other developers, who also rate that developer. GitHub's coding environment has instant messaging embedded within it, along with a distributed version control system (instead of a central code repository). In practice, what that means is you don't need a server; you have everything you need locally, and can start coding without first needing to get permission. And you can do so anywhere, even offline.

GitHub has successfully transformed the open source community by implementing virtually all of the ExO principles. The table below shows how the company has implemented an MTP, as well as SCALE and IDEAS:

MTP: "Social Coding"

Staff on Demand: GitHub can (and does) leverage the entire open source community for internal work.

Community & Crowd: Thanks to coding lessons and a collaborative environment, new developers (Crowd) are quickly turned into users (Community). In addition, GitHub has created a new office for any and all stakeholders to drop by and contribute or learn. There is open event space available for offline communities to gather and organize programs. GitHub explicitly doesn't use "lock-in" as a tactic, but rather focuses on respecting its users and being the best platform in the market space.

Algorithms: In GitHub's system, feedback is codified into algorithms and used for improved version control and workflow.

Leveraged Assets: GitHub doesn't own any of the projects hosted on its platform, which itself runs on the cloud. The company does use some of the software from various projects to enhance the platform itself—thus enlisting users into improving their own work environment.

Engagement: Game dynamics are extensively used, with leaderboards and a reputation system. This keeps users engaged without forcing their participation. Feedback on new code is accomplished in almost real time.

Interfaces: The company has customized a number of functions to support its developers, including instant messaging, rating and reputation systems, and software coding lessons. All are embedded within the platform. The core strength of the product is its highly automated control mechanism and workflow management, which integrates outputs of different external organizational attributes (such as software incentive competitions and gamification programs), as well as crowd and community deliverables.

Dashboards: GitHub monitors value metrics about the platform. This information is available internally via a sophisticated and intuitive control panel.

Experimentation: Due to its decentralized, responsive, transparent and self-organizing company culture, there is continuous and open iteration of new ideas in every department across the organization. To avoid chaos, GitHub has developed open, easy-to-use internal platforms and effective communication. Given the freedom employees have to join any project, they need ready access to training materials and documentation from across the organization; without them, switching projects creates too much friction as newcomers struggle to get oriented. In this way, new team members are able to be productive from the first day they join a project.

Autonomy: Authority and decision-making are completely decentralized. Teams self-organize, and the staff for any given project make the key decisions on that team's initiatives. That said, everyone in the company is encouraged to contribute to and act as advisor on decisions that are being made elsewhere in the organization. As a result, the recruiting process is primarily focused on self-starters who have passion, purpose, and potential. Within the company, this is called "open allocation," which essentially translates to: always work on stuff you are personally excited about or that you find fulfilling.

Social Technologies: With all employees across all departments using GitHub internally, social constructs and technologies are deeply embedded into GitHub's platform and culture. Indeed, it can be said that every aspect of the product has a social feature. Thus, the *de facto* office of the company is the chat room; email is used only for sending platform reminders and alerts about changes to the platform. This "conversational culture" boosts team morale and productivity. Senior management also has a motive for enforcing this culture: clear communication is a top priority in such an experimental, networked organizational model. Team members rely on face-to-face conversations, calls or Hangouts for strategic discussions, while using GitHub, chat or email for more operational work.

How well has GitHub done with this revolutionary, exponential, corporate culture?

In six years, the company has created a community of more than six million developers working collaboratively on more than fifteen million open source software projects. Even more important is that in Silicon Valley today, software developers' hiring prospects and even salaries are largely determined by their individual ratings on GitHub. And because of the power and influence of that rating system, developers are constantly adding code to GitHub projects in order to boost their personal ratings. This secondary benefit further adds value to the community and the company.

In short, GitHub is not only a great example of an Exponential Organization, but its product is also a powerful template for the ExO organizational model: collaborative, open, transparent, community-driven and peopled by staff well equipped and willing to self-select projects. It also offers 10x improvements across the board for different functions, jobs and departments. Bottom line: GitHub is an emergent organization driven by passion and purpose.

And although GitHub is currently optimized for developers, similar platforms will eventually emerge for lawyers, doctors, publicists and other professionals. The platform has already been extended into enterprise software development with a

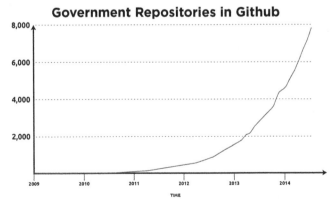

Credit: GitHub

successful paid business model, and can or soon will be used by governments, non-profits and educational institutions. GitHub charges users a monthly subscription—ranging from $7 to $200—to store programming source code. Andreessen Horowitz, one of the world's leading venture capital firms, recently invested $100 million in GitHub. It was the VC firm's largest investment round ever. To understand its rationale, see GitHub's usage by governments around the world (and please spot the exponential curve).

EXAMPLE 3: COYOTE LOGISTICS

We don't want to give you the impression that ExO principles only work on Internet companies or cute gaming firms. The example of Coyote Logistics shows that these principles can also apply to older, more established industries outside of social networking industries and places like Silicon Valley—in this case, the down-to-earth world of trucking and logistics.

Jeff Silver, a former executive at American Backhaulers, co-founded Coyote Logistics with Marianne Silver in 2006. The company took on the transportation and distribution of goods, and by leveraging ExO characteristics has managed to revolutionize an established, traditional industry. Currently employing 1,300 employees and serving 6,000 customers, including huge global clients such as Heineken, Coyote leverages a network of 40,000 contracted carriers across the country.

Coyote has successfully applied ExO principles in the following ways:

MTP: "Offer the Best Logistics Experience Ever"

Staff on Demand/Leveraged Assets: The 40,000 carriers operating under contract give Coyote extraordinary reach without the burden of managing a huge staff.

Community & Crowd: Coyote has transformed its 40,000 contracted carriers into a community that interacts with the core team via social media and mobile apps.

Algorithms: The core ExO innovation at Coyote is the use of complex, proprietary algorithms to eliminate the problem of empty trucks—known as deadheads— which are one of the industry's biggest logistical headaches. With more than 40,000 trucks in transit at any given time throughout the U.S., it is essential that Coyote pair empty trucks with cargo, and its algorithms give the company a competitive advantage over other trucking firms. Estimates suggest that in 2012 alone, Coyote Logistics eliminated 5.5 million empty miles, prevented 9,000 tons of unwanted CO_2 exhaust and contributed \$9 million back to its customers.

Interfaces: Coyote has created numerous customized processes for managing its contractors, customers and fleet. As shown above, these algorithms provide unique insights about matching trucks with cargo— Coyote's "secret sauce." For recruiting, the company prefers to hire young college graduates who show passion, attitude and personality, and who are completely new to the logistics industry. According to Coyote, this results in a workforce unencumbered by old industry standards and prejudices and open to new ideas and methods. To streamline this process, Coyote is adopting a data-driven selection management solution created by Hireology, and in 2012 hired 400 of 10,000 candidates using Hireology's platform. New employees receive extensive training and are informed of apprenticeship possibilities. In short, they are the vanguard of the company's future.

Dashboards: The data from all trucks, as well as from a proprietary company mobile app, are monitored in real time and are available both to company management and the drivers themselves to help all stakeholders better deliver on the company's mission and to achieve performance goals.

Social Technologies: Internally, the company makes

full use of social media. Employees are encouraged to communicate through social media such as Facebook, Twitter, YouTube and LinkedIn, and to support the community and charitable organizations through these accounts. Externally, Coyote has created its own mobile app, CoyoteGO, which streamlines all interactions among drivers, shippers and employees, creating the potential for Coyote to be in contact 24/7 with its carrier fleet, no matter where the trucks are located.

In 2012, Coyote Logistics enjoyed $786 million in revenues, and in 2010 was named the fastest growing logistics company in the Inc. 500. It was also ranked No. 1 and No. 4 in *Crain's* Fast Fifty, and currently holds the No. 26 spot on *Forbes'* America's Most Promising Companies list.

The MTP Coyote has embraced all but guarantees that it will remain highly customer driven. And it is continuously leveraging emerging technology to assure that its customer experience is as seamless and efficient as possible.

Most employees work in a single 100,000-square-foot company space, which looks nothing like a traditional trucking company headquarters. The vibe is hot young technology startup—fast moving, creative and spilling over with energy. The only difference is that Coyote is not in the business of delivering online games; instead, it delivers real physical goods, via truck, to stores and offices around the country. Coyote's attitude is reflected in the four brand characteristics the company confidently fosters: True, Tenacious, Tribal, and Smart. It is that attitude—cocky, communal and competent—that helps explain why Coyote Logistics has earned a spot on the *Chicago Tribune* Top Workplaces list four years in a row.

EXAMPLE 4: STUDIO ROOSEGAARDE

Founded by Daan Roosegaarde, who calls himself a "hippie with a business plan," Studio Roosegaarde was started in the Netherlands in 2007 with the avowed goal of building dreams. Indeed, Roosegaarde refers to his company as a dream factory (talk about an MTP). His studio is a special mix of art, design and poetry, as well as an array of interactive and exponential technologies.

Studio Roosegaarde creates contextual art installations using information-centric technologies such as sensors, nanotech and, most recently, biotech (synthetic biology). One example is a smart highway that responds automatically to weather changes. A second is a smog reduction project in Beijing that uses captured smog to create carbon rings as a wearable device. If all that sounds more than a little absurd, it's because it is…until the moment it all becomes real.

The studio's initial success was mainly due to its purpose, the physical and visceral nature of its projects, and the bold and unique nature of its ideas—what Roosegaarde calls MAYA (Most Advanced Yet Acceptable). Over a five-year period, the studio stabilized into a steady state. Revenues in 2007 were 50,000 euros (about $60,000) and over the following six years, the studio hovered around that revenue level. All studio work was handled internally by full-time employees—everything from idea generation and prototyping, to pilot and scaling. Processes had become institutionalized and strong habits were formed.

In 2012, Roosegaarde realized that the studio had lost its freewheeling artistic spirit and needed recalibration. He buckled down and transformed the enterprise, implementing several ExO characteristics, as shown in the following table:

MTP: "Opening the World with Techno Poetry to Humanize and Beautify the World"

Staff on Demand: Heavy dependence on SoD as a creativity booster.
Internships are key in SoD: desired attributes include passion and a self-starter mentality. Company has been built from the bottom-up and is based on its employees.

Community & Crowd: Original and smart ways to insource ideas and vendors to implement future art projects. The company first launches a simple idea in a low-profile magazine or newspaper via an interview. Next come inbound ideas launched via crowd, followed by a TV launch, and finally a launch via vendors who send inbound emails on how to build art projects. Art in general—and the studio's work in particular—has the power of pull and allows for sharing intentions that are manifested quickly (intention economy). Fewer resources and employees needed; most concept and vendor research is crowd-sourced, filtered by passion and commitment.

Algorithms: Early installations employed fuzzy logic. Later work personalized, based upon sensors and algorithms. No deep or machine learning.

Leveraged Assets: Labs in different universities (University of Zurich, University of Cambridge, Eindhoven University of Technology and Wageningen University). Shenzhen factories for prototyping and manufacturing/scaling.

Engagement: Studio Roosegaarde listens carefully to the community and crowd—not formally via online marketplaces, but via inbound emails and calls that feed directly to new ideas and experiments.

Interfaces: Three people manually process all inbound calls and emails to select the best press opportunities, people, ideas and vendors.

Dashboards: Real-time tracking of cash flow. Company aims for an eighteen-month runway of slack or play money. Number of ideas in every internal conversation are tracked and measured, along with emerging themes per conversation.

Experimentation: "Bowling vs. Ping-Pong." Studio Roosegaarde believes strongly in iteration and short feedback cycles, especially with clients and end users. Bowling is akin to slow, sequential development. Prototyping (Ping-Pong) is key.

Autonomy: No job descriptions. Staff can spend at

least 30 percent of work time on their own projects.

Hard to decentralize art due to its dependency on its visionary founder.

Moving towards implementing the Holacracy model (OKRs, Lean, open, transparent).

Social Technologies: Activity streams via Viadesk software and extensive use of wikis.

Connected 3D printers and advanced Cisco videoconferencing in Holland and China boost team bonding and creativity.

Google Trends and Social Media Monitoring (Lean Startup tool) personalize art installations or expositions by country (by culture or memes); such customization is called Copy Morph.

In 2012, Studio Roosegaarde won a high profile incentive competition at TEDx Binnenhof. That was an inflection point; the Studio subsequently won numerous national, European and global awards in 2013 and 2014, including a *Forbes* World's Most Innovative Companies designation. Today, the studio's focus is primarily on ideation and scaling with a much smaller core team, more staff on demand and a great deal of crowdsourcing.

Revenues in 2014 will top three million euros—a sixtyfold increase over 2007. For an art studio, with physical products that are less scalable and focused on an experiential authenticity, that is an impressive achievement indeed.

RETROFITTING AN ExO

These four examples help demonstrate that it is possible to embed ExO principles into pre-existing organizations—and then literally explode their performance. For any reader with lingering doubts about this approach, let's now look at the work of Robert Goldberg.

After spending a decade building out NBC's network Internet division and then running the pioneering incubator, Idealab, Goldberg put his skills at the service of others by becoming a venture capitalist and advisor to several startups and other funds. In 2009, he joined Zynga as its first business executive and headed up the game company's mergers and acquisition operation. As we noted in Chapter Four, over a two-and-a-half year period, Zynga grew from thirty employees to three thousand, making it one of the fastest growing companies ever. That growth was achieved as a result of forty acquisitions over just over ten quarters. Amazingly, 95 percent of those acquisitions proved successful—an almost unheard-of ratio.

So how did Goldberg do it?

The primary mechanism used by Zynga to manage growth without diluting its culture was the formal application of Objectives and Key Results (OKRs) to track teams and keep everyone synchronized. With his arrival, Goldberg took matters a step further by applying these processes to Zynga's new acquisitions…but with a twist.

Most acquisitions fail because the mother company intentionally slows the newly acquired operation in order to better understand it, adapt its internal operations to the new order, achieve integration synergies and inculcate the new employees into the company culture. It is an understandable impulse, but one that almost always confuses and frustrates the new team, resulting in what Goldberg calls "impedance mismatch." That is, the newly arrived team has a sense of being stuck at the starting gate—feeling forgotten, ignored or punished—a situation that often leads key people to depart the company.

Goldberg turned this model upside down. He not only refused to put the brakes on these new acquisitions, but also implemented, with their agreement, *exponential* OKRs. This torrid new pace not only kept the new teams engaged and excited, but they even began pulling Zynga forward towards more exponential results.

After Zynga went public, Goldberg returned to his investing roots. He created a new fund, GTG Capital Partners, to apply his landmark thinking to other companies and industries. GTG Capital Partners finds early-stage and mid-market companies that have stalled in their growth and applies the following

ExO attributes:

MTP: Company transforms mission statements and takes on grander visions.

Community & Crowd: Community heavily engaged.

Engagement: Online marketing and referral marketing used extensively to increase customer engagement.

Algorithms: Data science techniques implemented to extract new insights about customers and products.

Experimentation: Product redesigned with a Lean approach and features constant iteration.

Dashboards: Real-time value and growth metrics implemented to track external progress; transparent OKRs used across the board with the management team.

Social Technologies: Social mechanisms implemented both internally and externally.

Goldberg and GTG Capital Partners work with prospective startups and mid-market companies for a fiscal quarter, implementing some of the ExO techniques listed above. If, collectively, they are able to double the company's growth rate in that time frame (no mean feat), then an investment is made and a 10x growth target set. Over the last two years, GTG Capital Partners has raised a $100 million fund, systematized its approach and, to date, has applied its process to forty companies—an astounding number.

EXAMPLE 5: GOPRO

In 2001, Nick Woodman, a passionate surfer, started strapping cameras to his wrists to take shots from his surfboard. After some failed early experiments, Woodman realized he had to build the waterproof housing. By 2004, he was building his own cameras, and ultimately came to own the full customer experience. Although some success came via QVC, the television shopping network, sales soon stalled, and there was some minor panic in the face of the competing Flip Video camera's success.

The turning point came in 2006, when friends convinced Woodman to go fully digital, resulting in GoPro producing its first digital video camera. In 2008, GoPro introduced a wide-angle lens, but the excitement was short-lived; Steve Jobs' announcement that the iPhone would feature video brought on a second panic attack. Sales stalled once again and growth flattened. After seven hard years, GoPro had plateaued; the company seemed to be going nowhere. Meanwhile, Cisco bought Pure Digital, the maker of the Flip camera, for almost $600 million.

Woodman refused to surrender. Convinced that his market was out there, he continued iterating and innovating. His break finally came in late 2009 when he introduced high definition (HD) video in the GoPro HD Hero. Meanwhile, the cost of the camera had dropped exponentially to the point where mainstream customers could afford it. When BestBuy began selling GoPro cameras in 2010, sales tripled.

GoPro now has more than seven hundred employees (it had just eight in 2010) and is valued at $3 billion. In 2013, GoPro sold 3.84 million cameras and grossed $985.73 million (up 87.4 percent from 2012). GoPro is currently ranked No. 39 on *Fast Company's* World's 50 Most Innovative Companies list, and the company went public in July 2014, a culmination of a remarkable run.

So which ExO attributes did GoPro use in 2010 and 2011 to grow exponentially after its plateau?

MTP: "Help People Capture and Share Their Most Meaningful Experiences"

Community & Crowd: Users from all over the world share footage on GoPro's website and Facebook page, which currently has 7.5 million likes. Viewers see videos and are inspired to create their own. In addition, GoPro has become an open platform with open APIs. Third-party developers can create additional functionality for GoPro devices.

Algorithms: Extensive fuzzy logic embedded in

the camera.

Leveraged Assets: GoPro mostly uses manufacturers and suppliers in China to produce its equipment, relying in particular on Foxconn, which invested $200 million in GoPro in December 2012. Foxconn CEO Terry Gou is a GoPro advisor.

Engagement: GoPro held a "How will you GoPro?" contest. Participants used text and visual to share their dream adventures. Of thousands of entries, one winner received an all-expense-paid trip worth $30,000. A GoPro film crew accompanied the winner and helped create his motorcycle adventure. The company also has a daily incentive competition in which it gives away one of everything the company makes.

Experimentation: Pivots amongst camera quality (HD), where to use it (use cases), rights management and distribution outlets (Best Buy).

Social Technologies: Heavy use of YouTube, Facebook and the historic Felix Baumgartner space jump, which received 8 million views.

Although GoPro has done very well in the last four years, it still faces major challenges—not the least of which is the slow decline of Best Buy and other big box retailers, which are the company's primary distribution channels. But as an example of a flat company that leveraged ExO attributes to transform itself, it's hard to find a better example. GoPro easily qualifies as an ExO, having increased sales by more than 50x over a five-year period.

So, can established companies adopt ExO processes and produce 10x results? The answer, as we have seen in this chapter, is a resounding *yes*. But it is always challenging, and there is no well-marked path for getting there. When it comes to established companies, every ExO solution is a custom creation.

Experience has shown that transforming an existing enterprise into an Exponential Organization requires two things. The first is a company culture that can quickly adapt to rapid, often radical, change. Coyote Logistics succeeded thanks to its comparatively small and focused staff and the fluid nature of its clients. Robert Goldberg succeeded at Zynga because he was working with employees and operations brought on board as a result of acquisitions, which meant that the workers had no history with their new employer, and thus had no precedents to fall back on. And GitHub was almost entirely virtual from the start, so could easily change the requirements for participation. Needless to say, imposing the ExO model on a more traditional company—one with a hardened culture or a rigid managerial hierarchy—is much more difficult.

Still, it can be done. We are convinced that *any* stabilized environment or mid-market company can leverage ExO principles and transform itself to achieve exponential growth.

That leads us to the second requirement for turning an established company into an exponential one: a visionary leader who has the full support of the board and senior management. Accelerating a company to blinding speeds, empowering employees and customers, and emplacing a sophisticated and sweeping technical infrastructure takes a leader who not only thinks big and acts decisively, but who also has the backing of the most powerful people in the company—people who won't shut the whole thing down once things get scary, or when they get a nosebleed. Goldberg's success at Zynga came not just from his own talent and trust in his people, but also from the company's fearless top management. For established companies wishing to go exponential, the character and courage of the board of directors and executive row will often prove more decisive than their competence.

Perhaps the best example of such leadership today is Elon Musk. With the support of a strong board and visionary investors like Steve Jurvetson, Musk's tenacity and drive have carried him through extreme tests. Tesla, now ten years old, saw its growth level off in 2011 and 2012, and was on the verge of bankruptcy and layoffs for its five hundred employees. After an injection of funds from Jurvetson's DFJ fund, the company launched the Tesla S, which was named Car of the Year in 2013 by *Motor Trend* magazine and declared the safest car ever built. Not content to rest on his laurels, Musk next open sourced all company patents and is launching a new battery factory (an EExO) that will power other brands. From an ExO perspective, perhaps the most interesting example of 10x improvement is the leverage provided by an electric motor. The drivetrain of the Tesla S has just seventeen moving parts—compare that to the several hundred moving parts in a conventional car's drivetrain. By leveraging an MTP, opening the intellectual property to the community and taking advantage of accelerating technologies, Tesla revitalized itself from a stalled mid-market company. Its market cap in the last year has increased from $4 billion to over $30 billion.

A final word on managing fast-tracked growth comes again from Chip Conley, who created the Joie de Vivre chain of specialty hotels and is now part of Airbnb's senior management team. Conley found that the more information-based we become, the greater the need to rely on rituals and meaning to stabilize companies and keep teams motivated. Thus, as ExOs take on larger numbers of employees, individual tasks and functions increasingly need the gravity well of an MTP to provide purpose. Although that would seem to add to the burden of bigger companies trying to become ExOs, the fact that established companies are better at those rituals, stories and legends— the glue that holds organizations together—works to their advantage, especially when they are accelerating exponentially.

In the next chapters, we'll take on the toughest nut of all and look at what large organizations need to do to retrofit ExO thinking into their world.

CHAPTER EIGHT
EXOS FOR LARGE ORGANIZATIONS

Ramez Naam spent thirteen years at software giant Microsoft, leading early-stage development for new products, including Outlook, Internet Explorer and Bing. In that role, Naam was uniquely positioned to observe not just Microsoft, but many of its clients and competitors—and not just in their high-growth stages, but also as mature companies.

In 2008, Naam had an epiphany. The 20th century had seen the defeat of top-down structures, such as communism and managed economies, by bottom-up frameworks, including democracy and capitalism. And yet, he realized, despite this historic lesson, the structure of most corporations remained completely hierarchical and top-down.

Naam also observed that as a result of this top-down focus, the flow of information in large corporations inevitably followed a slow, circular motion. Information initiated from senior management and slowly cascaded down through the ranks. Eventually, frontline employees used this potentially obsolete information to perform a fixed set of scripted tasks. They then gathered the results and returned them to the flow, passing the tasks upward through layers of management until those results eventually reached the executive boardroom once more. There, new decisions were made—and again a new set of commands was sent down through the organization.

Besides the obviously glacial pace of this process, Naam also noted that it actually *increased* the distance between information and decision-making, resulting in the following structural failures:

- Information moved slowly and insights took a long time to be implemented.
- Reality, as with the game of "Telephone," became distorted at each point of transfer.
- The flow pattern of the information inevitably bypassed a tremendous amount of intermediary brainpower and experience.
- The process often caused organizations to behave in a sociopathic manner, ultimately forcing employees to do things against their better judgment.

We can generalize the many issues facing large organizations to the following three:

- Most focus and attention is internal, not external.
- Emphasis tends to be on technologies with existing expertise; converging technologies or adjacencies tend to be ignored and breakthrough thinking is punished.
- Reliance on innovation from inside rather than outside.

Naam wasn't the only investigator surprised by what he found in many modern corporations. Jason Yotopoulos, who spent several years at SAP as executive vice president of global research, interviewed senior executives at three dozen multinational companies, ultimately finding himself in agreement with the words of organizational theorist John Seely Brown: "Companies may promote the idea of new business creation, [but] in the end they are all in the business of reducing risk and building to scale—which is, of course, the antithesis of entrepreneurship and new ventures."

Along the way, Yotopoulos also discovered that the new-business teams at these companies were almost always staffed with internal company personnel, which almost guaranteed a conservative approach and more-of-the-same outcomes.

Yotopoulos' and Naam's observations underscore our overall thesis that traditional and large organizational structures simply do not fit the current (and certainly not the future) paradigm for organizations. This shouldn't be too surprising: disruptive new ideas *never* map onto the traditional organization chart, and mature companies, above all else, are all about org charts.

Salim came to the same conclusion back in 2007 as head of Brickhouse, Yahoo's internal incubator, specifically during a period when Yahoo was contemplating acquiring Twitter. The problem, he quickly realized, was that although the young social networking company could be force-fit into any of five different Yahoo business units, ultimately it wouldn't fit well anywhere. Why? Because Twitter's product and culture were just too alien to the more-established company. In addition, it was hard to figure out exactly what business Twitter was in— which is as true today as it was then. In the end, the decision not to follow through with the acquisition was more impacted by organizational considerations than strategic ones.

Think back to the Iridium layer story from Chapter One. Its message should serve as a wake-up call to all large and established companies. Already dinosaurs, they've been hit by a comet of information and are at increased risk of extinction. Nowhere is this more the case than among insular organizations, regardless of the industry, that rely heavily on manpower or are asset-based. All are subject to the extreme threat of disruption. As Peter Diamandis says, "If you are relying on innovation solely from within your company, you're dead."

As we enter what Dave Blakely of IDEO calls "a programmable world," what is a large and established organization to do? Answer: *Transform.*

Transformation isn't easy, however. A big company is like a supertanker: it takes a long time to turn. Nonetheless, it can be done. There are many examples of big companies morphing into new markets over time. For example, Nokia used to be a tire company, Samsung was once a trading company and Intel got its start in memory chips. GE, a company with a long and distinguished history, has repeatedly reinvented itself.

Few companies, however, are able to transform quickly.

Apple and IBM are two rare examples of large companies that have successfully undertaken an extreme transformation and executed it fairly quickly. And in both cases, inspiration grew out of desperation; each company was just a few months from running out of cash. At the same time, each also enjoyed a charismatic and bold leadership that was able to use dire circumstances as an impetus to turn the company around.

As economist Paul Romer has said, "A good crisis is a terrible thing to waste." But waste is exactly what most companies do, and the vast majority of eleventh-hour turnarounds don't end well. As we pointed out in the Introduction, the average lifespan of an S&P 500 company has fallen from sixty-seven years a century ago to just fifteen years today, and 40 percent of today's Fortune 500 companies won't exist a decade from now.

Clearly, it is not in the best interest of any established company, no matter its size or industry, to wait until disaster is at the gate to initiate transformative risks. However, many studies have revealed that the vast majority of corporate transformation projects fail. There are many reasons for these failures: complexity, long project timelines, lack of support from the top, exploding budgets and so on. However, a key structural reason is short-term thinking driven by stock prices and the pressure on quarterly earnings. When a CEO or senior management team is faced with attempting a risky, long-term transformation versus just keeping the boat steady until their stock options vest, the choice defaults to the do-nothing strategy. As a result, a key mitigating strategy currently used by many large organizations to slow this trend is regulatory capture. If you can lobby for favorable legislation, you can protect yourself from external disruption. In 1998, in what critics call the "Mickey Mouse Protection Act," the U.S. Congress voted to extend copyright protection by an additional twenty years—a blow to creativity, and certainly not in the best interest of the general public. Similarly, the cable and phone companies have aggressively pursued legal action to protect their regional monopolies, even going so far as to sue cities that propose giving away Internet access in an effort to spur economic development.

Indeed, the nonpartisan United Republic found that the return on investment for lobbying is astounding: 5,900 percent for oil subsidies, 22,000 percent for MNC tax breaks and an astounding 77,500 percent for keeping drug prices high. At these rates, it's actually fiscally irresponsible *not* to lobby.

However, we believe that in an ExO era, such tactics are unsustainable, particularly when it comes to the consumer domain. Why? Because of the amount of time they take. The pace of adoption over the Internet far outruns the regulatory process. For example, by the time taxi agencies and hotels around the country woke up to the threats posed by Uber and Airbnb, respectively, the public had already embraced the services enough to make lobbying against them that much more difficult; it was a case of swimming against the tide. The same is true of other industries, as well—just witness the tension between New Jersey car dealers and Tesla's direct sales model. (There's a delightful irony in listening to automobile dealerships loudly proclaim they're all about consumer protection.)

Along with delaying tactics, there is also a second, equally imperative reason not to wait until the last minute to initiate a turnaround: *the cure just might kill you*. It is our firm belief that a large company cannot suddenly implement the SCALE and IDEAS processes and turn itself into an ExO overnight. It is simply too radical a transformation, one that is likely to crush a company's core business before it has time to find a new one. And even if the company does manage to institute a new business, the internal stress caused by such radical change will be extreme.

At the same time, established companies must transform themselves or they will quickly become obsolete. Despite the well-documented difficulties in fostering innovation in large organizations, not to mention the endless number of innovation consultants waiting in the wings to give often bad and conflicting advice, a large company cannot sit by and do nothing. The newspaper industry tried to do just that and, well…look at the result.

In this new high-metabolism world, where accelerating

technologies are orthogonally impacting a greater and greater number of industries, large organizations need strategies to more closely align themselves with ExO thinking. We have identified four such strategies for large organizations to deploy in an accelerating business world while still keeping their core operational businesses intact:

1. Transform leadership.
2. Partner with, invest in or acquire ExOs.
3. Disrupt[X].
4. Implement ExO Lite internally.

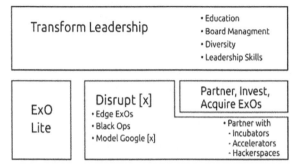

Let's now examine each of these efforts in turn.

1. TRANSFORM LEADERSHIP

There are four ways to transform the leadership layers of a big company:

Education

As we noted in Chapter One, the metabolism of the economy is accelerating, driven by a new breed of newly democratized, exponential technologies. If you're running a big company today and are not aware of these technologies—not to mention how they might impact your company—you are simply not doing your job. For any large organization, it is critical that its senior leadership bridges that gap to avoid becoming the next Kodak, Blackberry or Nokia.

In one answer to this need, Singularity University, in partnership with X Prize and Deloitte, set up a four-day workshop called the Innovation Partners Program (IPP). Every six months, eighty Fortune 500 C-Level executives receive two days of briefings on accelerating technologies, followed by two days of seminars introducing ExO-style organizational tools, including case studies, interviews and practice sessions on incentive prizes.

Before attending the program, 75 percent of the executives said they had little or no awareness of the technologies involved. After the program, 100 percent said they had already formulated immediate action items regarding those technologies. Even more dramatically, 80 percent of executives agreed that the newly understood breakthroughs would have a game-changing impact on their businesses within two years, with the remaining 20 percent confident the impact would be felt within five years.

> Recommendation: Bring in outside sources to update your senior management and board on accelerating technologies.

Board Management

The education requirement for senior leadership applies even more to board members, as they are even less likely to be technologically up to date. How can the board guide a CEO if it is not aware of the potentially disruptive changes the company faces?

Not surprisingly, smart CEOs are already setting up sessions geared toward helping board members come to grips with the new realities of an exponential world. In fact, one astute European CEO makes a point of sending his most staunchly traditional and backward-looking board members to training programs like those held at SU. His reasoning is that because the board members are the ones slowing progress, it is of the utmost urgency to disrupt their outmoded convictions and ideologies.

The good news is that not all board members hold such a narrow worldview; many, in fact, are remarkably enlightened. Yuri van Geest found that the forty most influential board chairs of large Dutch corporations were more aware of accelerating disruption than were their CEOs. He credited those board chairs with having a broader, pan-organizational perspective, noting that while CEOs need to focus on the business at hand, board members were free to look to the horizon and consider the larger picture.

The greater awareness among board members, especially once they've been trained, helps them to more fully support CEOs as they retool their organizations to adapt to an accelerating world. If a CEO isn't fully empowered by the board or given requisite cover, he or she will not be able to take the necessary steps to introduce change, and the resulting inaction will put the entire organization at risk.

The bottom line is that it takes everyone at the top, working together in full agreement about the threats facing the company, to achieve a shared vision and pull off a successful transformation of the organization.

A complement to board education is better management. As Jaime Grego-Mayor of Advisory Board Architects has noted, fully 95 percent of boards are not procedurally managed at all, despite the enormous value that well-connected board members can add. If ExOs are using OKRs to measure and track the performance of teams and senior management, then surely their board members, who arguably have the highest potential impact on the company, should be tracked and managed as well.

> Recommendations: Educate the board so that it is equipped to buy into the CEO's plan for radical change. In addition, track your board using OKRs.

Implement Diversity

The third level of transformation involves the actual composition of senior leadership.

It has been repeatedly shown that diversity in terms of gender, experience and age delivers better results. Yet most large organizations have painfully uniform layers of C-suite executives and board members, many of whom have attended the same business schools. Others come from an older generation and don't understand new technologies—including, sometimes, email.

Most Nobel Prize winners do their formative work in their mid- to late-twenties. The average age of the NASA engineers in the Apollo program was 27. Many of the founders of the dot-com era were in their early twenties. Yet most companies hold to the belief that the more senior the executive, the better understanding he or she has of the marketplace. In a fast-changing world, that supposition is no longer valid.

One of the recommendations Salim gives large-company CEOs is that they find the smartest 25 year olds in their organizations and have them shadow leadership positions to help close generational and technological gaps, accelerate their learning curve in management and provide reverse mentorship. Young leaders are desperately needed, and soon. In the new technology world, where organizations are dealing with market dynamics never before seen, experience as we've always defined it can hold a company back. Sebastian Thrun, CEO of Udacity and a driving force behind the Google car, recently said, "When I'm hiring employees today, imagination is much more important than experience."

Howard Schultz, CEO of Starbucks, showed his understanding of this concept by appointing Clara Shih to his board. Just thirty-one years old, Shih brings both a young perspective and deep experience of social media, ideal qualities as Starbucks struggles to better engage its customer base. She is a great example of the new phenomenon of "reverse mentoring."

Another dimension of diversity is gender. In 2012, the

Credit Suisse Research Institute finished a six-year study of companies with greater than $10 billion market capitalization.[1] One of its findings was that value of companies with all-male boards underperformed those of mixed-gender boards by an astounding 26 percent. Vivek Wadhwa, a noted journalist and co-author of the book *Innovating Women: The Changing Face of Technology*, has been championing this idea for several years now, fearlessly highlighting and showcasing companies with poor diversity ratios.

> Recommendations: Break up bastions of old-line thinking and replace them with individuals and teams offering diversity in terms of experience and perspective. Remember that one of the most important aspects of diversity requires putting young people into positions of power and influence. In addition, include more women on your board.

Skills and Leadership

While at SAP, Jason Yotopoulos observed that large companies often fail to recognize that there are different types of employees, and that each type is optimally suited for different roles within the company. These include:

- **Optimizers:** Run large businesses at scale and squeeze efficiency to maximize profits.
- **Scalers:** Take a proven model and grow it.
- **Evangelists:** Champion new ideas and move projects from the idea stage to initial commercialization.

Companies frequently make the mistake of taking their best performers from one area and moving them to another, expecting them to perform equally well. For example, a manager might ask an Optimizer to become an Evangelist, a role for which the

---

1   www.bloomberg.com/news/2012-07-31/women-as-directors-beat-men-only-boards-in-company-stock-return.html

employee may be utterly unsuited, either temperamentally or in terms of skills. The manager then wonders why a top performer failed so spectacularly. What is really required, however, is to tap those iconoclast Evangelists from the inside, the ones who know the corporation's unique assets and capabilities (which constitute the company's unfair advantage in entering new markets), and ask them to shape a new ExO at its edge.

Such arbitrary management decision-making—dropping people into slots for which they aren't suited—almost never works. And in the world of ExOs, it can be particularly catastrophic because successful leadership in an ExO world looks profoundly different from successful leadership in enterprises founded before, say, 2008. Rob Nail, CEO and Associate Founder of Singularity University, has examined leadership qualities in detail and determined six traits characteristic of ExO leaders:

1. **Visionary Customer Advocate:** In a period of rapid transition, it is easy for organizations and their products to stray from the originally successful connection they had with their customers/clients. Having the leader of the organization as the ultimate owner of this understanding and priority assures that it is consistently represented. Steve Jobs is a good example of a Visionary Customer Advocate who had access to extraordinary capabilities and new technologies, and who personally stayed involved in decisions regarding every aspect of the customer experience. If customers see their needs and desires being attended to at the highest levels, they are much more willing to persevere through the chaos and experimentation that often comes with exponential growth.

2. **Data-driven Experimentalist:** To create order out of high-speed chaos requires a process-oriented approach that is ultimately nimble and scalable. The Lean Startup approach can be applied at any scale to quickly iterate and build

institutional knowledge. We have many social tools and other vehicles to maintain incredible connections with our customers and community. When engaged properly, customers are not just likely to be flexible with the process, they may even be excited or demand to be part of it. However, without a data-centric approach, entailing rapid feedback and timely progression of a product or service, customers will become frustrated and, ultimately, disengage.

3. **Optimistic Realist:** When scaling rapidly, striving to understand and quantify the reality of a situation or opportunity is critical to navigation. When staring in the face of reality, however, some interpretation is always needed. Leaders able to articulate a positive outcome through any scenario, even downside scenarios, will be able to help maintain objectivity within their teams. Rapid growth and change may well be exciting for some, but most people generally find transformation disconcerting and difficult to adapt to. An overly pessimistic leader can exacerbate the fight or flight response, ultimately leading to poor decision-making.

4. **Extreme Adaptability:** As a business scales and its activities morph, so too must its management. For leaders to oversee long periods of accelerated growth, they must transform their focus and adapt their skills accordingly. It is rare to find a leader who can transform exponentially along with the technology and organization, so with disruption of business models comes the opportunity/ requirement to adapt/change the leadership. Constant learning is critical to staying on the exponential curve.

5. **Radical Openness:** A tremendous opportunity exists to embrace experts outside the organization.

Unfortunately, along with this opportunity comes the challenge of having to interact with a large and diverse community. Ultimately, engaging the crowd introduces a lot of noise and invites potential criticism and feedback. While many leaders and organizations ignore most of the criticism and suggestions, creating an open channel to the crowd and the mechanisms to determine signal from noise can provide new perspectives and solutions, allowing access to whole new layers of innovation.

6. **Hyper-Confident:** In order to live on the exponential curve and not get caught in the linear mindset of organizational bureaucracy, you must be willing to be fired or even fire yourself. Battles must be fought and naysayers overcome, and that requires extreme selflessness and self-confidence if a leader is to push to the edge. Two of the most important personality traits for an exponential leader to have are the courage and perseverance to learn, adapt and, ultimately, disrupt your own business.

Recommendations: Keep diversity in mind when appointing to governance and advisory boards. Regularly take your senior leadership through a personal transformation program. Examine your own leadership skill sets. Remove anyone who puts his or her own career ahead of the success of the enterprise.

2. PARTNER WITH, INVEST IN OR ACQUIRE ExOs

From 1990 to about 2005, there were at least five major disruptions in the retail or CPG industry. Three of them— EPOS systems with point-of-sale transactions, RFID tags for supply chain management, and customer loyalty cards—

produced a significant amount of new data that fundamentally changed the industry.

Marcus Shingles, a principal at Deloitte Consulting, and his research team spent most of 2012 helping the Grocery Manufacturer's Association (GMA) analyze the CPG industry for potential Big Data innovation disruptions of the same magnitude. To his surprise, he and his team identified hundreds of startups with industry-specific solutions, of which eighty had leveraged emerging technologies. Of those eighty companies, thirty were already showing signs of having a similarly disruptive impact as the three major disruptions outlined above.

In other words, while just a few major changes at the turn of the century turned the CPG industry upside down over the course of fifteen years, today there are *six to ten times* as many potential disruptions waiting in the wings, all of which have emerged in the last few years. To understand the importance of this sea change for the world of business—any business—it's important to keep in mind that the CPG field is generally less innovation-savvy compared to the larger and newer technology leaders, and is far removed from the hipster-driven, hyper-speed world of Silicon Valley. In this day and age, clearly, it's not just cutting-edge companies that need to watch their backs.

Shingles took the exercise a step further and looked at how the largest CPG incumbents viewed those thirty most-disruptive startups. He found that there were a few big companies—the 1 percent of industry players who are always ahead of the rest and continually innovating—that were not only tracking the startups, but had actually created partnerships with many of them. Meanwhile, the less forward-thinking CPGs hadn't even *heard* of the competitive threats, much less considered them. Not surprisingly, the asleep-at-the-wheel companies were astonished when GE partnered with Quirky in May 2013, a partnership that allowed Quirky inventors access to GE's prodigious patent portfolio. (In fact, GE led Quirky's $80 million investment round in November 2013.)

It's this type of thinking that separates leaders from followers within industries. Shingles and his Deloitte Innovation team are now talking to many industry groups about similar sweeps in their areas.

As we stated in Chapter Five, disruption is the new norm. Throughout every industry, the democratization of accelerating technologies is allowing hundreds of startups to attack and disrupt traditional markets: Bitcoin, Uber, Twitch, Tesla, Hired, Clinkle, Modern Meadow, Beyond Verbal, Vayable, GitHub, WhatsApp, Oculus Rift, Hampton Creek, Airbnb, Matternet, Snapchat, Jaunt VR, Homejoy, Waze, Quirky, Tongal, BuzzFeed—the list of disruptors is virtually endless. And while of course many newcomers won't succeed, their sheer number means that plenty will be around long enough to create a revolution.

Large companies must identify and track disruptive ExOs with the aim of observing, partnering with, investing in and/or acquiring them. And they must do so as early as possible to lower the investment threshold needed and to pre-empt the competition. The perfect moment to engage with an ExO is when the startup has real traction and is just emerging as a market leader. A classic example of such timing took place in 2005 when Google bought YouTube for $1.6 billion. YouTube had already out-executed Google Video and other competitors, and was gobbling up market share. Google picked up YouTube just before the company broke out, and was thus able to bring in its own muscle to help accelerate that once-threatening expansion.

As with the example of GE and Quirky outlined above, Allstate Insurance is another example of a traditional company in a mature industry that was forward-thinking enough to see the writing on the wall. A few years ago, after identifying and tracking the startups in Allstate's space, CEO Tom Wilson concluded that the biggest threat came from new online insurance companies like Geico and Esurance, which could seriously threaten Allstate's countrywide network of agents and offices. Instead of resorting to the watch-and-hope strategy most CEOs adopt, Wilson went out aggressively and acquired Esurance in 2011. Equally important, rather than trying to integrate the newcomer into its existing business, Allstate was smart—and brave—enough to leave it as an independent entity, and the bigger company is now learning from the startup.

The real question then is not *whether* to acquire an ExO, but *when* to partner with an ExO, *when* to invest in one and *when* to acquire it. Yotopoulos, who created the Acquisition Strategy group at SAP, describes the need to carefully select among the various "tools in the toolbox"—build, buy, partner and invest—when it comes to execution on disruptive market opportunities. Each opportunity is shaped differently, and for this reason, one size does not fit all. Instead, a more holistic approach is required.

A corporation should look to **create an internal ExO** when:

1. An opportunity is one to two adjacencies away from the company's core business—perhaps a different business model, buyer, user or go-to market.
2. Urgency is low—there is still time until the market's inflection point.
3. The company is able to hire the necessary talent. This approach typically maximizes control and minimizes costs for those markets that must be "owned" given their strategic nature.

Acquisition is usually the most appropriate path when a market is strategically imperative to "own" but you face the following obstacles:

1. It is difficult to hire the right talent.
2. The market inflection point is upon you.
3. The opportunity is too far removed (3+ adjacencies) from the corporation's prevailing model. In this case, you must judiciously manage the post-merger integration to ensure that the corporation's processes do not overwhelm the acquiree and destroy value.

When there is no immediate strategic need to own, a corporation can **partner** with an external ExO—akin to dating before marrying—to learn more about the market and the new model, as well as to gauge fit and synergy.

An **investment** in an external ExO may be the best move

in cases where it makes sense to test the waters—to watch and learn about an emergent opportunity with an eye toward partnership or acquisition in the future.

> Recommendation: Implement a program to identify, partner with, invest in or acquire the ExOs in your industry. Give it teeth.

3. DISRUPT[X]

A third strategy is for large organizations to leverage disruptive technologies themselves. As history has shown, this is a lot harder than it looks, given that the organizational structures of established companies exist to *suppress* disruptive influences.

But it can be done. Just consider HP's first scientific calculator, Apple's iPhone and Nike's FuelBand. The key is for senior management to embrace the idea of radical change—towards new markets—and then reward that acceptance throughout the organization. We call this Disrupt[X], a process that involves three important steps.

Inspire ExOs at the Edge

Creating ExOs at the edge of your organization is no easy task, as Google's Sebastian Thrun makes clear: "When you're in a company and your main product is search and every time you're doing an experiment you risk losing—I don't know—a few million or one hundred million people, then experimentation is really hard. Breaking out into fields that the company hasn't entered before is much easier."

When SAP bought TopTier in 2001, rather than trying to integrate founder Shai Agassi into the organization, where he would have been lost, the company instead put him at the edge of the organization and let him loose. Allowed to remain in his favored role as maverick, Agassi zeroed in on the SAP developer community, quickly realizing its untapped potential. Within two years he had created a two-million-strong developer network, a major asset for the company to this day.

In every organization, there are always changemakers like Agassi: highly creative, self-starting individuals who don't fit neatly into a box. Constrain them in that box and they can sow considerable chaos. Changemakers have brilliant ideas and vision—and are often fiercely loyal to the company—but they are frustrated by limitation. Eventually, after being held back by interminable management layers and bureaucratic processes, they get fed up and leave, or are fired. Prime examples of this phenomenon are ex-Google employees Ev Williams, Biz Stone, Dennis Crowley, Ben Silbermann and Kevin Systrom, all of whom founded startups (Twitter, FourSquare, Pinterest and Instagram, respectively) after leaving Google. Google is a hugely successful company, of course, but imagine where it would be today if those extraordinary individuals had stayed. (And Google has a better track record than most companies.)

It is critical, then, for big companies to locate change agents before their frustrations grow too deep, and re-assign them to the edges of the organization and give them free reign to build ExOs. This will not only leverage the strengths of the changemakers, it will also maintain stability at the heart of the organization. Furthermore, if the process is handled well and the outcome is positive, cutting-edge ExOs can serve as tugboats for the corporate supertanker, guiding it into new and profitable waters. Eventually, if successful, these fast-moving peripheral enterprises will themselves create a new center and, ultimately, replace the legacy business. Some retailers have successfully accomplished the creation of edge EExOs. Companies like Macy's, Burberry, Target and Wal-Mart all created ecommerce sites outside and independent of their core organization and only started integration once the EExO had reached critical mass. In fact, we recommend that once successful, the legacy bricks and mortar business should report into the EExO, as that is the clear future. Similarly, many luxury fashion brands have white labeled Yoox, the giant Italian ecommerce site, to get to market quickly.

John Hagel, co-chairman of the aptly named Center for the Edge, and his team have developed a promising new approach to large-scale organizational change that he calls "Scaling Edges."[1] The methodology behind Scaling Edges is built on the following basic guidelines:

- Find an edge in the form of an emerging business opportunity that has the potential to scale quickly and become a new core for the business.
- Line up a changemaker (or team of changemakers) who understands and embraces that edge opportunity.
- Place the changemaker/team of changemakers outside the core organization.
- Use the Lean approach and experiment with new initiatives to accelerate learning.
- Starve the team by providing little in the way of help, money or other resources.
- Encourage the team to seek leverage by connecting with other companies and participating in an ecosystem that can help accelerate growth.
- Point the ExO outward. The fledgling enterprise should create a new market or product area, NOT cannibalize the core product suite—at least in its early stages.

The rationale for these last three elements is that you do not want to awaken what Salim calls the immune response, so to speak, of the core organization. If the mother company senses that too many resources are being funneled to the new initiative, it will evoke a reaction (the notorious "corporate antibodies") and the body will attack and try to kill the startup.

One explicit step we would add to Hagel's list is to **leverage data**. Most large organizations have extraordinary insights and value locked up in their data stores, and leveraging those insights (which Hagel would label as an Edge) offer some low-hanging

---

1   www.deloitte.com/view/en_US/us/Insights/centers/centers-center-for-edge/scaling-edges/index.htm

fruit for edge ExOs to exploit. Wassili Bertoen, managing director of the Center for the Edge Europe, notes that in his seventeen years of dealing with corporate innovation, he has observed that most large companies have huge unlocked potential—in fact, they're begging for a structured outlet for it all.

When building out Yahoo's Brickhouse incubator in 2007, Salim put together a team of developers, some from within Yahoo, others from the outside. It was, briefly, one of the best development teams in the world (certainly everyone at Yahoo wanted to work there). But Yahoo wanted Brickhouse to build new products and services *for* the core organization rather than to create new markets for the company. Needless to say, within weeks of Brickhouse's launch, all vestiges of autonomy at Brickhouse had dissolved, and feelings of jealousy and resentment toward the newcomer swept through the company. ("Why do they get the best employees?" "Are they competing with *my* product?"). By the end of his tenure, Salim was spending 80 percent of his time fending off the company in an effort to protect his Brickhouse teams. Clearly a no-win situation for all parties.

Eventually, in 2008, in the wake of an attempted Microsoft purchase, Yahoo killed Brickhouse despite it having, against all odds, launched several products that truly pushed the edges of the consumer Internet. And although Yahoo's immune system won that particular battle, the company ultimately lost the war. (Since that time, however, Salim has spent time with the new senior management and is encouraged by what CEO Marissa Mayer and CMO Kathy Savitt are aiming for.)

Yotopoulos fared better at SAP because the new businesses created in that company's Global Business Incubator were fully sheltered throughout the tenure of three CEOs. Another factor contributing to their success was that the new companies also had a good sprinkling of ExO attributes, including:

- Full-decision autonomy with distinct processes and procedures.
- Small, agile and bootstrapped cross-functional

startup teams responsible for building new businesses from the idea stage through to commercialization.

- The ability to iterate on multiple types of innovation (business model, go-to-market, etc.) beyond traditional product level innovation.
- Iterative in-market testing of prototypes to customers with a goal of accelerated learning.

Ivan Ollivier, Director of Nissan's Future Lab, has similarly set up his unit in Silicon Valley, far away from headquarters, where he is exploring a twenty-year future of mobility for Nissan. The separation is critical, he maintains, for independence of thought and creativity.

> Recommendation: Move three proven changemakers in your enterprise to the edges of the organization and unleash them as ExOs to disrupt other markets. Learn how they interact with the mother ship, and then add more.

Hire a Black Ops Team

The traditional definition of a black ops team is a covert, disruptive operation that is clandestine and not attributable to the organization carrying it out. Another strategy, one that builds on the creation of Edge ExOs and partnerships with ExOs, is for a big company to assemble a team specifically designed to disrupt *itself*. The idea is to hire a team of young, digitally native, self-starting Millennials and charge them with the task of setting up a startup whose sole purpose is to *attack* the mother ship. Part of the assignment is that the team must interact with the external community to identify opportunities all-but-invisible from inside the company.

The cutting-edge design firm IDEO undertook just such an exercise a few years ago. Noting that the company's design processes and techniques were then widely understood by the market, the senior management team realized that the company was dangerously open to disruption. Thinking proactively, it invited Tom Hulme, one of its own managers, to form a team and take on the challenge of disrupting IDEO itself. The result was OpenIDEO, a fascinating open source version of the company that created an entirely new capability that, in the end, complemented IDEO's core offering.

Admittedly, this step requires a considerable amount of courage and gumption. But isn't that what leadership is all about? And if you are a big company, can you afford not to do this? Today, if you're not disrupting yourself, someone else is; your fate is to be either the disrupter or the disrupted. There is no middle ground.

In fact, we feel so strongly about this strategy that, in addition to an external disruption team, we suggest forming another, similar, internal team—a Red Team and a Blue Team, if you will, since the exercise is not unlike the military war games that test force-readiness. In this way, two perspectives are brought to the table and bets are hedged.

Cisco Systems, for example, has always operated in an environment of unpredictable standards, one in which the market can suddenly tip from one technology standard to another. As a hedging strategy, Cisco funds new internal businesses focused on the current standard that Cisco prefers. At the same time, Sequoia Capital, its original venture capital vehicle, finances an outside team—one often staffed by former Cisco employees—that is dedicated to pursuing the competing standard. (The alternate firm has a pre-agreed-upon purchase price from Cisco in case the market tips in the other direction.) In this way, Cisco both covers its bases and maintains its agility in an uncertain marketplace. And at Netflix, a system called Chaos Monkey deliberately and randomly disrupts the service's application infrastructure to ensure that developers have accounted for all possible error states.

> Recommendation: Hire both internal and external Black Ops teams and have them

establish startups with a combined goal of defeating one another *and* disrupting the mother ship.

Copy Google[X]

At a Singularity University event three years ago, Larry Page told Salim he'd heard good things about Brickhouse and asked whether Google should set up something similar. Salim's recommendation was no; he believed it would only evoke the same immune system response he'd experienced at Yahoo.

Page's response was cryptic: "What would a Brickhouse for atoms look like?" he asked.

We now know what he meant. In launching the Google[X] lab, Google has taken the classic skunkworks approach to new product development further than anyone ever imagined. Google[X] offers two fascinating new extensions to the traditional approach. First, it aims for moonshot-quality ideas (e.g., life extension, autonomous vehicles, Google Glass, smart contact lenses, Project Loon, etc.). Second, unlike traditional corporate labs that focus on existing markets, Google[X] combines breakthrough technologies with Google's core information competencies to create entirely new markets.

We strongly recommend that every big company attempt something similar by creating a lab that is a playground for breakthrough technologies. It should then conduct ongoing experiments with new products and services, with a goal of creating entirely new markets for the company. Equally important is protecting that lab (especially during slow times) from the "antibodies" within the organization, as they will inevitably argue that the lab—the alien body—has an insufficient ROI. Last but not least, *pay attention* to the lab's discoveries. Great ideas always come from crossing disparate areas.

The core competencies of a large organization combined with new technology breakthroughs create a potent force that can generate a new future for many big legacy companies.

Probably the gold standard in this respect is 3M, which over the years has delivered extreme autonomy to its researchers and, as a result, has repeatedly created breakthrough products in new markets—the ubiquitous Post-it note being a prime example.

The best part is that, thanks to the drastically lower costs of many accelerating technologies today, it doesn't cost all that much to set up an advanced laboratory. As outlined in our Chapter One table on falling technology costs, ten years ago it cost $100,000 to establish a DNA synthesis lab; today that price is down to about $5,000. And while an industrial robot would set you back a million bucks a decade ago, the latest model of that same robot (Rethink Robotics' Baxter robot) is now available for $22,000. In the realm of MEMS sensors, the outlay for accelerometers, microphones, gyroscopes, cameras and magnetometers has dropped 80 percent or more compared to five years ago, according to McKinsey. Finally, a 3D printer carried a $40,000 price tag seven years ago; today it costs just $100. In short, Moore's Law is the modern lab's best friend.

> Recommendation: Start an internal accelerating technologies lab, leveraging core competencies and aiming for moonshot innovations at a budget price.

Partner with Accelerators, Incubators and Hackerspaces

The last decade has seen an explosion of new business incubators and accelerators, ranging from Y Combinator (which created disruptive consumer Internet startups Dropbox and Uber) to the membership-based TechShop. Looking at large companies from an ExO perspective, let's consider four examples:

TechShop

We first examined TechShop's fascinating model in Chapter Three. Here we'll explore the chain's impact in further detail, focusing on how TechShop is helping large organizations, including Ford and Lowe's, two companies for which it has built individual facilities.

TechShop's CEO Mark Hatch offers Fortune 500 CTOs a compelling pitch: "Give me 1 percent of R&D and 1 percent of your staff and I'll return you 10x." It's a lofty goal, but Hatch's track record matches the rhetoric. The founders of Solum, Inc., which specializes in GPS-based nitrogen detection for agriculture, used TechShop's facilities to carry them from concept through four generations of product development, raising $1 million in just fourteen weeks. TechShop has seen several other business clients achieve $1 million in sales just *three months* after launch. To put that time frame into perspective, consider that some large organizations take three months just to approve *one step* of a stage-gate process.

Singularity University Labs

A steady stream of corporate executives pass through Singularity University in search of their Holy Grail: *any* mechanism to manage disruptive innovation. In response, SU has created a laboratory designed to enable corporate innovation teams to reside full-time at SU's open innovation campus so that they can collaborate and partner with SU's portfolio of startups and its faculty. Each SU startup aims to leverage accelerating technologies to positively impact a billion people. SU's faculty includes the world's leading experts, practitioners and researchers in eight accelerating technologies. Organizations already on board include Coca-Cola, UNICEF, Lowe's and Hershey's.

A comment from a recent participant captures the essence of the program: "Access to world experts in exponential technologies and organizations ensures we're thinking beyond next quarter's earnings report—way beyond. Most of the Corporate Innovation Exchange members are here to drive disruption within our own companies—before two kids in a garage do it for us."

mach49

Yotopoulos, who also created SAP's Global Business Incubator, has capitalized on that unique experience, combining it with his decade-long background as a Silicon Valley venture capitalist. He and Linda Yates, a seasoned CEO and public board member with over twenty years experience driving strategy and innovation in the Global 1000, are implementing several ExO principles to help global companies create new, "adjacent" businesses generated from within their organization. They intend to offer facilities, Valley networks and a seasoned team of executives familiar with both the corporate and startup worlds to jumpstart new corporate businesses—and to do so by leveraging resources that the corporation itself does not (and perhaps cannot) own.

Yotopoulos and Yates start by leveraging the corporation's crowd in an incentive competition to see which internal entrepreneurs propose the most compelling business opportunities. The winning teams get all-expense-paid trips to mach49's Silicon Valley facility. There, they are paired with non-competitive teams from other industries. All the groups are then immersed in Lean startup-style entrepreneurship and design thinking. The goal is to validate business opportunities through prototypes and in-market tests.

After working alongside the mach49 team and network, these small, multi-disciplinary teams of corporate intrapreneurs leave with defined, validated opportunities and a clear execution plan. They can then stay on in Silicon Valley to accelerate, be spun back into (or out of) the mother ship, or serve as pilots to pave the way to larger acquisitions or partnerships. While it's early days yet, we think the model holds extraordinary promise.

H-Farm (Treviso, Italy)

Maurizio Rossi, a seasoned entrepreneur, created H-Farm in 2005 with Internet veteran Ricardo Donadon. Their aim was to create an atelier for "digital artisans" at a countryside facility outside Venice. There, in forty-two buildings dotting a former farm, Rossi and Donadon run educational courses, hackathons and design competitions. The program has grown to house 450 entrepreneurs and developers, and the pair hopes to double that number within two years. The majority of their teams are made up of entrepreneurs, but about a third are composed of corporate accelerators who sign on for one-year memberships.

H-Farm also runs monthly hackathons for large companies, and winners are hosted onsite to build out their ideas. One creative H-Farm project comes from Porsche, which invites customers to the farm for pitch sessions in which Porsche owners can investigate and possibly even invest in great startups. Talk about the ultimate customer-purchasing bonus.

The incubator operations listed above are just a few examples of what is proving to be a broad trend. Similar ExO-oriented incubators are springing up in countries all over the world: Communitech and OneEleven in Ontario; SociaLab, with several offices throughout South America; Start-Up Chile, in Santiago; and Thinkubator, which is headquartered in Copenhagen. Google has been especially busy, partnering with Startup Weekend and Women 2.0 in the U.S., iHub in Kenya and Le Camping in France.

Everis, a multinational consulting firm based in Madrid, has partnered with two Spanish entrepreneurs, Luis Gonzalez-Blanch and Pablo De Manuel Triantafilo, to create mentoring software that matches executives in big companies with startups in their internal incubators. Everis, which intends to offer the service to hundreds of clients across Spain, is looking to push consulting into the new economy of open-talent, accelerating innovation, connected knowledge, Big Data, intelligent currency and pervasive entrepreneurship. In each field, a likely roadmap and database have already been created. In entrepreneurship, for example, the company has created the biggest B2B ICT startup database in the world. It lists 63,000 entrepreneur support organizations, is currently trawling through the APIs of over six hundred websites and has analyzed over half a million startups and SMEs.

Each partnership listed above is further evidence of our belief that large organizations can create successful partnerships with local, grassroots business accelerators. Business Integration

Partners (BIP), a global consulting firm based in Italy, even has a "Corporate Accelerator in a Box" service. BIP has helped several blue-chip clients set up their own operation with recruiting, VC connections and university partnerships. This service comes complete with process management and software to help run incentive competitions and manage open source projects.

Telefonica, the giant Spanish mobile phone operator, has taken matters a step further. Rather than just partnering with ExOs or creating one internal incubator, it has created a series of global incubators under the brand Wayra and is aggressively sponsoring the startup ecosystem in the countries in which it operates.

We were initially leery of Wayra when we realized that more than 80 percent of its startups were deemed "successful." Such a high number indicated to us a shortage of breakthrough thinking—that is, the company must be aiming too low. When it comes to startups we prefer to see an 80 percent failure rate, with 20 percent presenting game changing ideas. However, when we looked at the countries in which Wayra has spearheaded the creation of entrepreneurship communities—in many cases, emerging markets where none existed previously—the phrase "walk before you run" came to mind. By creating communities with multiple (albeit small) success stories, a platform is laid for future breakthrough thinking. After all, Silicon Valley itself took several decades to develop. Telefonica's approach gets high marks for the leadership role it is taking in an industry where one telco strategist expects a staggering 85 percent drop in revenues by 2020. Wayra has already spawned almost four hundred startups (out of 25,000 applications) over the past three years.

> Recommendation: Find an incubator or accelerator that is a good fit for your organization. Partner with it or, if it is of insufficient scale for your needs, fund it. If an incubator or accelerator doesn't exist, create one!

4. ExO LITE (THE GENTLE CYCLE)

Even when large companies must maintain their status quo and thus can't be turned into ExOs, that doesn't mean they can't take on some of an ExO's attributes, which can be implemented to accelerate company operations.

Here are IDEAS and SCALE attributes that we believe *every* large organization should put into place:

Migrate towards an MTP

Red Bull's tagline, "Giving you wings," is a far cry from a traditional mission statement. Our recommendation, however, is to follow its lead: Big companies need to move away from the old-school, predictable mission-and-vision statements currently sported by most Fortune 500 companies. Instead, they should migrate towards a Massive Transformative Purpose.

As we mentioned earlier, we predict brands will find and merge with aspirational MTPs that will steer them towards providing real value to society—in other words, to a triple bottom line. In order to inspire their teams, attract new top talent and create gravity wells for their communities, big companies should do the same and formulate their own, unique MTPs. This will not only establish the right image—based on reality—for the company's stakeholders, especially among younger workers within the organization, but it will also serve as a guiding principle when key decisions need to be made.

Allstate, for example, could have put together a perfectly serviceable mission statement along the lines of, "Deliver products and services that protect the financial future of our customers with a superior distribution network of agents and affiliates." Ugh…perfectly serviceable and perfectly awful. How much better, then, that they opted for the far more inspirational (and thus universally familiar) "You're In Good Hands With Allstate."

The following table shows how four major brands are launching initiatives that will nudge them towards an MTP:

Vodafone: Partnering with the Malala Fund to bring literacy to millions of women in developing countries. Vodafone aims to use mobile technology to lift 5.3 million women out of illiteracy by 2020.

Coca-Cola: Coca-Cola has partnered with entrepreneur and inventor Dean Kamen to leverage the Slingshot, Kamen's water purification device. One unit can provide enough drinking water for three hundred people daily. By 2015, Coca-Cola plans to bring one hundred million liters of water to 45,000 people across twenty countries.

Cisco: From 2008 to 2012, Cisco Israel invested $15 million to establish a healthy entrepreneurial ecosystem in the Palestinian territory of the West Bank. Thanks to this initiative, Palestinian ICT firms reported a 64 percent increase in international client work.

Unilever: Unilever launched a Sustainable Living Plan in November 2010 to highlight its sustainability goals for 2020. Objectives include helping a billion people take action to improve their health and well-being, enhancing the livelihoods of millions of people worldwide and reducing the company's environmental footprint by 50 percent.

Community & Crowd

Most large organizations are so busy managing their internals that they don't leverage their communities at all, let alone the much larger crowd. Most have improved a bit in recent years—almost by default, thanks to social media—but even now a company's online presence is mostly limited to a Facebook page half-heartedly managed by the marketing department.

How can companies rise above prosaic participation in the Web 2.0 world and create a truly *social business*? How can they cooperate with the sharing economy or with peer-to-peer startups to boost innovation internally? How can they build a vibrant community around their products that will enable them to use P2P forums to drive down support costs?

Zappos spends a great deal of time and money managing its community, and is an excellent example of a company that has launched a truly social business. The instant you declare yourself a fan of the company on social media, Zappos makes special deals available to you through its fans-only section. It's a relationship that quickly becomes a two-way street—Zappos calls it a "Like-Like" relationship—one that is designed to tie customers ever more tightly to the company and its services.

Similarly, software company Intuit has created the "Intuit Community," a place for users to post questions, each of which is assiduously answered by company representatives. Nearly half a million questions have been posted to date, creating a rich knowledge base that offloads support questions and drives product insights, all while greatly improving customer satisfaction.

Algorithms

These days every company finds itself generating mountains of data, little of which is actually put to use. That's a pity, because were companies to actually analyze some of the data they collect, they would gain extraordinary insight into their products, services, distribution channels and customers.

Yet another reason to use algorithms and data is that most new business models are information-based. Physical assets don't scale exponentially, but digitized assets lead to new use cases, partners, ecosystems, rules and business models. If you want to be truly disruptive, an information component is critical. Smart companies are already using services such as Kaggle, Palantir, Cloudera, DataTorrent, Splunk and Platfora for data insights; they're also using open source machine learning variations of Apache Hadoop. In fact, the possibilities are endless—if companies will just take advantage of them. Google certainly does: witness how it ruthlessly leverages data for almost every business function. The same is possible for most other companies as well. Data-driven insights also provide an important counterpoint (and reality check) for traditional intuition-based management decision-making.

To elaborate: Back in 2010, Jeremy Howard was the chief scientist for the Kaggle platform. Now an adjunct faculty member at Singularity University, he recently consulted for one of the world's biggest mobile phone companies. Howard ran a set of machine learning algorithms against that company's customer data to analyze credit-worthiness. In less than one month, he identified a jaw-dropping $1 billion of instantly implementable savings. (And yes, that's $1 *billion*...clearly he should have charged a percentage fee.) Howard has recently launched a new company, Enlitic, which uses algorithms to spot tumors in medical scans. Existing scans "shown" to those algorithms will serve as a training ground for future analysis, with no human intervention.

Engagement

The creation of games, contests and incentive competitions (preferably with MTP-congruent goals) is an easy way for big companies to quickly engage with their communities. In fact, a wide array of tools already supports such initiatives.

Gathering instant feedback from customers is also a critical driver of product development. This doesn't have to be external-only: Philip Rosedale, the creator of Second Life, has put into play some fascinating ideas in his recent startup, High Fidelity. For example, as noted earlier, Rosedale's employees vote each quarter on whether or not he should continue as CEO. (Apparently he should. Rosedale scored 92 percent the last time a vote took place.)

Unilever, one of the world's leading consumer goods companies, has two billion consumers worldwide consume one or more of its four hundred brands daily. In June 2013, Unilever announced a partnership with eYeka—a crowdsourcing platform that connects brands with 288,907 creative problem solvers from 164 countries. In total there have been 683 contests awarding 4.4 million in prize money on eYeka. Contestants for Unilever's competition had to design a Recycling Shower, a sustainable shower that saves water. Out of 102 contributors, five winners were awarded with a combined total of €10,000 in prize money. Unilever also leverages eYeka to host competitions for its portfolio brands, such as Clear, Lipton and Cornetto, among others.

Dashboards

Extending the notion that decision-making in companies should be driven by data rather than by intuition, Dashboards offer an intuitive way to present complex information in a simple and cogent way.

John Seely Brown and John Hagel have observed that although all of our large organizations are set up to scale efficiencies, in this new economy what we actually need to scale is *learning*.[1] And while some very good business intelligence (BI) systems exist out there, they are set up largely to measure scaling of efficiency. What is needed now are new dashboards that measure the learning capability of organizations. And if those learning dashboards don't emerge soon, big companies should consider requiring that their newly minted chief data officers (the hottest new C-Level position) build them.

What, exactly, should learning Dashboards track? Here are a few suggestions:

- How many (Lean Startup) experiments or A/B-tests did Customer Service run last week? Marketing? Sales? HR?
- How many innovative ideas have been collected over the past year? How many have been implemented?
- What percentage of total revenues is driven by new products from the last three years? The last five years?

---

1   dupress.com/articles/institutional-innovation/

Objectives and Key Results (OKRs) are also important metrics for corporations, even though OKRs are most important in new startups where high growth rates in employment necessitate a shorter feedback loop cycle. But big companies also need them because OKRs:

- Encourage disciplined thinking (major goals will surface).
- Increase effective communication (everyone learns what is important).
- Establish indicators for measuring progress (shows how far along company is).
- Focus effort (and thus synchronize the organization).

In 2008, Jeff Weiner, the new CEO of LinkedIn, introduced OKRs to the company, with a goal of enabling all employees to align themselves with LinkedIn's mission, as well as to provide a flexible, hands-off mechanism for tracking progress. This one move is widely regarded as a key reason why LinkedIn became a $20 billion company.

It is our opinion that in the future, the defining metric for organizations won't be ROI (Return on Investment), but *ROL* (Return on Learning). Kyle Tibbits recently took this notion to the level of the individual employee when he observed, "The most valuable compensation for working at a startup as opposed to a 'normal job' is a dramatically higher rate of learning (ROL)."[1]

Duleesha Kulasooriya of the Center for the Edge sees innovation in big companies as a measurement issue. Niall Daly, a former management consultant and Founder/CFO of Backpocket, concurs, noting that, "With disruptive innovation, you have to measure non-linear effects as opposed to linear accounting methods. That leaves more room for real innovation. Fuzziness is not accepted today in corporate environments." John Hagel believes that Edge thinkers in large organizations

1   www.kyletibbitts.com/post/83791066613/rate-of-learning-the-most-valuable-startup

should track metrics that will get the attention of the leadership at the core, but at the same time identify and ruthlessly track a new set of metrics relevant to ExOs.

One other approach to dashboards in large organizations is the Doblin Model. The Doblin Group spent thirty-five years researching innovation and recognized that most senior managers think of innovation largely as product features. However, they found there are nine other types of innovation to track in a balanced way across an organization:

1. **Profit Model:** How you make money
2. **Network:** How you connect with others to create value
3. **Structure:** How you organize and align your talent and assets
4. **Process:** How you use signature or superior methods to do your work
5. **Product Performance:** How you develop distinguishing features and functionality
6. **Product System:** How you create complementary products and services
7. **Service:** How you support and amplify the value of your offerings
8. **Channel:** How you deliver your offerings to customers and users
9. **Brand:** How you represent your offerings and business
10. **Customer Engagement:** How you foster compelling interactions

Apple's iPod and iTunes, for example, integrate eight of the ten types—a telling indicator. In fact, companies using the Doblin Model to track and balance their innovation portfolios have reported a multiple times ROI for their efforts. We believe the Doblin Model, used in conjunction with an ExO diagnostic, provides an excellent scorecard for any large organization.

The global retail Spanish firm Zara, which has nearly 2,000 stores in ninety countries, heavily leverages real-time statistics and dashboards.[1] The retailer bucked the trend of trying to achieve success via economies of scale and instead focused on small, unique batches and a nearly real-time production process. For example, almost half of Zara's garments are manufactured centrally, a decision that allows it to move from new design to distribution in less than two weeks. It also helps explain why fully 75 percent of the company's displayed merchandise turns over each month. In the end, shoppers visit Zara stores seventeen times a year on average, more than four times the number of visits to Zara's competitors.

Experimentation

Perhaps the attribute most critical to a learning organization is Experimentation, which is particularly hard for big organizations, since they tend to focus on execution rather than innovation. But any large company can implement techniques like the Lean Startup approach, as well as continually test assumptions. Indeed, in a world of increasing volatility, any organization's understanding of the outside world needs to keep pace with reality. And that requires taking risks—though risk-taking, of course, also means facing an increased likelihood of failure.

You may recall the "failure awards" we mentioned in Chapter Four. Such awards, of course, are nothing new: in the 1970s David Packard famously gave a "Medal of Defiance" to employee Chuck House, who had ignored orders and built what was ultimately a successful new product. But while "failure awards" are great in principle, the fact remains that most large organizations punish failure quite severely. It is our strong recommendation that risk awards and experiment tracking become a key component of the recognition process employed by large companies. To track its innovation portfolio, for example, Amazon records exactly how many experiments any department runs, as well as its success rate.

GE has done something even more ambitious with its

---

1   www.slideshare.net/amritanshumehra/zara-a-case-study

FastWorks program, in which Lean Startup expert Eric Ries was invited to train eighty coaches.[1] Backed by GE's top management (including CEO Jeffrey Immelt) the program has exposed nearly 40,000 GE employees to Lean Startup principles. As a result of the FastWorks program, one of the biggest initiatives ever undertaken at GE, more than three hundred projects have been launched globally. One example is the PET/CT scanner, the development of which would normally cost millions and take two to four years. Thanks to fast iterations with the customer in the loop, however, the development time was halved and the prototype developed for ten times less.

Social Technologies

While it may seem as though social technology initiatives have already been adopted by every company for every product possible, Michael Chui of the McKinsey Global Institute estimates that as much as *80 percent* of the true value of social media may have yet to be captured. Even more dramatically, Jonah Berger of Wharton calculates that "only 7 percent of word-of-mouth is online." Needless to say, their conclusions indicate enormous upside potential for prope[...] products and services.

Internally, social technologies focus mainly o[...] tools such as Dropbox, Asana, Box, Google Drive [...] Starting with non-mission critical data, internal te[...] file sharing and then conduct live discussions on [...] Remember our GitHub case study in Chapter [...] at through the lens of collaboration, a good q[...] is: Which advanced social technologies withir[...] corporations implement in a controlled manner?

More on the topic of collaboration: *VentureB[...]* more than 80 percent of Fortune 500 companies [...] social software such as Yammer.[2] However, [...]

[handwritten margin notes: Linda follow up: internal design principle?]

---

1   www.gereports.com/post/82723688100/the-bigg[...] ries-and-ge-team-up-to

2   venturebeat.com/2011/08/22/yammer-salesforce-integration/

Altimeter Group's Charlene Li and Brian Solis, only 34 percent of 700 executives and social strategists surveyed felt their social efforts had an effect on business outcomes.

Similarly, *Computing* magazine recently surveyed one hundred senior IT professionals and found the following:

- 68 percent said their organization is using some sort of collaboration.
- Just 12 percent said they had an enterprise-grade collaboration suite.
- Only 17 percent allow or deliberately ignore the use of consumer products (e.g., Evernote, Dropbox).[1]

Change expert Dion Hinchcliffe of Adjuvi calls the implementation of social structures via IT departments "a shift in emphasis from systems of record to systems of engagement," and has documented several examples of large organizations seeing outstanding results after deploying collaborative technologies.

CEMEX, the Mexican concrete giant, is one such example, and is a particularly inspiring one due to the high average age of its workforce. Hinchcliffe's research showed that within a year of introducing collaboration tools, fully 95 percent of CEMEX's employees were using them. Why? Because the pilot program to introduce the tools was designed exclusively for senior management, who typically lag in adopting them. By getting everyone enrolled early on, later success was all but guaranteed.

CONCLUSION

As we noted in Chapter Five, when building an ExO it is not realistic to expect to implement all eleven attributes. However, when it comes to big companies, we believe it is important to take on several—and to take them on *today*. Remember, the information comet has already hit, so adaptation to this new world

---

1   www.computing.co.uk/ctg/news/2344575/organisations-embracing-online-collaboration-tools

has to happen fast. And the keys to adaptation are MTP, IDEAS and SCALE. One reason we're optimistic about this approach is that it solves the "Big Bet" stigma of betting the farm on an unproven strategy. Experimenting at the edges and growing ExOs there allows large companies to launch numerous low-cost, high-potential spinoffs that pose no threat to Wall Street or executive bonuses. It's one reason that GE, Coca-Cola and other large companies are so rapidly embracing Experimentation.

Apple is a good example of how a large company approaches this challenge. Apple's core competency has always been design, and how it launches that design follows a set path. In short, Apple's formula has been to:

1. Leverage core design capabilities.
2. Form small teams of changemakers extracted from the larger organization.
3. Send those teams to the edge of the organization.
4. Combine design with cutting-edge new technology.
5. Utterly disrupt a legacy market.

That's not a bad template to follow. Starting with the iPod, which disrupted music players, then iTunes, which fragmented music delivery, then the iPhone, and most recently, the iPad, Apple has demonstrated what an ExO can do at the edge of an existing organization. It has also demonstrated just how big the payoff can be. In 2012, for example, an astounding 80 percent of Apple's revenues came from products that were fewer than five years old. Those new revenues helped to make Apple the most valuable company in the world.

Amazon represents another archetype of this philosophy. Jeff Bezos has repeatedly shown the courage to proactively cannibalize his own businesses (e.g., the Kindle at the expense of physical books), launch edge ExOs (Amazon Web Services), buy companies that disrupt his own (Zappos) and pursue transformative technologies (delivery drones). Such bold leadership is critical in the age of the ExO.

While large organizations may struggle to adapt structurally to this new age, they still have one key advantage: *intellectual capital.* Large companies didn't get big by accident. Most of the world's global brain trust is running these organizations, and that brain trust has the capacity to come up with some amazing ways to capture or adapt ExO principles. What's needed is vision and will. Or—failing those—fear.

In the next chapter, we'll take an in-depth look at some examples of how large organizations are adapting to the ExO era.

CHAPTER NINE
BIG COMPANIES ADAPT

Let's now look at how forward-looking companies are implementing the ideas discussed in the previous chapter. Some are building ExOs at their edges; some are acquiring or investing in ExOs in their current market space; still others are implementing ExO Lite.

A common saying around Silicon Valley is *execution eats strategy for breakfast*. So, before we dive in, let's first look at what can go wrong when a company leaps into the ExO universe. This isn't idle speculation. While researching companies whose initiatives were producing positive results, we also found a number that had lost their way. For example, we are convinced that one of Blackberry's biggest mistakes was that it never had an MTP, while Blockbuster's downfall can be traced to the fact that it never leveraged its community (not to mention its considerable hubris when Netflix begged for a partnership deal).

Bridgewater – Burning Bridges

We also found organizations that, while they didn't completely fail, did attempt some ExO principles—only to experience adverse consequences.

One such company is the hedge fund Bridgewater Associates, which uses radical transparency to try to achieve a culture of ultra-honesty, one that is free of negative traits. While there is no question that the firm is phenomenally successful, there is also no question that it suffers from a very high employee turnover rate annually, a problem we attribute to its uncompromising commitment to "perfect transparency."

For example, *every* conversation, phone call and meeting at Bridgewater is recorded and available to *all* employees, who are empowered to challenge *anyone* in the firm. Not only are employees free to question fellow workers, they are also encouraged to attack one another's ideas.

But that's not all. Employees subject to the greatest number of attacks receive smaller bonuses. As you might imagine, Bridgewater's practice doesn't actually result in greater honesty. Instead, it promotes an environment of antagonism, betrayal and hidden partnerships. (Word-of-mouth accounts suggest that departing employees take up to a year to recover from Bridgewater's intense culture.)

Our assessment is that Bridgewater is a company without a purpose—that is, it has no MTP. And without that greater, unifying purpose, the aggressiveness that the company instills in its employees ends up misdirected; employees simply turn on one another. Their only aspiration is to be less beat-up than their peers, resulting in a Hobbesian all-against-all scenario that, if left unchanged, will prevent Bridgewater from ever becoming a fulfilling place to work.

The following examples show how some big companies are adapting to an ExO age.

THE COCA-COLA COMPANY – EXPONENTIAL POP

Coca-Cola, one of the biggest and most geographically distributed corporations in the world, is particularly vulnerable in an age of ExOs, given that the company owns vast assets and has 130,000 employees.

However, Coca-Cola didn't achieve industry eminence and then hold onto it for more than a century without being forward thinking and adaptive. In keeping with its tradition of aggressive goal setting, Coca-Cola is currently halfway through an ambitious, exponential target: to double its revenues between 2010 and 2020. To achieve this goal, the company has taken on several elements that correlate well with ExO thinking. (Frankly, to hit those numbers, the company doesn't have much choice.)

One of the biggest clues that Coca-Cola has adopted an exponential way of thinking is that it has taken on an MTP: "Refresh the World." A component of the company's new Open Happiness marketing campaign, "Refresh the World" is certainly Massive, it could be Transformative and it has real Purpose. While at first glance the phrase may sound like just another marketing tagline, it has in fact already begun to galvanize the company. For example, after Typhoon Haiyan hit the Philippines in 2013, Coca-Cola allocated its entire ad budget for the country to disaster relief. Now that's walking the walk. The MTP served to clear an internal path at Coca-Cola for non-traditional thinking.

Coca-Cola also has determined how best to juxtapose itself with the startup community. It realizes that the best ideas most often come from outside the organization and its supply chain, and that the company's core strengths are leveraging assets, creating network effects, planning and executing. As David Butler, Coke's vice president of innovation and entrepreneurship, said recently, "That has become our vision—to make it easier for starters to be scalers and scalers to be starters."

To deliver on this startup philosophy, Coca-Cola is working with Steve Blank and Eric Ries to implement their Lean Startup philosophy across the entire corporation [Experimentation]. Multiple small efforts, each with an MVP (Minimum Viable Product) will iterate assumptions and make this approach available to anyone in the company via an initiative called Open Entrepreneurship. The effects of Experimentation have been immediate: Butler reports that due to the initiative, Coke's sustainability goals have already improved by 20 percent.

Coca-Cola also has become a founding member of Singularity University Labs, where disruptive teams can, away from the mother ship [Autonomy, Leveraged Assets], work with startups on next-generation products and services. And to further ensure that new ideas can evolve away from existing legacy thinking, Coca-Cola is creating new companies that are completely separate from current cash-cow businesses. These new companies enjoy full autonomy from Coke's existing tax, legal, finance and HR systems [Autonomy, Dashboards].

That said, there is one notable departure for Coca-Cola relative to the ExO philosophy: the transparency of its disruptive innovation. It is our thesis that disruptive innovation efforts work best when they operate in stealth mode, divorced from the rest of the company, so as to avoid triggering an organizational immune system response. Instead, Coca-Cola, taking the long view, has created transparent disruption innovation teams with the avowed goal of openly changing the culture of the larger company. The company has even publicly taken a strategic stance to integrate disruptive innovations into its very core.

It is an audacious experiment and we're watching keenly to see how it pans out. We believe that if Coke's core business is infected by the Lean Startup meme in time, the company will see the value of this innovation approach and become even more open to disruptive innovation efforts at the edges.

In short: corporate innovation at Coca-Cola is not so much about the success of any individual internal startup, but more about the sustainability or repeatability of the innovation business model itself. Certainly within its industry, Coke is a standout example of a company tackling a disruptive future.

Our assessment of Coca-Cola's Exponential Quotient—62 out of 84.

MTP	S	C	A	L	E	I	D	E	A	S
✓				✓	✓			✓	✓	

[Note: all assessments in this chapter were made by the authors using the Exponential Diagnostic Survey found in Appendix A. Twenty-one questions are scored from one to four. A score over 55 indicates an ExO.]

HAIER – HIGHER AND HIGHER

One of the biggest concerns we hear about from companies implementing ExO thinking is that "It might work in Silicon Valley, but it just won't work in London, or Budapest or Milan."

In his book *The New Geography of Jobs*, Enrico Moretti argues just that: where a company is based does indeed matter. For example, if you're trying to build a global company in Italy, your primarily Italian speakers at company headquarters won't have a global perspective. Thus, it's no accident that most of the ExOs we've found are based in Silicon Valley, or at least in English-speaking countries. That said, in our research we *did* find several large enterprises in non-English-speaking locales that are successfully implementing ExO principles.

Perhaps the most remarkable of these is Haier, a Chinese appliance maker (formerly known as Qingdao Refrigerator Company), which has 80,000 employees and which recorded $30 billion in sales for 2013 alone.

Bill Fischer, co-author with Umberto Lago and Fang Liu of the book *Reinventing Giants: How Chinese Global Competitor Haier Has Changed the Way Big Companies Transform*, makes the important observation that the "business model and corporate culture are inextricably linked."[1] The authors tracked Haier for over a decade, along the way identifying four key stages that large organizations must navigate to reinvent their cultures:

- Build quality
- Diversify
- Re-engineer the business process
- Reduce distance to customer

Zhan Ruimin, a former Haier administrator who was appointed CEO by the Chinese state in 1984, implemented the quality-building step early on in his tenure. A famous anecdote has him handing out sledgehammers and joining staffers in destroying a few dozen subpar refrigerators. His next move

---

1   www.forbes.com/sites/stevedenning/2013/05/13/the-creative-economy-can-industrial-giants-reinvent-themselves/

was to diversify into other home appliances. In 2005, Zhan decided to shred Haier's entire middle management layer and reorganize the company's 80,000 employees into 2,000 ZZJYTs, a Chinese acronym for independent, self-managed units, each having a P&L, where team members are paid on performance [Autonomy]. These units have several fascinating characteristics:

- Employees are able to switch between units.
- Each unit has a P&L, and team members share profits, have their own performance-based incentives and are paid on performance.
- Customer-facing employees are given maximum flexibility and full decision-making capabilities.
- Instead of following set orders from the company, a team's primary responsibility is to increase customer demand.
- Anyone can propose new products, which are then voted on not just by employees, but also suppliers and *customers*, who collectively determine which projects are funded [Experimentation, Community & Crowd].
- Whoever proposes a winning idea becomes a unit leader, empowered to recruit team members from across the organization.
- Every quarter, each team has the opportunity to vote its unit leader out [Autonomy].
- Performance is tracked on a daily, real-time basis [Dashboards].
- Haier's community management system, known as HOPE (Haier Open Partnership Ecosystem), is an open innovation ecosystem across which 670,000 users communicate with suppliers and other customers searching for new business opportunities [Engagement]. Anyone can contribute ideas or compete in contests [Engagement: incentive competitions].
- Haier launched a global Green Home Vision

contest and a global slogan contest on Facebook. In its first year, four winners (out of 200,000 slogan entries) won a trip to China. [Community & Crowd, Engagement].

Haier has been named the most valuable brand in China for the past thirteen years. Both *Fast Company* magazine and the Boston Consulting Group recently labeled it one of the most innovative companies in the world. In fact, despite being overseen by the Chinese government, Haier is amazingly innovative. For example, the company is currently working on a cutting-edge nanorefrigerator that will allow consumers to create food inside a refrigerator over several days, using advanced lighting and mathematical models of plant growth.

Haier's revenues have increased fourfold over the last fourteen years. Sales grew to $29.5 billion, in 2013, when Haier sold more than 55 million home appliances. From 2011 to 2014, the market cap of Haier tripled from $20 billion to $60 billion, largely due to its implementation of Autonomy and Experimentation. Not surprisingly, the company gets high scores as an ExO.

Haier's Exponential Quotient—68 out of 84.

MTP	S	C	A	L	E	I	D	E	A	S
		✓			✓	✓	✓	✓	✓	✓

XIAOMI – SHOWING YOU AND ME

It's hard to fully capture the incredible ascent of Xiaomi Tech, another Chinese company. Founded in June 2010 and focused on low-end Android smartphones, the company sold twenty million handsets in 2013, recording annual revenues of more than $5 billion.

Lei Jun, one of the founders, is seen as a Chinese Steve Jobs. That's not just because he's been heavily inspired by Apple's design, marketing and supply chain management, but also because of Xiaomi's intense focus on performance, quality and customer experience—characteristics that Lei Jun wants to make available to everyone at affordable prices.

Xiaomi offers a curated Apple smartphone experience with the software development, speed and processes of Google Android, all at a low price. The company currently outsells Apple in China and is closing in on Samsung. Its products are available in four Asian countries and the company plans to expand to ten more emerging markets, including India and Brazil. Needless to say, Xiaomi features a full complement of ExO characteristics.

Xiaomi has an extremely flat structure consisting of core founders, department leaders and about 4,300 employees, a system that enables short-line communication and decision-making in a fast-paced organization [Autonomy]. Some 3,000 employees, including 1,500 people working at a call center, perform e-commerce, logistics and after-sales. The rest of the workforce (1,300 employees) works in R&D, which, at 30 percent of the workforce, is significant.

The culture of the individual teams is that of a traditional clan or tribe—family-like and focused on mentoring, collaboration and adhocracy [Autonomy, Experimentation]. Dynamic and entrepreneurial, with a focus on risk taking, Xiaomi only hires people who are passionate about their work and who are experts in their respective fields. Job incentives are available in the form of profit sharing and job rotation, which means employees are free to switch jobs at any moment.

A big difference relative to Apple is how extensively Xiaomi leverages its ecosystem [Community & Crowd]. Lei is convinced that customers are the company's best source in terms of product design and services. As a result, Xiaomi employees are required to spend at least thirty minutes a day interacting with customers on user forums and social networks. Xiaomi also holds special events for its community of almost ten million fans, and stages elaborate product launches, much as Google and Apple do.

Xiaomi's most loyal followers are called "Mi fen" (米粉 in Chinese), which in addition to translating as "Xiaomi fan" also means "rice flour," a play on Xiaomi's name, which means millet or "little rice." During its 2014 Mi Fen Festival, fans bought $242 million worth of products in just twelve hours. Xiaomi came up with a game for the festival called Kings of Knockout, in which users could win discount coupons [Engagement]. The game was heavily promoted on the Chinese social network site Weibo, as well as on Twitter, Facebook and Google+. Recently appointed global vice president Hugo Barra, ex-VP of Google Android, thinks that this type of informal and playful engagement is the biggest reason for Xiaomi fans' loyalty to the brand.

As Lei predicted, the community also helps with product development. Of the twenty-five languages currently available on its OS, Xiaomi developed just three; the rest were created by users [Community & Crowd]. This user community of almost ten million helps the company not only with products but also with support. Xiaomi has a fully peer-to-peer customer service platform that is driven and organized by the users themselves. On top of that, the company's marketing costs are relatively low, since Xiaomi sells its products directly online, using no resellers. In fact, all marketing is done via social media, with consumers spreading the word virally, at no cost to the company. Although it was initially very difficult for Xiaomi to find manufacturing partners for its smartphones, the company now uses Foxconn and other partners for its product lines [Leveraged Assets]. Xiaomi also discloses the names and parts numbers of all its suppliers, which helps protect those suppliers from the many counterfeit devices flooding the Chinese market.

Imagine selling twenty million smartphones in just three years—from a standing start. Xiaomi, which has done just that, embodies ten of the eleven ExO attributes.

Xiaomi's Exponential Quotient—74 out of 84.

MTP	S	C	A	L	E	I	D	E	A	S
✓	✓	✓		✓	✓	✓	✓	✓	✓	✓

THE GUARDIAN
– GUARDING JOURNALISM

For the past fifteen years, the newspaper industry has been suffering from classic innovator's dilemma. Its traditional engine was for editorial content to drive readership and for readership to drive advertising revenue, which in turn funded the newsroom.

As consumers increasingly shun print publications in favor of the Internet and other media, the traditional newspaper business model has not translated to the online world, a devastating blow that is resulting in many newspapers winding down. Some premium news organizations, such as the *New York Times* and *Wall Street Journal*, have thus far avoided that fate thanks to paywalls or freemium models. But few have actually changed their fundamental model.

Meanwhile, a plethora of new media startups have entered the field, among them Medium, Inside, BuzzFeed, Mashable, Blendle and Correspondent.

The *Guardian*, a UK-based newspaper best known for unleashing Edward Snowden's revelations onto the world, has been furiously innovating on the traditional model of newsgathering. Advised by industry icons Jeff Jarvis and Nicco Mele (who describes the *Guardian's* model in his recent book, *The End of Big: How the Internet Makes David the New Goliath*), the *Guardian* has been audacious in its efforts to reinvent journalism. Here are some of the paper's initiatives:

- In 2007, the *Guardian* offered a free blogging platform for thought leaders and created online forums and discussion groups [Community and Crowd].
- Developers offered an open API to the paper's website so they could leverage content on the site [Algorithms].
- Investigative reporting for the millions of WikiLeaks cables fully crowdsourced [Community & Crowd].

The *Guardian* has institutionalized the crowdsourcing of investigative reporting and has successfully used that approach on several occasions, including after obtaining public documents from Sarah Palin's tenure as governor of Alaska. Similarly, in 2009, when the UK government bowed to public pressure and released two million pages of parliamentary expense reports, the *Guardian* asked its readership to find any newsworthy needles in that vast haystack of words. In response, its readers analyzed more than 20 percent of the total volume in just over three days.

We believe that journalism will increasingly follow the *Guardian's* lead and shift to an ExO model, much like Medium's efforts to become a platform. And that is good news, because a free and *healthy* press (with investigative journalism being the tip of that spear) is critical both for democracy and in guarding fundamental individual freedoms.

The *Guardian's* Exponential Quotient—62 out of 84.

MTP	S	C	A	L	E	I	D	E	A	S
✓	✓	✓			✓	✓	✓			✓

GENERAL ELECTRIC – GENERAL EXCELLENCE

It is no accident that GE is one of the most admired companies in the world. Over the decades, the company has repeatedly and successfully reinvented itself—something it seems to be doing once again by aggressively partnering with ExO companies.

We have referenced Quirky several times throughout this book and will now focus on its MTP, which is "Make Invention Accessible." General Electric early on saw the huge potential of the new crowdsourced model of product development. It subsequently partnered with Quirky in 2012 on incentive competition [Engagement], whereby the Quirky community was tasked with dreaming up innovative everyday products. The submissions would then be put to a community vote, with the winning invention manufactured by GE.

Out of a total of 1,500 submissions, the Quirky community selected the Milkmaid, a smart container that alerts users when milk begins to spoil or run low, as the top product. Each subsequent phase of the Milkmaid's production, including product design, name, tagline and even price, was crowdsourced as well [Crowd], resulting in a total of 2,530 contributions from the Quirky community for a single product.[1]

Although the Milkmaid was just a pilot [Experimentation], the project was deemed a huge success, and in 2013, GE and Quirky announced the next stage of their innovative new partnership: GE gave Quirky's 900,000 community members open access to GE's most promising patents and technologies. It also started a co-branded Internet of Things initiative called "Wink: Instantly Connected," dedicated to building a line of smart home devices.

GE, which invested $30 million in Quirky, chose to open up its patents in order to accelerate the creation of new, innovative products—something GE determined the crowd could accomplish more quickly than it could do on its own. That decision is clearly paying off. In addition to the four connected-home products currently available in Quirky's online store, GE and Quirky expect to release more than 30 more such products over the next few years.

At about the time GE announced its partnership with Quirky, the company also opened a new makerspace in Chicago called GE Garages, which is powered by TechShop and works in partnership with Skillshare, Quirky, Make and Inventables [Leveraged Assets, Staff on Demand]. As with the Quirky relationship outlined above, GE began with a pilot program in 2012, launching GE Garages as mobile pop-ups traveling around the United States. A year later it opened its Chicago makerspace, where contributors have full access to manufacturing tools such as CNC mills, laser cutters, 3D printers and molders. GE also

---

1   www.quirky.com/products/327-The-Milkmaid-smart-milk-jug/
    timeline

provides workshops and demos.[1]

In February 2014, GE extended its ExO initiatives even further by announcing a partnership with Local Motors to launch a new model for manufacturing called First Build. This partnership will source collaborative ideas from an online community of engineers, scientists, fabricators, designers and enthusiasts who will focus on identifying market needs and solving deep engineering challenges in the hopes of unlocking breakthrough product innovations. The most popular of these innovations will then be built, tested and sold in a specialized "microfactory." This facility will focus on testing, rapid prototyping and small-volume production.

In conjunction with Alaska Airlines, GE provides yet another example of using ExO partnerships to leverage Engagement. In November 2013, the two companies partnered with Kaggle to create Flight Quest, an incentive competition in which contestants were challenged to create algorithms that could predict airplane arrival times more precisely. Each reduced-minute per flight can save $1.2 million in crew costs and $5 million in annual fuel savings. GE provided contestants with two weeks of FlightStats data. Out of 173 entries, five winners were awarded a total of $250,000. The winning algorithm proved 40 percent better at predicting arrival times than current technologies.[2]

GE is a perfect example of how a large organization can leverage exponential startups such as Kaggle, Quirky, Local Motors and TechShop to extend itself past its own organizational boundaries and scale.

GE's Exponential Quotient—69 out of 84.

MTP	S	C	A	L	E	I	D	E	A	S
	✓	✓		✓	✓	✓	✓	✓	✓	✓

---

1   www.ge.com/garages/press.html

2   www.gequest.com/c/flight

AMAZON – CLEARING THE RAINFOREST OF "NO"

In describing his notion of "impedance mismatch," Robert Goldberg noted that in large organizations, just one out of fifty managers can resist an idea—and in doing so, kill it. By comparison, if just one of fifty *investors* likes a startup, it's off to the races.

Along with the many ExO attributes Amazon has implemented, the company has also addressed the ease with which anyone in a big company can say no. One of the more intriguing organizational innovations to come out of the company is what CEO Jeff Bezos and CTO Werner Vogels call "The Institutional Yes."

Here's how it works: If you're a manager at Amazon and a subordinate comes to you with a great idea, your default answer must be YES. If you want to say no, you are required to write a two-page thesis explaining why it's a bad idea. In other words, Amazon has increased the friction entailed in saying no, resulting in more ideas being tested (and hence implemented) throughout the company.[1]

Jeff Bezos is perhaps the most underrated CEO of the last couple decades. Not only has he made that rare transition from founder to large-company CEO, but he has also consistently avoided the short-term thinking that so often comes with running a public company—what Joi Ito calls "nowism." Amazon regularly makes long bets (e.g., Amazon Web Services, Kindle, and now Fire smartphones and delivery drones), views new products as if they are seedlings needing careful tending for a five-to-seven-year period, is maniacal about growth over profits and ignores the short-term view of Wall Street analysts. Its pioneering initiatives include its Affiliate Program, its recommendation engine (collaborative filtering) and the Mechanical Turk project. As Bezos says, "If you're competitor-focused, you have to wait until there is a competitor doing something. Being customer-focused allows you to be

1   www.hbr.org/2007/10/the-institutional-yes/ar/1

more pioneering."

Not only has Amazon built ExOs on its edges (such as AWS), it also has had the courage to cannibalize its own products (e.g., Kindle). In addition, after realizing that Amazon's culture wasn't a perfect fit with the outstanding service he wanted to offer, Bezos spent $1.2 billion in 2009 to acquire Zappos. His goal? To improve the customer service culture throughout Amazon (after all, Zappos' MTP is "Provide the Best Customer Service Possible") and help implement Autonomy.

Amazon's Exponential Quotient—68 out of 84.

MTP	S	C	A	L	E	I	D	E	A	S
✓		✓	✓	✓	✓	✓		✓	✓	✓

ZAPPOS – ZAPPING BOREDOM

It took just eight years for Zappos, which got its start selling shoes online in 1999, to hit $1 billion in annual sales. In 2007 Zappos expanded its business to clothing and accessories, which now account for 20 percent of its annual revenue.

We've already seen some of the ways Zappos uses ExO attributes: an emphasis on customer service [MTP: "Provide the Best Customer Service Possible"]; its creation of a community around common passions and a common location in the Las Vegas Downtown Project, and its managed communities through Like-Like relationships [Community]; and its use of the Face Game to improve internal culture [Engagement: gamification].

To that list add the fact that Zappos employees answer 5,000 calls a month and 1,200 emails a week (and even more during the holiday season, when call-frequency increases significantly). Call center employees don't have scripts and there are no limits on call times; in fact, the longest Zappos call reported is ten hours and twenty-nine minutes [Autonomy, Dashboards].

50 percent of a new recruit's probationary review is based on his or her cultural fit with the company. Each recruit spends

four weeks shadowing experienced employees [MTP], and at the end of that period is offered $3,000 to *leave* the company—further weeding out cultural misfits.

Instead of performance reviews, Zappos managers conduct cultural assessments [Dashboards]. They evaluate employees based on their fit within the company culture and offer suggestions on how to improve that fit. To be eligible for raises, employees must pass skill-based tests. Zappos also regularly holds internal incentive competitions and hackathons, most relating to company data and APIs. In 2011 Zappos opened its competitions to the external developer community as well (the API Developer Challenge[1] and the Winter Hackathon), and awarded money and gift certificates to the winners [Engagement].

In December 2013, CEO Tony Hsieh adopted the Holacracy approach and shook up the 1,500-person organization by moving to full Autonomy. After six months, 225 employees had been transitioned from the old hierarchical model, and Zappos is currently stripping all job titles and management layers—eventually, even the CEO job will disappear. This is an extraordinary move for a large firm, perhaps the largest such transition ever attempted.

A key question that often comes up with Zappos is, "How does it hire without job descriptions?" In 2014, despite the fact that Zappos planned to expand its workforce by a third, from 1,500 employees to almost 2,000, no job postings went up anywhere. In order to apply, candidates were required to join a social network called Zappos Insiders. By continually monitoring the activity of candidates and how they interfaced with existing employees, Zappos recruiters maintained an always-on pool of candidates. Zappos also used Ascendify, an online platform that runs Q&A sessions and incentive competitions, to filter for skills and cultural fit. With the success of this hiring process, Zappos may very well revolutionize the corporate HR function. For all these reasons, Zappos gets a high score on our ExO diagnostic.

---

1   developer.zappos.com/blog/first-zappos-developer-contest

Zappos Exponential Quotient— 75 out of 84.

MTP	S	C	A	L	E	I	D	E	A	S
✓		✓	✓		✓	✓	✓	✓	✓	✓

ING DIRECT CANADA (NOW TANGERINE) – BANKING AUTONOMY

Another major concern often expressed about implementing ExO principles is, "Well, it might work in Silicon Valley or for a cute gaming company, but it won't work in a real operational environment."

Enter ING Direct Canada, a bank with fiduciary obligations and regulatory requirements—in notoriously regulatory Canada, no less. Originally part of ING Group, headquartered in the Netherlands, ING Direct Canada was founded in April 1997 by Arkadi Kuhlmann. It was the first test market for ING Group's direct banking business model, which provided more favorable rates to customers by removing brick and mortar branches altogether.

Kuhlmann started ING Direct Canada with the MTP "Save Your Money," and added three key complementary values: Simplify, Be challengers, Be the good guy.

Kuhlmann took the concept of Autonomy to its full extent by completely flattening the organization and getting rid of all job titles, seniority levels, management layers, formal meetings and even offices. Employees worked together and identified themselves by their responsibilities.

In 2008, Peter Aceto became CEO of ING Direct Canada and continued what Arkadi had started. In fact, after a year in the role, he took a page from Philip Rosedale's book and had his employees vote on whether or not he should stay on as CEO. Aceto also has no office, and to this day continues to share as much information as possible internally about the performance of the company. In doing so, he has stimulated a culture of trust, sharing, transparency and vulnerability. Named Toronto's Communicator of the Year in 2010, Aceto is known as "the social media CEO" and even responds to customer queries on weekends.

ING Direct set up four "cafés" (a term ING prefers to branches) across Canada. These locations served as touch points for customers to enjoy face-to-face interaction with bank representatives, or to simply grab a cup of coffee. Kuhlmann's primary purpose with the cafés was to reassure customers and build the brand. Increasingly, however, ING cafés have become places to hang out and talk to other people about money. Local community groups even organize Tweetups.[1]

In 2010, ING invited 10,000 Canadians to be part of a beta group to test THRiVE, a new free checking account service. Their feedback helped improve the service prior to launch, and in 2011, THRiVE was named Financial Product of the Year by global market researcher TNS Global.

Scotiabank acquired ING Direct Canada in August 2012. Now known as Tangerine, it remains a stand-alone business, with Aceto still at the helm.

Tangerine staff still operate with considerable Autonomy. If an advertising promotion proves successful, employees operate on a beehive philosophy and those with customer service experience swarm to the phone banks. At regulatory reporting time, those same employees might cluster around fulfilling that requirement. A combination of real accountability (the company's chief risk officer has regulatory accountability) and a flexible work staff gives the organization the best of both worlds.

How well has it worked? While an average Canadian bank has about 250 customers per employee, Tangerine handles 1,800 per employee—a 7x improvement. On average, Canadian banks manage about $10,000 in deposits per employee; Tangerine handles $40,000 per employee—a 4x improvement.

---

1   www.thefinancialbrand.com/15550/ing-direct-cafe-us-canada-photos/

Tangerine's Exponential Quotient—69 out of 84.

MTP	S	C	A	L	E	I	D	E	A	S
✓		✓			✓	✓		✓	✓	✓

GOOGLE VENTURES
– THE ALMOST PERFECT EExO

In March 2009, Bill Maris launched Google Ventures, Google's own corporate venture capital fund, with a $100 million capital commitment. Now, after five years, the company has emerged as one of the most active and successful VCs, with sixty employees (all partners) and $1.5 billion under management. Now that is an ExO move, one that represents a 15x increase over five years.

Google Ventures already has completed more than twenty successful exits, with returns far exceeding market averages for venture capital funds. Indeed, its emergence as one of the top financiers of startups may be a first for a corporate venture fund. While tech companies have long backed startups, their venture arms have a history of terribly subpar returns, mainly because there was no real independence from the parent company.

Google Ventures has invested in more than 225 portfolio companies encompassing all stages and industry sectors, including such rising stars as Uber, Nest, 23andMe, Cloudera, Optimizely, TuneIn, Homejoy and High Fidelity. As a result of its many successes, Google Ventures opened a London office in 2014, with $100 million to invest in European startups.

Although Google provides the funds for Google Ventures, invested companies don't have to benefit Google. That means portfolio companies stay independent and can be acquired by competitors. A downside of this structure, of course, is that Google Ventures might well remain in the dark about potential deals being undertaken by its parent company. In fact, this is what happened when Google acquired Nest, creator of smart thermostats and smoke alarms, for $3.2 billion in January 2014.

Nonetheless, although the possibility of such an outcome is a show-stopper for many large organizations, we believe the benefits of independence far outweigh the occasional costs.

Google Ventures contributes more than money. In addition to providing design services (10x faster than traditional design agencies), it hosts workshops where founders and employees of portfolio companies hone their product management or operational skills. The company also helps with marketing, recruiting, and engineering, often tapping Google's vast resources to do so.

A key differentiator for Google Ventures is its use of data analytics and algorithms to assess deals. The company employs seven data scientists who collect and analyze as much data as possible before deciding where to invest. As Maris said, "We have access to the world's largest datasets you can imagine. Our cloud computer infrastructure is the biggest ever. It would be foolish to just go out and make gut investments." Other firms, such as Sequoia Capital and Y Combinator, are taking note and adapting quickly.

It's important to note that the data informs but does not decide. Like most VCs, Google Ventures invests in people over products. If the data shows a potentially great company but the founding team doesn't feel right about some aspect of it, no investment will be made. The fund uses OKRs extensively to track the progress of its portfolio companies and relies heavily on real-time metrics—everything is quantified. The portfolio companies are initiated into this way of thinking via GV's Startup Lab, a private program that is part incubator, part hackathon and part co-working space.

To find potential companies, Google Ventures leverages Google's 50,000 employees. Employees are encouraged to refer stealth startups or founders; if an investment is ultimately made, the employee gets a $10,000 finders fee. In addition, portfolio companies not only have full access to GV's partners, they also have the option of connecting with specific Google employees. In fact, this is one of the biggest perks Google Ventures offers: unique access to some of the best engineers, scientists and technology in the world. A community portal connects the GV team with Google employees and peers from other portfolio companies. Hiring for the portfolio companies is also facilitated by Google Ventures' ability to tap Google's extensive database of resumes, which number over a million a year.

Like any worthy ExO, Google Ventures is even willing to disrupt itself. In 2014 it led a $28 million financing round in AngelList, a Craigslist-like marketplace that matches entrepreneurs and angel investors. AngelList introduced a new funding model called syndicates, in which lesser-known angels pool their dollars with those of investors with established track records. The model essentially allows better-known investors to build mini-funds for specific deals. Remarkably, this puts those investors in direct competition with Google Ventures, especially over seed-stage deals, which account for about half of its investments. Nonetheless, Google Ventures is willing to accept the possibility of competition, putting the company firmly on the disruption side of Clayton Christensen's Innovator's Dilemma.

Google Ventures boasts ten ExO attributes out of eleven (and the eleventh, the MTP, is inherited from its parent).

Google Ventures' Exponential Quotient—76 out of 84.

MTP	S	C	A	L	E	I	D	E	A	S
	✓	✓	✓	✓	✓	✓	✓	✓	✓	✓

GROWING WITH THE CROWD

In December 2013, Jeremiah Owyang, a social media strategist, launched an industry group called Crowd Companies. According to Owyang, Crowd Companies is a "brand council" whose activities include introductions, educational forums and networking with relevant startups, many of which are ExOs. Several dozen major brands have already joined the group, and Owyang believes that as this new breed of companies leveraging crowd dynamics spreads out across the world, they will in turn spark what he calls a Collaborative Economy (outlined below). Owyang has identified seventy-five crowd-based startups operating in six vertical markets. Lisa Gansky's Mesh Labs takes this model to a much more granular level, listing nine thousand crowd-based startups in twenty-five categories.

Such adoption of social media is not a fad. In fact, the social business movement (tagged #socbiz on Twitter) represents a foundational step towards a future landscape filled with ExOs. Currently, one hundred twenty business leaders and thirty-four Fortune 500 companies are council members of Crowd Companies and, according to Owyang, over eighty global brands have experimented with these techniques.

Owyang isn't alone in his thinking: Shel Israel, co-author of the book *Age of Context: Mobile, Sensors, Data and the Future of Privacy*, noted recently that there have been many such labels attached to this new movement: the Sharing Economy, the Mesh Economy, Collaborative Consumption and the Collaborative Economy.

We actually think Exponential Organizations works quite well as a label. But whatever the ultimate designation, it is clear that ExO attributes can and are being implemented by large organizations. In fact, as we wrote this book we were surprised to see how fast that implementation is occurring. What was little more than a loose theory when we sat down to outline the book has now taken on the trappings of a global movement. Large organizations everywhere are realizing that to remain competitive they must address their historic biases and impose a new reality, one that willingly jettisons anachronistic business practices—no matter how effective they were in the past—in favor of new ones that are better equipped for an ever-faster moving world.

Over the last four years, Juan Manuel Rowland of Azteca (Mexico), the largest Latin TV studio, has been transforming Azteca's approach to digital content. Initially a consultant responsible for migrating all Azteca novellas and programs to digital video streams, Rowland was tapped by Azteca CEO Mario San Román to join the company and do something bold. Rowland noticed that although streaming existing programs

Collaborative Economy Honeycomb Version 1.0

The Collaborative Economy enables people to efficiently get what they need from each other. Similarly, in nature, honeycombs are resilient structures that efficiently enable many individuals to access, share, and grow resources among a common group.

In this visual representation, this economy is organized into discrete families, sub-classes, and example companies. To access the full directory of 9000+ companies visit the Mesh Index, at meshing.it/companies managed by Mesh Labs.

By Jeremiah Owyang
@Jowyang

KEY MARKET FORCES

SOCIETAL DRIVERS
- DESIRE TO CONNECT
- SUSTAINABLE MINDSET
- POPULATION INCREASE

ECONOMIC DRIVERS
- FINANCIAL CLIMATE
- UNTAPPED IDLE RESOURCES
- STARTUPS HEAVILY FUNDED

TECHNOLOGY ENABLERS
- INTERNET OF EVERYTHING
- MOBILE TECHNOLOGIES
- SOCIAL NETWORKS

CROWD COMPANIES
www.crowdcompanies.com

< MAKER MOVEMENT >

LOANER PRODUCTS
RESOURCE GOODS
SHARED FOOD
PERSONAL SERVICES
PRE-OWNED GOODS
MEAL SHARING
SHARED FOOD DELIVERY
CROWDFUNDING
PROFESSIONAL SERVICES
CRYPTO CURRENCIES
MONEY LENDING
TRANSPORTATION SERVICES
SPACE - WORK SPACE
PLACE-TO-STAY

EMPOWERED PEOPLE
MAKERS, CO-CREATORS, CROWDFUNDERS, PEERS, CUSTOMERS

FOOD
GOODS
SERVICES
MONEY
TRANSPORTATION
SPACE

With input from:

Neal Gorenflo (@gorenflo).
Lisa Gansky (@instigating).
Shervin Pishevar (@shervin).
Mike Walsh (@mwalsh).
Brian Solis (@briansolis).
Alexandra Samuel (@awsamuel).
and Vision Critical (@visioncritical).

Design by Vladimir Mirkovic www.transartdesign.com
May 2014. Creative Commons license: Attribution-NonCommercial.

yielded little revenue for the company, Latin YouTube stars were getting millions of views for their videos. Moving to the edge as requested, he acquired a big house and installed a dozen young YouTube enthusiasts, all tasked with producing videos under a new brand called ContenTV. Reveling in the off-brand culture and the opportunity to live and work in a creative, take-no-prisoners space, the kids thrived. Within a year, ContenTV videos were getting more than ten times the views than those of Azteca (again, talk about an ExO!). In the second year, Rowland and his team developed a business model and put a sales team on it. After some growing pains and tensions with the flagship brand, ContenTV was reabsorbed into Azteca, but it remains a stand-alone property. Having learned from their experience, Rowland and San Román are reapplying their original vision to a new model.

Who drives the decision to become an Exponential Organization? We can see from the Azteca example that it is the *senior managers*, the men and women at the C-Level such as San Román, upon whom the fate of the enterprise ultimately rests. They will soon be experiencing tremendous pressure to adapt, just as they will ultimately be responsible for the results. It is to this group, then, that we turn in our final chapter.

CHAPTER TEN
THE EXPONENTIAL EXECUTIVE

The ExO concept—the new organizing principle for the information age—is just a few years old and thus still evolving into its final form. By necessity then, this book has been very much a series of messages from the front lines of business competition.

As we noted at the beginning of the book, this is not the first time such a revolution has taken place. Indeed, business transformations have arrived like clockwork almost every decade for the last century, each time driven by the appearance of some new and important enabling technology. Thus, the "virtual" economy we live and work in today was made possible twenty years ago by the rise of the Internet and, more recently, by the impact of mobile technologies. Here is an example of how one company's senior management is facing that future:

Case Study: Exponential Innovation Within Citigroup

Interest Rates is one of the major market-facing divisions of Citigroup's investment bank. With hundreds of employees globally, more than fifty separate sub-businesses and billions of dollars in yearly revenue, it is a large organization by any measure—and not the sort normally associated with disruptive innovation.

The company was staffed with a lot of very smart people drowning under a deluge of data—price movements, economic releases, client data and news—far more data than any human could reasonably consume and analyze.

Andy Morton, the division's global head and a self-described "numbers guy" (famous in the financial world as one of the three creators of the Heath-Jarrow-Morton interest rate framework), had long believed that a new generation of smart algorithms could exponentially improve the productivity of his organization. In 2014, he hired Arjun Viswanathan, an interest rate option trader with twelve years of experience using computational market techniques, to help him realize this vision. Viswanathan's task was to find a way to embrace and use data effectively.

Viswanathan (like Morton, a mathematician/computer-scientist-turned-trader), had been exposed to the concept of Exponential Organizations at the 2013 Singularity Summit in Budapest, and wanted to implement ExO ideas internally. He and Morton carefully designed their experiment: Viswanathan would report directly to Morton and would have access to all Rates' resources and data. He also had a mandate to form fluid teams with other senior people within the business. Resources would be used on demand, while applications would be tested and iterated rapidly via an internal group of employees. Apps would be small, intuitive, fun and visual—in short, they would be designed to get information into employees' minds as quickly as possible. AI, Machine Learning and data analytics would be extensively used to free up human thinking. The idea was to put the right people, resources and ideas together and wait for something magical to happen.

Something did. Within just three months, the new setup resulted in several key problems being solved, including predictions concerning client behavior, market moves and pending economic releases, as well as market regime classification. There were also several other chunky problems that, in the old world, would have taken multi-person teams a year of more to implement.

All issues on the table, however, were solved within weeks, using one-twentieth the resources, time and cost as before—an outcome that would have seemed impossible as recently as 2012. Real applications now sit on key desks, answering in seconds questions that previously took days to answer—or simply could not be answered at all. The apps themselves were beautiful, and employees were enjoying using them in ways not originally imagined; data was once again fun. Today, this paradigm is catching on elsewhere within Citigroup, with other divisions investigating how they can kick-start similar change within their own operations.

Why did the new setup work so well for the Rates group? Success grew out of a strong combination of the following:

- Support for the project at the highest level. Morton is an intellectually curious business head willing to disrupt his organization.
- Reliance on a coordinator with both domain and machine learning expertise.
- A well-connected network of people within the business who actively embrace algorithmic augmentation of human roles and are quick to exchange ideas.
- An understanding and implementation of ExO techniques.

LIFE AT C-LEVEL

Today, a new wave of revolutionary technologies have begun to make their mark: cheap analog sensors, Bitcoin, 3D printing, neuro-marketing, AI, robotics, nanotech and Big Data. And these technologies are just the vanguard of an era of unprecedented innovation. Not only can they change the way businesses organize and operate, they *must* do so. Merely adopting any of these new technologies will force fundamental changes in how we work. In particular, by their very nature, these technologies will accelerate the pace of the commercial world—and not just incrementally, but *exponentially*. And for all that we've been through over the last half-century of the technology revolution, this acceleration will be unlike anything we've ever known before.

In time, we are all going to experience this astonishing new pace of change…but no one sooner, or ultimately more, than corporate executives. These so-called C-Level executives, including the CEO, CMO, CTO, CFO etc., and the newly-emerging Chief Data Officer (CDO), are going to find themselves under enormous pressure to either "go exponential"—as we've already seen, a difficult task for any established enterprise—or deal with the threat presented by new, exponential competitors. The decisions they will make, often under pressure and on the fly, will likely determine not just whether their companies succeed, but whether or not they *survive*. Once again, this isn't the first time corporate executives have faced an existential challenge wrought by a technological/organizational revolution, but this time around the window of opportunity will be briefer than ever before. There will be no time to hesitate—much less time to ponder—before making major strategic moves.

For that reason, we are dedicating this final chapter to understanding the Exponential Executive, a new leader destined to emerge from this transformed economy. And by the end of the chapter, we hope to have answered the following:

- Which technologies will have the most impact on the C-Suite?
- What new organizational developments must an Exponential Executive track and be ready for?
- What questions and issues will the ExO Executive face in the next five to ten years as a result of this collective and accelerating change?

We begin by touching on a sample of five major technologies and some meta-trends that will drive change across many industries. Then we'll examine how the CEO, CMO, CTO and other executives need to deal with these technologies in the very near future.

Let's begin with the transformative technologies (with many thanks to the faculty at Singularity University, who suggested or reviewed many of the ideas below):

Likely Breakthrough Technologies

Sensors and the Internet of Things

Description: We'll see a leap from eight billion Internet-connected devices today to fifty billion by 2020. Anything and everything will have sensors embedded, from wearables and packages to even food.

Implications: Infinite computation (as Moore's Law continues) and infinite storage, both essentially free; the Quantified Employee; AaaS (Analytics as a Service); hardware as the new software via developments such as Arduino; new business models based on connected products.

AI, data science and analytics

Description: Ubiquitous usage of Machine Learning and Deep Learning algorithms to process vast caches of information.

Implications: Algorithms driving more and more business decisions; AIs replacing a large percentage of knowledge workers; AIs looking for patterns in organizational data; algorithms embedded into products.

Virtual/augmented reality

Description: Avatar-quality VR available on desktop in 2-3 years. Oculus Rift, High Fidelity and Google Glass drive new applications.

Implications: Remote viewing; centrally located experts serving more areas; new practice areas; remote medicine.

Bitcoin and block chain

Description: Trustless, ultra-low-cost secure transactions enabled by distributed ledgers that log everything.

Implications: The blockchain becomes a trust engine; most third-party validation functions become automated (e.g., multi-signatory contracts, voting systems, audit practices). Micro-transactions and new payment systems become ubiquitous.

Neuro-feedback

Description: Use of feedback loops to bring the brain to a high level of precision.

Implications: Capacity to test and deploy entirely new classes of applications (e.g., focus@will); group creativity apps; flow hacking; therapeutic aids, stress reduction and sleep improvement.

These new technologies will, in turn, underpin the appearance of five likely **meta-trends:**

Perfect knowledge

Implications: With the Internet of (Every)thing, sensors, low Earth orbit (LEO) satellite systems and unlimited sensors, users will be able to know anything they want, anywhere and at any time.

Virtual worlds

Implications: Philip Rosedale notes that Hollywood special effects migrate to the desktop after five years. Avatar is now three years old and will soon be available on the Oculus Rift. Almost perfect VR is around the corner, and will deliver experiential reality and transform retail, travel, and living and working environments.

3D printing

Implications: 3D printing (and soon 4D) will not radically change big manufacturing, but it will enable an entirely new class of products that will displace traditional manufacturing. A Kinko's model of local 3D printing of virtually anything will appear shortly and the technology will have a major impact on warehousing and transportation. U.S. manufacturing will be revitalized as recent offshoring trends reverse.

Disruption of payment systems

Implications: In 2012, Visa and MasterCard credit card purchases totaled more than $1.5 trillion in the U.S. alone. Payment systems and money transfer mechanisms haven't changed for decades, but with Square, PayPal and now Clinkle and Bitcoin, this domain is ready for a major transformation. One form will come via mobile/social wallets and seamless transactions. A second will come via micropayments (probably via the block chain). The ability to move infinitesimal transaction amounts will underpin entirely new business models.

Autonomous vehicles

Implications: In September 2014, California will issue the first license plates for driverless cars. Starting with delivery vehicles and then taxis, predictions call for existing road capacity to increase 8-10 times once a critical mass of AVs is reached. Ridesharing is an intermediate step toward fully automated transportation, which may have a bigger visible impact on society than anything else, including sustainability, urban planning (almost no parking lots) and fewer traffic fatalities.

Note that most of these technologies and trends were unknown a decade ago, and all were non-existent thirty years ago. No doubt even more technologies and trends, as yet unknown, will emerge in even the next five years as convergences and intersection points drive an ever-faster pace of change. For five decades, predictions around Moore's Law have promised acceleration, and we are now seeing what that really means.

It is important to stress that the two lists above represent just a small sample of what is racing our way. It's also worth revisiting the findings of the Innovation Partners Program survey, detailed in Chapter Eight, of the eighty Fortune 500 C-Level executives:

- Before the event, 75 percent of the C-Level attendees had little or no awareness of accelerating technologies.
- After the program, 80 percent of the attendees agreed that the technologies and strategies would have a "game-changing impact" on their industries within two years, and *all* agreed that the impact would occur within five years.
- All of the executives—100 percent of them—had a list of urgent-action items upon returning to their offices.

Note that second statistic. **80 percent of Fortune 500 CxOs agreed that their industries would experience game-changing transformations due to disruptive technologies within two years**. Just two years. That pitifully short time frame is what is keeping Exponential Executives awake at night—a fate soon to be shared by every corporate executive on Earth.

We'll next turn our attention to the major challenges facing C-Level executives, and how Exponential techniques can help them reach solutions.

CEO – CHIEF EXECUTIVE OFFICER

For leadership of any kind, but especially for CEOs, it is becoming increasingly apparent that their duties—especially those that are externally facing—are shifting from operating in a predictable world, where the scaling of efficiencies is the dominant strategy, to a world in which adaptability and disruption represent higher-order competitive advantages. This will present tremendous opportunities—and at the same time considerable pressure—for change, especially when it comes to legacy businesses.

The Exponential CEO must constantly be on alert for disruptive startups emerging out of nowhere; competition won't just come from existing players. The best strategy in most industries won't be to fight those disruptors—but to join them. Thus, juxtaposing with startup ExOs is a major priority.

Key Opportunity	Implications and Actions
Migrate to an MTP	Change or expand your brand or mission statement to encompass an MTP, which is critical if you want to leverage a community and keep your team focused externally.
MTP communities	In many industries, interest-based communities (e.g., Quantified Self, Maker Faire, DIYbio, TechShop, Bitcoin) are growing fast. Join them, sponsor them and learn from them—before your competition does.
Disruptive ExOs in your industry	As Marcus Shingles found in the CPG world, several dozen disruptive ExOs are already in operation in every industry. Find them and then partner with, invest in or acquire them.
Leveraged Assets and Staff on Demand	If you have a large workforce or asset base, develop strategies to mitigate inertia and "old" thinking by moving to Staff on Demand and Leveraged Assets, as well as leveraging Community & Crowd. This will increase the (innovation) metabolism and adaptability of your company.
Information-based products and services	Find new products and services that are (fully) information-based for scalability. If they aren't yet available, develop them.
Death of the five-year plan	Strategic planning is giving way to data-driven predictive analytics, a strong product vision and purpose (MTP). Increasingly, the past cannot be extrapolated to the future. Constant experimentation at the edges of the organization will drive just-in-time

(cont.)	planning functions. Move to a one-year planning cycle.
External innovation	As Peter Diamandis has said, "If you are relying on innovation solely from inside your organization, you are dead." Find ways to leverage Community and/or Crowd for innovation; investigate co-innovation and Crowd Companies and let your employees loose.
Explore new business models	Micropayments will enable entirely new business models to appear in established industries. The same is true for the emergence of the DIY (Maker) and P2P (Sharing) movements. Finally, as data becomes the new oil, many business models will be transformed from hardware to software to services.
Explore other innovation types	Most CEOs see innovation as product innovation. But there is also process innovation, social innovation, organizational innovation, management innovation, business model innovation, etc. Technology and products are no longer the only drivers for innovation. [See Doblin's 10 Types of Innovation, briefly outlined in Chapter Eight.]
Accept that there are limits to quantification, data and rationalization	There remains a place and role for intuition, personal vision and gut feelings. Because the future is to a large degree unknowable, most key strategic decisions still rely on intuition. Gut feelings can sometimes serve as a compass in an uncertain world, especially when solving a problem you're passionate about.
Automate and measure different processes in all departments	Using free code/algorithms optimized within the GitHub or GitLab social platforms and the vast data available, classic throughput or process-based models will be substituted by performance-based models (e.g., cost per sale).

Perhaps the most critical guidance we can give an Exponential CEO is to beware of Orthogonal Information Effects (OIEs); in other words, watch out for the unexpected value of seemingly peripheral data. Remember the example in Chapter One of the Buenos Aires car wash, which saw a 50 percent drop in revenues due to better weather forecasting? That wasn't an anomaly. Everywhere you look, industries are being reshaped by heretofore hidden information-driven changes—largely as a result of new data that is being gathered all the time. And as we also saw with our Argentinean car wash, although data is often readily available, it isn't always being interpreted.

For example, consider focus@will, which offers streamed music and sounds designed to put listeners in the "zone" when they need to get work done. The website is currently *averaging* five hours per visit per user! If/when focus@will takes off, it won't just impact a thin sliver of folks trying to improve their study habits. If you are the CEO of Red Bull or Starbucks or just about any coffee growing company, you need to be concerned about this non-caffeinated attention-enhancer.

Today it is more critical than ever for each and every CEO to consider that his or her company's market might be materially affected by innovation in an adjacent space. The lesson? If you don't watch out for OIEs…they're liable to become OVs (oy veys).

CMO – CHIEF MARKETING OFFICER

Marketing roles have seen considerable disruption over the past decade thanks to the global phenomenon of mobile and social media. Over the next few years, that disruption will take on a number of new and different forms.

Todd Defren, CEO of Shift Communications, a public relations firm based in San Francisco, and a thought leader in the PR space, has described a bifurcation in his industry where agencies are either becoming creative visual storytellers working on logos, games and branding or they are becoming analytics firms helping to manage their clients' sales funnels.

Key Opportunity	Implications and Actions
Product personalization	Complete personalization of products and services based upon individual customers (right size, taste, language, behavioral data, contextual data, sensor data, transactional data and, possibly, DNA or neuroprofile). Neuromarketing should not only be used to measure attention, motivation, intention, brand and effectiveness, but also as a way to personalize in areas like entertainment, sports and food.
AI monitoring of social media	AI monitoring of your company's social media designed to provide FAQ/help, information, communication and personal assistance when needed. It also alerts the right people when further action is necessary. (See Ekho.me as an example.)
Real-time behavioral dashboards	Real-time aggregated customer data providing insights into the behavior and emotions of customers, enabling matching of products and services with those customers (hyper-narrowcasting) and gauging demand for new concepts. Social and mobile media as the zeitgeist and thus the triggers for validated innovation.
MTP Community as sales force	If you can align with an MTP community, that community can then operate as a sales force for your organization. This implies a convergence of MTPs across the whole ecosystem of a company over time and results in a company with a MTP congruent with the MTPs of all of its external communities.
Vendor Relationship Management— extension of intention economy	The age of CRM is over, replaced by Vendor Relationship Management (VRM), a term coined by Doc Searls from Harvard University. VRM is an extension of the intention economy, and VRMs offer the ultimate in customer-driven.

(cont.)	marketplaces (e.g., Uber, BlaBlaCar). Consumers own their own personal data and expose demand and purchasing intentions with different vendors in the cloud, mostly in real time. CRM is initiated by companies, VRM by customers
Differential real-time pricing models	Real-time monitoring will allow for the institution of real-time pricing to maximize pricing based on real-time demand (e.g., airline tickets). AIs will prove extremely valuable in this transition.
Crowdsourced online marketplaces for marketing materials	Using online marketplaces to crowdsource TV commercials (Tongal), logos and banners (99 designs), or any marketing expertise (Freelancer).
PR & marketing will have to aim a lot further out to place business memes	Due to accelerated pace of change it is mandatory to look further into the future to launch marketing and PR campaigns by identifying when a meme is booming (predictive planning) or, even better, when it first emerges.
Lean Startup prototyping and testing	Using the Lean Startup method to test and validate assumptions around new campaigns and new products via advanced testing and prototyping forms, such as A/B-testing concepts in Google AdWords and landing pages, social media monitoring, neuro-feedback in retail stores of test groups, customer development interviews, crowdfunding, and testing in virtual worlds such as High Fidelity. In sum: a data-driven and continuous testing approach to marketing.
New revenue models	More subscriptions versus one-off sales due to access versus ownership trend; more apps; more connected products and more cradle to cradle and Circular Economy; more freemium models (free and paid—e.g., the horribly named.

(cont.)	"tryvertising"). New fee models, such as API fees, platform licensing, syndication fees and virtual goods

CFO – CHIEF FINANCIAL OFFICER

The finance function, although historically very conservative and cautious, is about to face radical disruption from several technologies, including AI (Deep Learning), sensors and Bitcoin (the underlying block chain protocol in particular).

Key Opportunity	Implications and Actions
AI accounting	Automatic A/P, A/R software-enabling automatic reminders and payment, automatic tax management, and AIs watching for errant behaviors in transaction flows.
Taxation without borders	Governments are getting their act together regarding tax havens, which will likely continue to face ever-closer scrutiny in the coming years.
Digital payment solutions	More than 60,000 merchants already accept Bitcoin, which we predict will hit Wall Street in late 2014 and will most likely be mainstream by 2016. This is in addition to the growing impact of Square and PayPal. Micro-transactions will drive orders-of-magnitude increases in the sheer number of transactions needing to be processed, tracked and audited.
Crowdfunding / crowdlending	New ways of getting financed for products or services by leveraging the crowd (e.g., Gustin, Kickstarter, angels and Lending Club), especially to demonstrate market demand for a product or service.
Cash flow measurement	Discounted Cash Flows will be replaced by Options Theory as a preferred mechanism.

We are seeing an overall unbundling of the financial arena, and the digital payments sector is particularly ripe for transformation. Quicken and Quickbooks have both had a major impact on traditional accounting firms. Now, similar to Mint for personal finance, Wave Accounting offers 100-percent-free small business accounting, although its real business model is to mine the data buried within those transactions. A little further out, the Bitcoin phenomenon continues to unfold. The smartest five VCs we know are all building or investing in between fifteen and twenty Bitcoin companies *each*. These investments could prove to be unimaginably disruptive. In fact, Salim believes Bitcoin to be the single biggest technology-enabler of the above list.

Leading Bitcoin investor Brock Pierce frames it thusly: While the Internet is a medium for open communication—on top of which a layer of secure transactions has been attempted with great difficulty—the block chain itself is an ultra-low-cost infrastructure of secure, guaranteed transactions over which all manner of applications can be laid (currency being just one of them).

Note that pretty much everything in the modern world is a transaction, be it communications, social agreements and, not least, commerce. For example, in an accounting system layered on the block chain, the *entire* audit function disappears.

CTO/CIO – CHIEF TECHNOLOGY/ INFORMATION OFFICER

In the past, CTOs mostly had two tasks: to deal with large software packages and services, and to ensure only officially sanctioned devices operated inside the organization. Now they will need to deal with a growing number of devices, technologies, services and sensors brought in by the workforce, which is increasingly demanding electronic access from everywhere. This will lead to increased hacking and other security issues that the CTO/CIO position was largely created to address.

Marc Goodman, a futurist for the FBI, estimates that just

6 percent of all corporate security breaches are detected by IT departments. Goodman recommends that CIOs run Red Ops teams to find hidden breaches before external agents can exploit them, pointing to a study showing that if you leave a thumb drive in an office parking lot, 60 percent of employees will plug it into their corporate computers to see what is on it (thus instantly compromising security). If the company logo happens to be printed on the thumb drive (an absurdly easy ruse), a whopping 90 percent of employees will plug it in.

Does your company's CIO ban all thumb drives and work overtime to alert all employees (not to mention contractors, who are the potential Edward Snowdens on your payroll) to this particular danger?

Key Area to Track	Implications and Actions
BYOx	Bring your own devices, technology, services and sensors to the company, providing a lot more data and resulting in more possibilities and innovation.
Cloud access	Access to social technologies, data and services everywhere, independent of location (cloud access).
AI assistants	Artificial intelligence to manage appointments, planning, information, help/FAQ, etc. (Google Now, Watson, Siri).
Big Data security	The world is becoming rapidly digitized, making it highly hackable, which in turn results in an explosion of security threats. For this problem, Big Data solutions (e.g., Palantir) are needed to detect breaches and make data secure.
Quantum computing and security	Leveraging quantum computing for security (decoding encryption with, paradoxically, secure quantum encryption).
Legal	Many industries (including banking, medicine and the law) mandate that client information be kept within

(cont.)	enterprise walls and on enterprise servers. The developments listed above will place extreme, even unbearable, stress on this requirement.

CTO/CIOs need to enable personalization of the workforce (which expects cutting-edge technologies and services) without compromising the security of the organization—a tall order indeed. Worldwide, the CIO position today is perhaps the most challenging corporate executive role. One example: large software implementations, such as ERP systems, are being replaced to a certain degree by specialized SaaS startups that align horizontally with other software offerings via open APIs. As ExOs scale beyond their traditional boundaries, the number of integration and data handoff points is set to explode, making fault traceability increasingly difficult.

CDO – CHIEF DATA OFFICER

Brad Peters, co-founder and chairman of Birst and a columnist at Forbes.com, has defined the chief data officer as a newest C-Level profession. Throughout the course of this book we've mentioned data extensively: billions of sensors churning out data for algorithms, Big Data solutions, data-driven decisions and value (or Lean) metrics. All organizations today have a dire need to manage and make sense of all this data and to somehow do so without breaching privacy and security laws and customer trust.

Meanwhile, within the organization, CIOs have gravitated towards managing the increasingly large information infrastructure. As a result, the job of managing all of the newly generated data has fallen upon the marketing department, for which the task can never be more than a side activity. Hence the need for the chief data officer, whose primary focus is managing data, finding the actionable information within, and then delivering it quickly, securely and in a useful form to every stakeholder in the organization.

Key Opportunity	Implications and Actions
Externally driven IT	Leverage external community (developers) and partnerships (startups, SaaS, companies) for new services/ products and open platforms with open APIs (remix datasets, open source standards) and provide own metadata (access, remixing).
Business intelligence (BI)	Data management systems that use methodologies, processes, architectures and technologies to transform raw data into meaningful and useful business information (more effective strategic, tactical and operational insights and decision-making). A key heuristic: if you operate in a highly uncertain environment, make it simple (not too many variables); if you operate in a predictable environment, make it complex (use more variables to manage BI).
Realignment of customer data ownership	Customers will own their own data (such as Personal or Respect Network) and then provide access to parts of it (for relevant and beneficial services) only to those authorized to receive the information.

The chief data officer is a relatively new executive function, but we see it as an essential part of any exponentially growing organization. Big Data solutions (especially Machine Learning and Deep Learning), data management systems and Dashboards will help greatly with real-time data gathering, sorting, filtering and remixing, as well as with creating a more personalized and effective organization.

CIO – CHIEF INNOVATION OFFICER

Note the following distinction carefully: this CIO, the chief innovation officer, is not to be confused with the other, better known, CIO, the chief information officer. The latter manages the enterprise's IT apparatus, the former the company's creative development. Innovation is key when growing a sustainable Exponential Organization. More than ever, chief innovation officers need to rely on external sources to keep up with the growing pace of change. The key is to leverage the entire ecosystem, which is driven by the MTP and consists of the community, hackerspaces, hackers, developers, artists, startups and companies.

Key Opportunity	Implications and Actions
Open Source R&D	Leverage community and crowd for R&D and product development (e.g., Quirky) as well as the collective intelligence and assets from hackerspaces, such as TechShop and BioCurious (Leveraged Assets, JIT supply).
Leveraging M&A	Invest in, partner with or acquire startups/companies and leverage them to enable R&D and product development (big companies as investment funds).
VRM R&D	Based on an intention or idea, a completely automated R&D and product development process can be fully driven by the community (collective purpose), just like CRM for sales purposes.
Brain-stimulated ideation	The use of brain stimulation technologies (tDCS, TMS, tACS) and hybrid learning (the brain directly connected to the cloud) to improve ideation and enhance capabilities (the optimal brain state: flow hacking, reduce/relieve stress, think faster, improve working and learning memory). A futuristic concept that is quickly becoming real.
Virtual reality testing	The use of virtual worlds to test, prototype, experiment and learn, such as Philip Rosedale's High Fidelity. Leveraging tools like Oculus Rift for. visualization, Gravity Sketch tablets for

(cont.)	design and Leap Motion for interaction. The arrival of disruptive 3D printers for testing in virtual worlds with gesture interfaces
Constraint-based design (AI)	Letting AIs design innovation, within particular constraints.

More than any other C-Level player, the chief innovation officer will come to lean heavily on many exponential technologies. The CIO needs to stimulate the innovation process both internally and externally, especially in terms of coherence and synchronicity. He or she must also encourage risk-taking and allow failure to flourish.

COO – CHIEF OPERATING OFFICER

As the heart of any organization, the chief operating officer's job is to just get things done. The COO has to take into account the growing trends of security and privacy risk, decentralization, localization and Leveraged Assets, as each will greatly affect the organization. When dealing with physical products, more so than with digital products, technology will impact production and the supply chain due to fast-moving developments in nanotechnology, 3D and 4D printing, sensors, artificial intelligence, robots and drones.

Key Opportunity	Implications and Actions
Decentralized or outsourced production	Digital production and unbundling of production steps, freeing the company to focus on its core competencies (customer relationships, R&D, design and marketing). Accomplished by leveraging OEMs (e.g., PCH International, Flextronics, Foxconn) or through the use of 3D printers, robots and nanotech/stacks (see Tesla).

Recyclable materials / circular economy	Production materials that can be recycled and reused multiple times. Salvaging of faulty products through the systematic extraction of raw materials. This feeds on the decentralized production model above. Using bio-nanocomposites and nanocellulose for biodegradable packaging.
Nanomaterials and nanomanu-facturing	Manufacturing and using materials made from engineered atoms and molecules (e.g., carbon graphene and carbyne), designed with specific shape, size, surface properties and chemistry to enhance reactivity, strength and electrical properties. The Materials Project as an open source database of materials and their properties.
3D and 4D printing	Self-assembly of products on location; quick prototyping and repair services.
AI production monitoring	Leverage sensor data, algorithms and AI to detect early faults in production and resolve them long before the product comes to market, thus radically reducing repairs, returns and recalls.
Customizable and programmable robots	Easily programmable and customizable robots for manufacturing, helping workers or removing the need for them to do repetitive and heavy tasks altogether (e.g., Baxter, Unbounded Robotics, Otherlab).
Sustainable production and logistics	Greener and more self-sufficient production driven by robo-transport, sensors, AI, flexible solar panels and perovskite solar cells. Nanomaterials (graphene) that can be added to buildings, vehicles, machines and equipment. Transformation in Logistics (road, water and air transport).
Autonomous transport and delivery	Leveraging autonomous vehicles (e.g., Google's self-driving car) and drones (e.g., Matternet) for the transport and.

(cont.)	delivery of supplies and products, especially in remote areas
Full supply chain tracking/ monitoring	Internet of Things sensors used to monitor the entire supply chain. Location, status, preservation and safety of most substances can be monitored (chemical substance traces, pollution, quality of life).
Biological production	Biology has the unique trait of being software that can create its own hardware. Leverage bio-based materials and synthetic biology as alternative means of production. Bio-production remains difficult to scale, but in the medium term promises to transform current production methods.

It is important to note that the need for long-distance transport will drop over time due to the rise of localized production and a growing circular economy (recycling). More and more products will be produced on the spot through local partners (Leveraged Assets), access to 3D printers and cheap labor provided by highly customizable robots. Since customers prefer to receive products the moment they decide they need them, they will be increasingly receptive to locally assembled products for two reasons: ethics (jobs and sustainability) and practicality (lower delivery costs, improved customer service, etc.). An average American meal today travels 2,500 miles to reach the table but local farming and techniques, such as vertical farming, can and will reduce that number considerably (for example, already 7 percent of the vegetables currently sold in Singapore are vertically farmed).

CLO – CHIEF LEGAL OFFICER

The ExO revolution poses a whole new set of hurdles for the legal function, making it both an exciting and stressful time to be a CLO. The legal system is the collective repository of societal values and is thus often incompatible with rapidly advancing progress. The stress on the system today is greater than ever before—thereby prompting one of Salim's favorite questions: *How will regulatory and legal frameworks cope as technology accelerates away from us?* No matter how challenging the obstacles, however, CLOs won't have the luxury of sitting back and waiting for the problems to resolve themselves. And while the concept of an Exponential legal department may strike you as an oxymoron, that doesn't have to be the case.

Issues that ExO legal executives should be aware of are detailed in the table below:

Key Opportunity	Implications and Actions
Fractional IP	IP will become more and more relevant due to the speed of new developments and devices, resulting in fractional IPs (patents for small portions).
Open sourcing patents	Just like Tesla did with its electric car patents, open sourcing IP will enable the creation of a much larger innovation ecosystem in which, by default, your organization will be the center. It pre-empts competition and insources innovation.
Reduced IP relevance	In an accelerating world, by the time you file a patent, it's out of date.
Rise of IP insurance	Formalized structures to protect against IP infringement.
Smart contracts	Legal clauses embedded as code; instant activation of consequences and outcomes; personalized legal systems.
Fluid legal contracts	Flexible and real-time legal contracts, constantly adapting to new data, stats and insights (e.g., current SCRUM contracts but more advanced).
Dangerous regulatory structures	As technology outpaces our ability to regulate, regulatory agencies become irrelevant; even worse, they become neo-Luddites.

Regulation as an economic development mechanism	Huge advantages will be conferred on those countries or regions that drive the future of regulatory systems. For example, if a small country fully legalized robotic cars, a great deal of R&D would be transferred there. ExOs will lobby their governments heavily for competitive regulatory environments.
Regulatory capture	Big organizations with deep pockets will increasingly resort to lobbying for favorable legal environments to create walls around their domains. Although lobbying is the prevalent escape route for large organizations today, it is not a sustainable strategy.

Due to emerging exponential technologies, it's become increasingly clear that intellectual property, privacy and property laws, and contractual mechanisms will be transformed in the coming years. It will be interesting to watch how regulatory frameworks keep pace. We expect any region or country (e.g., China, particularly its free zones) that adopts a forward-thinking regulatory environment will offer ExOs a major competitive edge.

CHRO – CHIEF HUMAN RESOURCES OFFICER

The accelerating pace of exponential technologies will not spare the HR world either. Developments in biotechnology (employee DNA profiles), neurotechnology (employee neuroprofiles), sensors and Big Data (the quantified employee) will provide unprecedented insights into the workforce. We also see a shift in recruitment techniques, collaboration and employee development as these all become increasingly digitized.

This is all likely to result in some unexpected, and surprising, changes in both recruiting and team leadership. For example, Google recently demonstrated that its best employees were not Ivy League students, but rather young people who had experienced a big loss in their lives and had been able to transform that experience into growth. According to Google, deep personal loss has resulted in employees who are more humble and open to listening and learning. Finally, Rate of Learning will become a mainstream measure to gauge the progress of an individual, team or even a startup.

Key Opportunities	Implications and Actions
Digital job interviews and meetings	Job interviews and collaboration leveraging video (Skype), telepresence (Double Robotics) or virtual reality (Oculus Rift or High Fidelity) for virtual meetings, as well as testing to enable the growing global Staff on Demand workforce. Social networking skills will increase in importance, as will internships and a focus on real life skills testing.
Hire employees who ask the right questions	We're moving into a world of open data, open APIs and even open source (deep learning) algorithms. If all that is free, what is unique? Machines (AI) are great for providing answers, but humans are better at asking the right questions. HR policies will focus on people who can ask them and cultivate an environment where questions, perspectives, art and culture are more deeply respected.
Hire based on potential, not just on track record and/or resume	Due to accelerated change, work experience will prove much less important. A prospect's potential is more important than IQ, features or competencies. Potential is tracked by intrinsic motivation, purpose (match with MTP), engagement, determination, curiosity, insight and risk literacy (statistics). It is also about (un)learning and adaptability. Over time, these tools can also be applied to Staff on Demand (e.g., Tongal) and Community & Crowd.

DNA/neuro recruitment and team formation	Recruitment and team formations based on DNA profiling (suitability for the job based on particular hormones, neurotransmitters and health risks) and neuro profiling (right attitude, emotions, focus, truth-telling, passion, avoiding cognitive bias). AIs will recommend which people should work together and how to form teams for different tasks.
Peer learning and coaching	Programming software schools such as MIT and France's Ecole 42 have no faculty, relying instead on peer learning; such institutions are highly cost-effective. HR will copy these models for better knowledge-creation and skills-transfer between employees.
P2P reputation systems	Internal and external reputation measured by communities (Mode, GitHub, LoveMachine, Klout, LinkedIn, etc.).
Personal development dashboards and MTP alignment	Dashboard with data analytics, serious gaming and predictive insights into the development of the workforce, such as the OKRs, serendipity or learning KPIs, performance reviews, P2P reputation systems, MOOCs, etc. Big Data leveraged to identify anomalies, including outlier ratings by colleagues. Gamification leveraged for Engagement and alignment with the corporate MTP will be measured/tracked.
Quantified Employee/teams	Employee and team health monitoring provides actionable insights based on body health (fatigue, concentration, movement, rest and relaxation), thus helping to avoid mistakes, stress, productivity loss and burnout. Employee DNA, biome and biomarkers used to minimize health risks, resistance to flu, etc.

Neuroenhance-ment	Neurotechnology used to improve mood, employee capabilities (accelerated learning, focus, reading, sleep, mental state, avoiding cognitive bias) and help combat social phobias (nervousness and fear of contact or connection). Tools and services that help with the mental well-being of employees, such as Happify and ThriveOn. Combined with sensors, these tools teach wellness, resilience and other core life skills; they also measure their impact.

Virtual Reality (VR), currently in limited use with Oculus Rift and Google Glass, and slated for future initiatives such as High Fidelity, will not only profoundly affect recruitment and collaboration, but will also have the potential to disrupt work as we know it today. Think about leveraging VR for Experimentation, inviting customers to test your products virtually even before a prototype is created with a 3D printer. We are also entering an age in which HR will be critical in effectively managing not only core FTEs, but also the larger Staff on Demand (as well as crowdsourced inputs), which will now operate on a global scale. Managing the ExO attributes Interfaces and Staff on Demand will be key new requirements for the HR function.

THE WORLD'S MOST IMPORTANT JOB

It should also be clear by this point that when it comes to large organizations, major transformation is in store for senior management roles worldwide. There is no question that given the multiple transformational technologies converging at numerous intersection points, existing corporate executives will experience extreme stress. And as we've said, nowhere will this impact be more deeply felt than in the office of the CEO. Indeed, it is very likely that a decade from now, the job of the CEO will be so completely revolutionized as to deserve a new title: *Chief Exponential Officer.*

All hail the CXO! And best of luck to that remarkable individual. Because the CXO (not to mention the rest of us) is in for a wild and scary but ultimately exhilarating ride as we enter the age of the Exponential Organization.

EPILOGUE
A NEW CAMBRIAN EXPLOSION

Two key questions we asked ourselves at the beginning of this journey were: Are ExOs for real? And if so, will they last?

Put another way, is the ExO paradigm sustainable or is it just a flash in the pan?

The following table shows the market cap of some top ExOs from when we first started writing this book. We're confident it answers the above questions loud and clear.

	Age (years)	2011 valuation	2014 valuation	Increase
Haier	30	$19 billion	$60 billion	3x
Valve	18	$1.5 billion	$4.5 billion	3x
Google	17	$150 billion	$400 billion	2.5x
Uber	7	$2 billion	$17 billion	8.5x
Airbnb	6	$2 billion	$10 billion	5x
Github	6	$500 million (est.)	$7 billion	14x
Waze	6	$25 million	$1 billion (in 2013)	50x
Quirky	5	$50 million	$2 billion	40x
Snapchat	3	0	$10 billion	10,000x +

What a difference thirty-six months make—more importantly, this kind of multiple would never show up in any five year strategic plan. Remember our Iridium moment. Although its is a relatively new paradigm that is evolving quickly, there is no question in our minds that ExOs are here to stay—business innovator Nilofer Merchant calls them "800-ounce gorillas." Leveraging SCALE elements allows ExOs to extend themselves beyond traditional boundaries, and the IDEAS elements help retain control and some semblance of order. In fact, we are seeing a fascinating development in companies like Amazon, Facebook and Google who have full implementation of the IDEAS elements: *they become depoliticized*. By making data-driven, objective decisions (Experimentation), self-directed teams (Autonomy), constant shared awareness (Social) and Dashboards, teams focus on the end result rather than internal politics.

And for existing organizations, the Chapter Ten example of Arjun Viswanathan at Citigroup shows how dramatically you can make an impact by applying ExO thinking into an existing organization. Ian Chan, a partner at Deloitte Canada whose enviable title is "Disruption Leader", has already formed a team to implement ExO principles for their clients.

Their extreme performance and scalability comes as a result of either dominating new markets with information services, or attacking existing ones by dropping the cost of supply and virtually taking out the denominator in the revenue/cost equation.

Here's another tangible example: In 1979 General Motors employed 840,000 employees and generated $11 billion in earnings (in 2012 dollars). Now, let's compare GM to Google, which in 2012 employed 38,000 (less than 5 percent of GM's 1979 workforce) and generated $14 billion in earnings (120 percent of GM's). What a difference an information-based environment can make! In fact, the recent book by Eric Schmidt and Jonathan Rosenberg, *How Google Works*, maps almost completely to our IDEAS elements.

So, now that we know ExOs are here to stay, here are a few new questions to think about: How far into the general economy will ExOs penetrate? How many industries and markets will they upend? How many established and (currently) successful companies will disappear in the face of exponential competitors? And finally, how would an ExO economy change the way we live and work?

In addition to the extraordinary financial progress achieved by the organizations listed above, we have also tracked their organizational progress as they systematically implemented each of the ExO elements (MTP, SCALE and IDEAS). (And we'll continue to track their evolution at **www.exponentialorgs.com**.) Along the way, we've come to appreciate that the best analogy for an ExO is the Internet itself. The Internet is a distributed, decentralized architecture, with open standards and innovation occurring at the edges. Startups with ExO attributes mirror that same set of characteristics. After twenty years of being the edge of innovation, the Internet is now the foundation of almost all innovation. As enterprises grow more exponential, it is our belief that they will become distributed, decentralized platforms leveraging communities with open APIs. We also believe they will operate with a balanced mix of open and protected data, encouraging constant and disruptive innovation at their edges.

In the same way that Internet communications have seen costs drop to near zero, we expect to see internal organizational and transactions costs also fall to near zero as we increasingly information-enable and distribute our organizational structures. Ultimately, in the face of such low transaction costs, we anticipate what we're calling a *Cambrian Explosion* in organizational design—everything from community-based structures to virtual organizations (see Ethereum) that will be small, nimble and extensible.

It is also becoming increasingly clear that, like the Internet, the ExO paradigm is not just for business. It can just as easily be applied to all sorts of enterprises and organizations, from academia to non-profits to government. In short, it is not just a system of commerce, but also a *philosophy of action*.

For example, what would an exponential government look like? Entrepreneur and technology strategist Andrew Rasiej believes governments should be *platforms* for civic engagement. Jerry Michalski, founder of the Relationship Expedition (REX), notes that the true task of government should be to manage the commons—the cultural and natural resources that belong to all members of a society—a system more effectively handled by MTP-driven communities than by elected, corruptible officials with often-suspect motives.

Frankly, from the right perspective, traditional representative government can be seen as just a rudimentary version of an ExO. That is, it has an MTP (its country or region), leverages community and crowd (tax collection as coerced crowdfunding), is decentralized, gathers and leverages data and insights, puts the community first (in theory), leverages engagement (civics and elections), and has extensive assets (public lands) and staff on demand (the armed forces and reserves).

So the real question is not whether governments can become ExOs—in a crude way, they already are—but whether or not they are able to fulfill their destiny to be true, fully functional, technology driven, high-performance modern ExOs. In fact, here's what we really should be asking ourselves: What would such a government look like?

The opportunity for governments to fulfill that destiny certainly exists. In fact, a couple of ExO-style governmental systems have already been realized. The protection of the Lesser Prairie Chicken, an endangered species in the Southern Great Plains of the U.S., has ironically had a negative effect on anyone trying to erect a wind turbine in the region. The process to assess habitat impact was taking over six months. Each aspect of an assessment required approval at every step. Finally, a group of agencies, including Wildlife & Parks, created a GIS system that encoded all the sensitive areas. Now, the system approves a new location instantly and offers alternatives if there's a problem. That's an almost millionfold improvement in elapsed time, and all with minimal effort.

Successful implementation of ExO strategies within a governmental organization can also be found in the UK. Mike Bracken, head of the Government Digital Service, runs his department as if it were an ExO. Constant experimentation with users, fast iterations, citizen-centered design and the use of GitHub repositories have resulted in a 90 percent approval rating for the department's latest app. (When was the last time any government service saw approval numbers like that?)

Aside from government, we believe ExO principles will transform other siloed areas as well. Take scientific research, which, bizarrely, is still fiercely attached to the "publish or perish" mantra.

"A strong publishing record is key to getting grant funding," says Sarah Sclarsic, a biotech executive with Modern Meadow who has been researching this issue. The problem, however, is that top scientific journals favor sensational studies with positive-correlation findings. As a result, she says, scientists feel pressure to produce those sensational outcomes, regardless of whether or not the science is sound. Sclarsic notes that when researchers at Amgen recently tried to reproduce the results of fifty-three landmark cancer papers, they were only able to substantiate six (11 percent).[1] "This [publishing] bias undermines the open inquiry and objectivity that lie at the heart of science, and which is critical for the discipline's success."

Thankfully, new initiatives like figshare and the Public Library of Science (PLOS) are breaking down this archaic structure. Researchgate, an ExO, is an open, community-based website where researchers can publish all results—and scientists and researchers are flocking to the site in droves. Now over five million strong, the ResearchGate community alone might well multiply scientific and technological progress by orders of magnitude.

JOBS AND THE ECONOMY

Other, equally important questions to contemplate as we move into an ExO environment: What kind of economy would an ExO world produce? What happens as we information-enable more and more processes and products?

Paint a picture of an information-enabled world and you're liable to elicit a typically dystopian scenario: robots and other

---

1   www.nature.com/nature/journal/v483/n7391/full/483531a.
    html#t1

forms of artificial intelligence obviate the need for our jobs and we collapse into crisis and social chaos. The effect of technology on the economy is hardly a new conversation. The McCormick reaper in the 1870s, the assembly line in the early twentieth century, the computer in the 1950s—we've heard it all before. Marc Andreessen has pointed out that the robots-will-take-our-jobs argument first took place in 1964, relying on the exact same terminology and engendering the same fears we're seeing in the press today. In a recent discussion with Salim, noted economist John Mauldin said he stands with Andreessen in not believing in a zero sum game. Instead, he holds that the economy will simply expand to include new activities that could never have been imagined before. (That said, Mauldin also believes there are two opposing tensions at play in the bigger economics picture, at least in the short term: governments making unsustainable promises regarding pensions, healthcare, etc., and increasing productivity as a result of technology.)

Mauldin has criticized economists for their tendency to assess the economy based on an assumption of equilibrium, pointing out that they almost never realize that the information revolution inevitably disrupts this equilibrium. As W. Brian Arthur recently said: "Complexity economics is a different way of thinking about the economy. It sees the economy not as a system in equilibrium but as one in motion, perpetually 'computing' itself—perpetually constructing itself anew. Where equilibrium economics emphasizes order, determinacy, deduction and stasis, this new framework emphasizes contingency, indeterminacy, sense-making and openness to change. Until now, economics has been a noun-based rather than verb-based science."

We believe very much in the optimistic Andreessen/ Mauldin worldview. For example, in 1980, only ninety-two craft brewers existed across the U.S. When our co-author Mike Malone's father was writing about the beer industry in the 1980s, these "hobby" breweries were considered little more than novelties, unable to maintain consistent quality and targeted to a niche audience. Then, as technology drove costs lower, making the industry accessible to anyone and everyone, hobbyists and small brewers suddenly found themselves in a position to run increasingly sophisticated, high quality microbreweries. Today there are almost 3,000 microbreweries in the U.S., the most in over a century. Among them, they have created 110,000 jobs across the country.

But that's not all. A 2010 study conducted by the Kauffman Foundation found that over the past forty years, big companies have created *zero* new net jobs. Instead, 100 percent of new job creation has come via startups and entrepreneurs. After tracking the popular Maker Movement, pioneered by Dale Dougherty, *The Grommet* uncovered similar results, reporting that small businesses have created eight million new jobs since 1990, while large ones have eliminated four million positions.

As we mentioned in Chapter Five, the democratization of technology allows individuals and small teams to follow their passions, be it drones, DNA synthesis or beer. We believe MTP communities leveraging accelerating technologies could dramatically create new economic opportunities, and we expect to see an abundance of new occupations in the near future—albeit very different from the kind of work we're doing today. The question we may soon ask one another is, "How do you occupy yourself?" rather than, "What's your job?" Bottom line: the Cambrian Explosion is already underway.

FROM SCARCITY TO ABUNDANCE

Futurist Paul Saffo has noted that humanity started out as a producer economy, transformed into a consumer economy and is now moving towards becoming a creator economy. Over the centuries, money and commerce have been the main modes of discourse around the world. Today, however, information is rapidly supplanting money to become the main mode of discourse (note that information is already largely fungible). Perhaps the easiest way of framing this macro shift is as a move from scarcity to abundance. Jerry Michalski notes that in the past, scarcity meant *value*. That is, without scarcity, you didn't have a business. Now that notion has been upended. Dave Blakely of IDEO thinks about ExOs in the following way: "These new organizations are exponential because they took something scarce and made it abundant." Nokia bought Navteq, trying to buy, own and control scarcity, only to be leapfrogged by Waze, which managed to harness abundance.

Basically, Exponential Organizations are about managing abundance, and an information-based world drives us towards that abundance. (As outlined earlier, Steven Kotler and Peter Diamandis' book *Abundance* demonstrates the likelihood of this outcome.)

Thus, the triumph of the Exponential Organization begins to look inevitable. In his 2014 book *The Zero Marginal Cost Society: The Internet of Things, the Collaborative Commons, and the Eclipse of Capitalism*, Jeremy Rifkin presents a central thesis that strongly correlates with our "Drive to Demonetization" notion, presented in Chapter Five, in which we point out that ExOs push marginal costs to near zero. Rifkin, however, makes a much bigger point. He believes that what we're seeing is a new economic system emerging for the first time since the rise of capitalism, a new world of very low or zero marginal costs, one that he refers to as the Collaborative Commons.

As you can imagine, this new economic system represents an enormous threat to capitalism. Ironically, the very rise and ascendance of capitalism (to make goods and services ever cheaper) has been so successful that, Rifkin believes, it will ultimately eat its creator, thereby destroying capitalism itself. The key driver for this dynamic? Goods and services being information-enabled on a global scale.

Only time will tell if Rifkin is correct, or at least partially correct, as this new paradigm comes to dominate large sectors of modern life. But what is certain is that Exponential Organizations are the key to managing the new age of the Collaborative Commons and the economies of Abundance. Unfortunately, and ironically, there is a scarcity of guidance for this new paradigm. Almost every business school case study today is now out of date, since each teaches (abundantly) how to optimize and manage scarcity. Correspondingly, most management practices, which predominantly focus on scaling efficiency, are also out of date. There is no MBA course that demonstrates Interfaces and no management consultant who can advise Uber about implementing algorithms.

We've noted that when ExOs get big, they become platforms that spawn other, smaller ExOs, much like a healthy and growing coral reef spawns all number of interesting creatures at its outer fringes. As industries become increasingly information-enabled, we believe they will inevitably consolidate to a few big platforms per industry, each hosting a multitude of small ExOs at their vents and fissures.

However all this plays out, one thing, we hope, is clear. The Exponential Organization is the future for any enterprise with a strong information component—which is, of course, *every* enterprise. You can enter this new world now or later. But, in the end, you will enter it.

Your responsibility to your employees, investors and customers demands that you not wait. The instant a part of your business or industry is information-enabled, marginal costs will start to disappear and your organization will either take on ExO dynamics or disappear. Hesitate too long and you may soon watch your competitors accelerate away, leaving your company a mere footnote in their corporate histories.

There is no need, however, to end up a historical footnote. Think again about the many examples of how exponential thinking and action have not only enabled disruptive new companies, but also driven stunning progress and change in all kinds and sizes of organizations. You now have the instruction manual for recreating yourself as an Exponential Organization. We invite you to start down that path today.

Salim Ismail
Mike Malone
Yuri van Geest

As is clear from our "Top ExOs" chart at the beginning of the Epilogue, ExO attributes are evolving quickly. If you are interested in staying current on news, tips and tricks, and case studies, please join us at **www.exponentialorgs.com**.

AFTERWORD

So there you have it, the blueprint for building an Exponential Organization. Whether you're a three-person company, or a 30,000 person company, reinventing your company around the intrinsic and extrinsic attributes identified in this book are critical.

We can all point at companies we think of as linear (say GM) and companies we think of as exponential (say Google), but now we can actually measure that difference and know how and why they operate at a 25-fold performance differential in revenue per employee, as Salim points out in the epilogue. Part of that 25x difference comes from the productivity tools (i.e. exponential technologies) now available. And granted they operate in different industries, but it indicates directionally the broad shift from a material-based world to an information-based one.

We have arrived at this perspective from our experiences at Singularity University, where for the last six years, we've been learning from the top thought leaders, researchers and practitioners in accelerating technologies. What's critical to note however, is that we literally are still at the very beginning of the coming age of disruptive technologies. We haven't seen anything yet. In the next decade or two, these accelerating tools will continue to grow in utility, and winner-take-all network effects will accelerate Exponential Organizations to record heights.

The reality is that during this time of exponential change you *must* evolve your company—you are either disrupting yourself or someone else is—sitting still equals death.

To give you a better picture of the tsunami of change coming our way, allow me to paint the picture of four levels of convergence set to unfold in the near future.

Level I: First, we have the continued acceleration of specific exponential technologies riding on top of computation, which continues to double (a.k.a. Moore's Law). This is occurring in areas such as Infinite Computing, Networks/Sensors, Artificial Intelligence, Robotics, Digital Manufacturing and Synthetic Biology. You have seen the tables in Chapter One showing dramatic progress in all these areas.

Level II: The convergence of these technologies—the intersection of Networks, AI and 3D printing—will soon allow anyone to describe their thoughts. We will have AI enabled design software listening to you describe beautiful, detailed 3D printable designs, which will then be printed and delivered to your doorstep. Every one of us, with or without skills, becomes a master designer and manufacturer, in much the same way that Microsoft Word makes us all perfect spellers.

Level III: As mentioned in the book, in this decade the number of digitally connected people on Earth will grow from two billion in 2010 to at least five billion by 2020. The addition of three billion new minds entering the global economy will have a powerful impact, but importantly, three billion people will be fully empowered with dematerialized, demonetized and democratized technologies ranging from mobile phones to Google to online 3D printing, AI techniques, medical diagnostics and synthetic biology. They will have access to technologies that only a decade ago were only available to the largest corporations and government labs. What will that enable? What will they build?

Level IV: We have seen that the rate of innovation on Earth increases as a direct effect of people concentrating in cities (moving from the rural areas). Five years ago, the proportion of urban dwellers globally crossed the 50 percent threshold for the first time in human history. To paraphrase Matt Ridley, author of the important book *Rational Optimist: How Prosperity Evolves*, ideas are having sex, mating and recombining at a faster and faster rate, driven by urbanized people in close proximity exchanging and iterating ideas. Soon, the global mind of five billion connected people will drive the most rapid iteration of technology ever seen. Innovation cycles on new products will go from years, to months, to weeks. How will the intellectual property system and global governance systems keep up? How will corporations with large scale linear thinking manage? What happens when the rate of change is faster than the patent process? Will corporations and governments be able to handle this rate of change?

It is these four levels of disruption that will be driving the tsunami of change ahead of all of us. Ultimately, this book was created to help you learn to surf on top of that tsunami instead of being crushed by it.

Both Salim and I have spent the past two years crisscrossing the globe keynoting, coaching and advising corporate and national leaders who are waking up to fact that exponential technologies are here to stay, and these technologies are, in fact, accelerating. Those who thought the "Internet thing" was an isolated incident from the last decade, have finally realized it was only the beginning of *everything*.

I wish you all the best, in taking your company, your organization, perhaps even your country, from a linear thinking entity to an Exponential Organization.

Peter H. Diamandis
Founder and Chairman, XPRIZE Foundation
Co-Founder and Exec. Chairman, Singularity University
Santa Monica, CA

APPENDIX A

WHAT IS YOUR EXPONENTIAL QUOTIENT?

Each question is scored 1-4 (total 84).
ExOs achieve scores over 55/84.

Human Resources and Asset Management

1) To what extent do you use full time employees vs. on demand contractors?*

❑ We only use full time employees *(1 point)*

❑ We use mostly full-time employees with some on-demand contractors in non-mission critical areas (e.g. IT, event production, etc.) *(2 points)*

❑ We use some on-demand contractors to augment mission critical areas (e.g. operations, production, HR, etc.) *(3 points)*

❑ We mostly use on-demand contractors in addition to a small full-time core team *(4 points)*

2) To what extent do you leverage external resources to perform business functions?*

❑ Most business functions are handled by internal employees

❑ We outsource some administrative and support functions (e.g. AP, AR, help desk, facilities, etc.)

❑ We outsource some mission critical functions (e.g. Apple & Foxconn)

❑ We emphasize agility - even mission critical functions are outsourced as variable costs rather than fixed costs

3) To what extent do you own vs. rent the assets in your organization?*

    ❏ We own all assets except peripheral equipment (e.g. copiers)

    ❏ We access some key equipment/services on demand (e.g. cloud computing)

    ❏ We use on-demand assets in multiple business functions (e.g. Hackerspaces or shared offices vs. leasing or buying office space; Using Netjet vs. buying a jet)

    ❏ We use on-demand assets even in mission critical areas (e.g. Apple & Foxconn)

Community & Crowd

4) To what extent do you manage and interact with your Community (users, customers, partners, fans)?*

    ❏ We have very passive involvement with our community (i.e. we use some social media)

    ❏ We leverage our community for market research and other listening activities

    ❏ We actively use the community for outreach, support and marketing

    ❏ The community heavily influences our organization (e.g. product ideas, product development)

5) How do you engage your Community?*

    ❏ No engagement beyond standard customer service (e.g. traditional CRM)

    ❏ Our community is centralized and communication is "one to many" (e.g. TED.com, Apple)

    ❏ Our community is decentralized and communication is "many to many" but passive & single purpose (e.g. LinkedIn, Facebook)

    ❏ Our community is decentralized, communication is "many to many" and drives peer-to-peer value creation (e.g. DIY Drones, GitHub, Wikipedia)

Engagement of Community & Crowd

6) Do you actively convert "the Crowd" (general public) into Community members?*

- ❏ We use standard techniques like PR to increase awareness
- ❏ We leverage social media for marketing purposes
- ❏ We use gamification and incentive competitions to turn crowd into community
- ❏ Our products and services are inherently designed to convert crowd into Community (e.g. shareable memes like the Lyft mustache or Hotmail signature)

7) To what extent do you use Gamification or Incentive Competitions?*

- ❏ We use gamification/incentive competitions for internal motivation only (e.g. salesperson of the month)
- ❏ We use basic gamification externally (e.g. loyalty programs, frequent flyer programs)
- ❏ We build gamification/incentive competitions into our products and services (e.g. Foursquare)
- ❏ We use gamification/incentive competitions to drive ideation and product development (e.g. Quirky, Kaggle)

Information & Social Enablement

8) To what extent are your products/services inform-ation based?*

- ❏ Our product/services are physical in nature (e.g. Starbucks, Levi's or most traditional retailers)
- ❏ Our products/services are physical, but their delivery and/or production is information-based (e.g. Amazon)
- ❏ Our products/services are physical, but services are information based and revenue generating (e.g. iPhone/App store)
- ❏ Our products/services are entirely information-based (e.g. LinkedIn, Facebook, Spotify, Netflix)

9) To what extent is Social functionality and collaboration a central element of your product/service offering?*

❑ No social/collaborative aspect is designed into our products/services (e.g. buying a lawnmower)

❑ We have bolted social/collaborative structures onto existing products/services (e.g. products have a Facebook page or Twitter feed)

❑ Social/collaborative functionality is used to enhance or deliver product/service offerings (e.g. 99Designs, Indiegogo, Taskrabbit)

❑ Social/collaborative inputs actually build our products/services offering (e.g. Yelp, Waze, Foursquare)

Data & Algorithms

10) To what extent do you use algorithms and machine learning to make meaningful decisions?*

❑ We don't do any meaningful data analysis

❑ We collect and analyze data mostly via reporting systems

❑ We use Machine Learning algorithms to analyze data and drive actionable decisions

❑ Our products and services are built around algorithms and machine learning (e.g. PageRank)

11) Do you share strategic data assets internally across the company or expose them externally to your community?*

❑ We don't share data, even between departments

❑ We have data shared between departments (e.g. use internal dashboards, activity streams and wiki pages)

❑ We expose some data to key suppliers (e.g. EDI interfaces or via APIs)

❑ We expose some data to our external ecosystem via open APIs (e.g. Flickr, Google, Twitter, Ford)

Interfaces and Scalable Processes

12) Do you have specialized processes for managing the output of externalities within your internal organization? [by externalities, we mean Staff on Demand, Community/Crowd, Algorithms, Leased Assets and Engagement]*

❑ We don't leverage externalities or we have no special processes to capture or manage externalities

❑ We have dedicated staff to manage externalities (e.g. X Prize creates one-off prizes, TEDx applications handled manually)

❑ We have automated processing of one externality (e.g. Elance or DonorsChoose)

❑ We have automated processing of several externalities (e.g. Indiegogo, Github, Uber, Kaggle, Wikipedia)

13) How replicable and scalable are key processes outside your core organization?*

❑ We have traditional, mostly manual processes (usually confined by SOP - Standard Operating Procedure)

❑ Some of our processes are scalable and repeatable, but only inside the organization

❑ Some of our processes operate outside the organization (e.g. TEDx events, XPRIZE or franchise structures)

❑ Most core processes are self-provisioning and executed outside the organization via a scalable platform (e.g. AirBnB or Adsense)

Real-time Dashboards and Employee Management

14) Which metrics do you track about your organization and your product innovation portfolio? (e.g. Lean Startup Analytics?)*

❑ We only track traditional KPIs monthly/quarterly/annually (e.g. sales, costs, profits)

❑ We collect some real-time, traditional metrics from

transactional systems (e.g. ERP)
❏ We collect all real-time, traditional metrics and use some Lean Startup metrics
❏ We collect real-time traditional metrics and Lean Startup (value and learning) metrics like repeat usage, monetization, referral and NPS

15) Do you use some variant of Objectives and Key Results (OKRs) to track individual/team performance?*

❏ No, we use traditional quarterly/annual performance reviews or 360 reviews or stack ranking
❏ We have implemented OKRs in innovation areas or at the edges of the organization
❏ OKRs are used across our organization (e.g. LinkedIn)
❏ OKRs are used across our organization with full transparency (e.g. Google—everyone can view each others' performance)

Experimentation & Risk

16) Does your organization constantly optimize processes through experimentation, A/B testing and short feedback loops? (e.g. Lean Startup methodology)*

❏ No, we use traditional business process management (BPM)
❏ We use the Lean approach (or similar) for customer facing areas like marketing
❏ We use the Lean approach for product innovation and product development
❏ We use the Lean approach for all core functions (innovation, marketing, sales, service, HR, even legal!)

17) To what extent do you tolerate failure and encourage risk-taking?*

❏ Failure is not an option (NASA) and is a Career Limiting Move (CLM)

❑ Failure and Risk are encouraged, but in name only and not tracked or quantified

❑ Failure and risk-taking are allowed and measured, but sandboxed in skunkworks or very defined boundaries (e.g. Lockheed Skunk Works)

❑ Failure and risk-taking are expected, pervasive, measured and even celebrated across the organization (e.g. Amazon, Google, P&G Heroic Failure Award)

Autonomy & Decentralization

18) Does your organization operate with large, hierarchical structures or small, multi-disciplinary, self-organizing teams?*

❑ We have a traditional corporate hierarchy with large, specialized groups operating in silos

❑ We have some small, multi-disciplinary teams operating at the edges, away from the core

❑ We have some small, multi-disciplinary teams accepted and embraced within the core organization

❑ Small, multi-disciplinary, networked, self-organizing teams are the primary operating structure across the organization (e.g. Valve)

19) To what extent is authority/decision making decentralized?*

❑ Our organization uses traditional, top-down command & control

❑ Decentralized decision-making happens in R&D, innovation and product development

❑ Decentralized decision-making happens in all customer-facing areas like marketing, sales, etc. (e.g. Zappos)

❑ All key decisions are decentralized (except purpose, culture and vision, e.g. Valve)

Social Technologies & Social Business

20) Do you use advanced social tools for knowledge-sharing, communication, coordination and/or collaboration (e.g. Google Drive, Asana, RedBooth, Dropbox, Yammer, Chatter, Evernote)?*

❑ No, email is our primary communication vehicle

❑ Some teams use social tools, but not across the organization

❑ Most business units use social tools (and some external vendors/partners, though often unauthorized)

❑ Use of social tools is mandated across the organization as policy

21) What is the nature and focus of your organizational purpose or mission?*

❑ Our Mission focuses on delivering the best products and services

❑ Our Mission focuses on our core values as an organization, extending beyond delivering products and services

❑ Our Mission is broader than serving end customers; it aims to bring positive change to our entire ecosystem of vendors, partners, suppliers and employees

❑ We have a transformational purpose that goes beyond a Mission Statement. We aspire to deliver significance to the whole world

APPENDIX B
SOURCES AND INSPIRATIONS

All the books below were extensively reviewed, analyzed and cross-referenced with the ExO model.

Anderson, C. (2006). *The Long Tail: Why the Future of Business Is Selling Less of More*. Hyperion.

Anderson, C. (2009). *Free: The Future of a Radical Price*. Hyperion.

Anderson, C. (2012). *Makers: The New Industrial Revolution*. Crown Business.

Blank, S. (2005). *The Four Steps to the Epiphany*. Cafepress.com.

Blank, S., & Dorf, B. (2012). *The Startup Owner's Manual: The Step-By-Step Guide for Building a Great Company*. K & S Ranch.

Botsman, R., & Rogers, R. (2010). *What's Mine Is Yours: The Rise of Collaborative Consumption*. HarperBusiness.

Brynjolfsson, E., & McAfee, A. (2012). *Race Against The Machine: How the Digital Revolution is Accelerating Innovation, Driving Productivity, and Irreversibly Transforming Employment and the Economy*. Digital Frontier Press.

Brynjolfsson, E., & McAfee, A. (2014). *The Second Machine Age: Work, Progress, and Prosperity in a Time of Brilliant Technologies*. W. W. Norton & Company.

Catmull, E., & Wallace, A. (2014). *Creativity, Inc.: Overcoming the Unseen Forces That Stand in the Way of True Inspiration*. Random House.

Christakis, N. A., & Fowler, J. H. (2009). *Connected: The Surprising Power of Our Social Networks and How They Shape*

Our Lives. Little, Brown and Company.

Christensen, C. M. (2000). *The Innovator's Dilemma: When New Technologies Cause Great Firms to Fail*. HarperCollins Publishers.

Christensen, C. M., & Raynor, M. E. (2003). *The Innovator's Solution: Creating and Sustaining Successful Growth*. Harvard Business Review Press.

Christensen, C. M., Dyer, J., & Gregersen, H. (2011). *The Innovator's DNA: Mastering the Five Skills of Disruptive Innovators*. Harvard Business Review Press.

Collins, J. (2001). *Good to Great: Why Some Companies Make the Leap...And Others Don't*. HarperBusiness.

Collins, J., & Porras, J. I. (2004). *Built to Last: Successful Habits of Visionary Companies*. HarperBusiness.

Collins, J. (2009). *How the Mighty Fall: And Why Some Companies Never Give In*. JimCollins.

Collins, J., & Hansen, M. T. (2011). *Great By Choice: Uncertainty, Chaos, and Luck - -Why Some Thrive Despite Them All*. HarperBusiness.

Cooper, B., & Vlaskovits, P. (2013). *The Lean Entrepreneur: How Visionaries Create Products, Innovate with New Ventures, and Disrupt Markets*. Wiley.

Cowen, T. (2013). *Average Is Over: Powering America Beyond the Age of the Great Stagnation*. Dutton Adult.

Cusumano, M. A. (2001). *Strategic Thinking for the Next Economy*. Jossey-Bass.

Cusumano, M. A. (2010). *Staying Power: Six Enduring Principles for Managing Strategy and Innovation in an Uncertain World*. Oxford University Press.

Davidow, W. H., & Malone, M. S. (1992). *The Virtual Corporation: Structuring and Revitalizing the Corporation for the 21st Century*. HarperCollins Publishers.

Diamandis, P. H., & Kotler, S. (2012). *Abundance: The Future Is Better Than You Think*. Free Press.

Eggers, W. D., & Macmillan, P. (2013). *The Solution Revolution: How Business, Government, and Social Enterprises Are Teaming Up to Solve Society's Toughest Problems*. Harvard Business

Review Press.

Ertel, C., & Solomon, L. K. (2014). *Moments of Impact: How to Design Strategic Conversations That Accelerate Change.* Simon & Schuster.

Ferriss, T. (2009). *The 4-Hour Workweek: Escape 9-5, Live Anywhere, and Join the New Rich.* Harmony.

Fischer, B., Lago, U., & Liu, F. (2013). *Reinventing Giants: How Chinese Global Competitor Haier Has Changed the Way Big Companies Transform.* Jossey-Bass.

Furr, N., & Dyer, J. (2014). *The Innovator's Method: Bringing the Lean Start-up into Your Organization.* Harvard Business Review Press.

Hagel III, J., & Brown, J. S. (2005). *The Only Sustainable Edge: Why Business Strategy Depends On Productive Friction And Dynamic Specialization.* Harvard Business Review Press.

Hagel III, J., Brown, J. S., & Davison, L. (2010). *The Power of Pull: How Small Moves, Smartly Made, Can Set Big Things in Motion.* Basic Books.

Hamel, G., & Prahalad, C. K. (1994). *Competing for the Future.* Harvard Business Review Press.

Hamel, G., & Breen, B. (2007). *The Future of Management.* Harvard Business Review Press.

Hamel, G. (2012). *What Matters Now: How to Win in a World of Relentless Change, Ferocious Competition, and Unstoppable Innovation.* Jossey-Bass.

Hill, D. (2012). *Dark Matter and Trojan Horses: A Strategic Design Vocabulary.* Strelka Press.

Hinssen, P. (2004). *The New Normal: Great Opportunities in a Time of Great Risk.* Portfolio Hardcover.

Hoffman, R., & Casnocha, B. (2012). *The Start-up of You: Adapt to the Future, Invest in Yourself, and Transform Your Career.* Crown Business.

Hoffman, R., Casnocha, B., & Yen, C. (2014). *The Alliance: Managing Talent in the Networked Age.* Harvard Business Review Press.

Horowitz, B. (2014). *The Hard Thing About Hard Things: Building a Business When There Are No Easy Answers.*

HarperBusiness.

Johansson, F. (2004). *The Medici Effect: What You Can Learn from Elephants and Epidemics*. Harvard Business Review Press.

Kahneman, D. (2011). *Thinking, Fast and Slow*. Farrar, Straus and Giroux.

Kanter, R. M. (1989). *When Giants Learn to Dance*. Simon & Schuster.

Kapp, K. M. (2013). *The Gamification of Learning and Instruction Fieldbook: Ideas into Practice*. Pfeiffer.

Kawasaki, G., & Welch, S. (2013). *APE: Author, Publisher, Entrepreneur - How to Publish a Book*, Nononina Press.

Keeley, L. (2013). *Ten Types of Innovation: The Discipline of Building Breakthroughs*. Wiley.

Kelly, K. (2011). *What Technology Wants*. Penguin Books.

Kim, W. C., & Mauborgne, R. (2005). *Blue Ocean Strategy: How To Create Uncontested Market Space And Make The Competition Irrelevant*, Harvard Business Review Press.

Kurzweil, R. (2006). *The Singularity Is Near: When Humans Transcend Biology*. Penguin Books.

Kurzweil, R. (2013). *How to Create a Mind: The Secret of Human Thought Revealed*. Penguin Books.

Lencioni, P. M. (2012). *The Advantage: Why Organizational Health Trumps Everything Else In Business*. Jossey-Bass.

Malone, M. S. (2007). *Bill & Dave: How Hewlett and Packard Built the World's Greatest Company*. Portfolio Hardcover.

Malone, M. S. (2009). *The Future Arrived Yesterday: The Rise of the Protean Corporation and What It Means for You*. Crown Business.

Maurya, A. (2012). *Running Lean: Iterate from Plan A to a Plan That Works*. O'Reilly Media.

McGonigal, J. (2011). *Reality is Broken: Why Games Make Us Better and How They Can Change the World*. The Penguin Press.

McGrath, R. Gunther (2013). *The End of Competitive Advantage: How to Keep Your Strategy Moving as Fast as Your Business*. Harvard Business Review Press.

Mele, N. (2013). *The End of Big: How the Internet Makes David the New Goliath*. St. Martin's Press.

Merchant, N. (2012). *11 Rules for Creating Value In the #SocialEra*. CreateSpace Independent Publishing.

Mintzberg, H. (1994). *Rise and Fall of Strategic Planning*. Free Press.

Moretti, E. (2012). *The New Geography of Jobs*. Mariner Books.

Osterwalder, A., & Pigneur, Y. (2010). *Business Model Generation: A Handbook for Visionaries, Game Changers, and Challengers*. Wiley.

Osterwalder, A., Pigneur, Y., Bernarda, G., & Smith, A. (2014). *Value Proposition Design: How to Create Products and Services Customers Want*. Wiley.

Owens, T., & Fernandez, O. (2014). *The Lean Enterprise: How Corporations Can Innovate Like Startups*. Wiley.

Pistono, F. (2012). *Robots Will Steal Your Job, But That's OK: how to survive the economic collapse and be happy*. CreateSpace Independent Publishing.

Radjou, N., Prabhu, J., & Ahudja, S. (2012). *Jugaad Innovation: Think Frugal, Be Flexible, Generate Breakthrough Growth*. Jossey-Bass.

Ries, E. (2011). *The Lean Startup: How Today's Entrepreneurs Use Continuous Innovation to Create Radically Successful Businesses*. Viking.

Rifkin, J. (2014). *The Zero Marginal Cost Society: The Internet of Things, the Collaborative Commons, and the Eclipse of Capitalism*. Palgrave Macmillan Trade.

Rose, D. S. (2014). *Angel Investing: The Gust Guide to Making Money and Having Fun Investing in Startups*. Wiley.

Schmidt, E. & Rosenberg, J. (2014). *How Google Works*. Grand Central Publishing.

Scoble, R., & Israel, S. (2013). *Age of Context: Mobile, Sensors, Data and the Future of Privacy*. CreateSpace Independent Publishing.

Searls, D. (2012). *The Intention Economy: When Customers Take Charge*. Harvard Business Review Press.

Shirky, C. (2010). *Cognitive Surplus: Creativity and Generosity in a Connected Age*. The Penguin Press HC.

Sinek, S. (2009). *Start with Why: How Great Leaders Inspire Everyone to Take Action*. Portfolio Hardcover.

Solis, B. (2013). *What's the Future of Business: Changing the Way Businesses Create Experiences*. Wiley.

Spear, S. J. (2010). *The High-Velocity Edge: How Market Leaders Leverage Operational Excellence to Beat the Competition*. Mcgraw-Hill.

Taleb, N. N. (2007). *The Black Swan: The Impact of the Highly Improbable*. Random House.

Taleb, N. N. (2012). *Antifragile: Things That Gain from Disorder*. Random House.

Thiel, P. & Masters, B. (2014). *Zero to One: Notes on Startups or How to Build the Future*. Crown Business.

Tracy, B. (2010). *How the Best Leaders Lead: Proven Secrets to Getting the Most Out of Yourself and Others*. AMACOM.

Wadhwa, V., & Chideya, F. (2014). *Innovating Women: The Changing Face of Technology*. Diversion Books.

Zook, C., & Allen, J. (2012). *Repeatability: Build Enduring Businesses for a World of Constant Change*. Harvard Business Review Press.

In Dutch only:

Kwakman, F., & Smeulders, R. (2013). *Groot Innovatie Modellenboek*. Van Duuren Management.

Mandour, Y., Brees, K., & Wenting, R. (2012). *Groeimodellen: Creëer nieuwe business*. Van Duuren Management.

ABOUT THE AUTHORS

This book is a joint collaboration involving Salim Ismail, Michael S. Malone and Yuri van Geest, with key ideas and framing provided by Peter Diamandis, along with consultation from the faculty of Singularity University.

Ismail and Diamandis became business partners when they founded Singularity University, an institution created to study the impact of exponentially growing technologies on companies, industries and humanity's grand challenges. Van Geest has been involved in the collaboration, writing, researching and thinking of this book for almost the entire three years of its creation. Malone is considered by many to be the writer of record for Silicon Valley and has written two dozen books, several of which identify key new milestones in the history of organizations.

SALIM ISMAIL is the founding Executive Director at Singularity University, where he moderates most academic programs, and is its current Global Ambassador. Before that, as a vice president at Yahoo, he built and ran Brickhouse, Yahoo's internal incubator. His most recent company, Angstro, was sold to Google in August 2010. He has founded or operated seven early-stage companies including PubSub Concepts, which laid some of the foundation for the real-time web. He also spent several years as a management consultant with CSC Europe and later with ITIM Associates. Ismail holds a BSc in Theoretical Physics from the University of Waterloo in Canada.

MICHAEL S. MALONE is one of the world's best-known technology writers. He has covered Silicon Valley and high-tech for more than thirty years, beginning with the *San Jose Mercury*

News as the nation's first daily high-tech reporter. Malone's articles and editorials regularly appear in the *Wall Street Journal*. He was editor of *Forbes ASAP*, the world's largest-circulation business-tech magazine, at the height of the dot-com boom. Malone is the author or co-author of nearly twenty award-winning books and television series, notably the bestselling *The Virtual Corporation*, *Bill and Dave: How Hewlett and Packard Built the World's Greatest Company*, and *The Future Arrived Yesterday: The Rise of the Protean Corporation and What It Means For You*. Malone holds an MBA from Santa Clara University, where he is currently an adjunct professor in professional writing. He is also an associate fellow of the Saïd Business School at Oxford University, and is a Distinguished Friend of Oxford.

YURI VAN GEEST is an international keynote speaker, boardroom consultant, the managing director of the Singularity University Summit Europe, the Dutch Ambassador for Singularity University and a double alumnus of Singularity's programs. He holds a MSc degree in strategic management and marketing from Erasmus University Rotterdam and has been a key figure, firestarter and organizer in the global Lean Startup, Quantified Self, TEDx and Mobile Monday movements. He has consulted for Google, ING Bank, Vodafone Group, Adidas Global, Philips Global, Heineken Global, Friesland Campina, Samsung and MIT, and was a key member of the Topteam Creative Industry within the Dutch Ministry of Economic Affairs, Agriculture and Innovation for two years.

PETER H. DIAMANDIS is a serial entrepreneur having co-founded fifteen companies, most notably the X Prize Foundation, Singularity University and Planetary Resources. He has a molecular biology and aerospace engineering degree from MIT and an MD from Harvard. He is also the co-author of the *New York Times* bestselling book, *Abundance: The Future Is Much Better Than You Think*, which is recommended pre-reading for those interested in Exponential Organizations. CNN and *Fortune* just named Peter Diamandis one of "The World's 50 Greatest Leaders."

ACKNOWLEDGMENTS
(FROM SALIM, YURI AND MIKE)

We've realized it doesn't just take a village to complete a project like this—it takes a whole town. A small portion part of the help we received is gratefully acknowledged below:

First, to Paul Saffo, who suggested that Salim write this book. (Though it is unclear to Salim whether Paul meant well or not, as this project almost finished him.)

Second, to Peter Diamandis, who dove in and helped frame many of the major concepts and how they were articulated in a way only Peter can.

Third, to Michiel Schuurman, whose relentless research and analytics laid a solid foundation on which the ideas could rest.

Fourth, to Sarah Sclarsic, whose prodigious brain helped frame some key insights that emerged from the book.

Our editor, Lauren Cuthbert, comes with halo attached and cleaned up what seemed like every second word. Similarly, Joe DiNucci and Atiya Davidson from Enabling Thought Leadership, who managed the process from end to end.

Thanks to Mary Cummings, Laura Duane and their colleagues at Diversion Books along with James Levine, Kerry Sparks and the whole team at Levine Greenberg Rostan Literary Agency.

Thanks also to the following readers, who reviewed the book and provided valuable insights, commentary and feedback. Without their input, the book would have been finished in half the time (and would have been a tenth as good): Dave Blakely, ErnstJan Bouter, Leen Breevoort, Marc van der Chijs, Martin Voorzanger, Wassili Bertoen, Erwin Blom, Kees van Nunen,

Louise Doorn, Gerd Leonhard, Ajit Jaokar, Paul van Liempt, Jan Fred van Wijnen, Rutger Bregman, Joe Pine II, Anders Hvid, Pepijn Vloemans, Wouter van Noort, Marc Fonteijn, Raymond Perrenet, Bart van de Laak, Pascale Scheurer, Hood Whitson, Nicoletta Iacobacci, Sonal Shah, Michelle LaPierre, Nilofer Merchant, Yonatan Adiri, Vince Daranyi, Jabeen Quadir, VJ Anma, Joel Richman, Kent Langley, Nathalie Trutmann, Gulay Ozkan, James Donnelly, Johnny Walker, Eitan Eliram, Eric Ezechielli, Howard Baskin, Andrew Vaz, Russ Howell, Lawton Langford, Steve Leveen, Diane Francis, Sasha Grujicic and Carin Watson.

To our community at Singularity University, who continue to inspire, inform and guide us in our thinking. Specifically, we want to thank faculty members Neil Jacobstein, Brad Templeton, Raymond McCauley, Rob Nail and Marc Goodman, who added mightily to the ideas in Chapter Ten.

And finally, our wives, for their infinite patience through this entire process. Salim, especially, gratefully acknowledges his wife Lily, for her heroic support and numerous interventions.

9 781626 814233